Water
Management
& Agricultural
Development

Water Management & Agricultural Development: A CASE STUDY OF THE CUYO REGION OF ARGENTINA

KENNETH D. FREDERICK

Published for RESOURCES FOR THE FUTURE, INC.
by The Johns Hopkins University Press
Baltimore and London

Resources for the Future is a nonprofit corporation for
research and education in the development, conservation, and
use of natural resources and the improvement of the quality
of the environment. It was established in 1952 with the
cooperation of the Ford Foundation. Part of the work of
Resources for the Future is carried out by its resident staff;
part is supported by grants to universities and other nonprofit
organizations. Unless otherwise stated, interpretations and
conclusions in RFF publications are those of the authors;
the organization takes responsibility for the selection of
significant subjects for study, the competence of the
researchers, and their freedom of inquiry.

This book is one of RFF's Latin American studies, which are
prepared under the direction of Pierre R. Crosson. Kenneth
D. Frederick is a Research Associate in the Latin American
program. The manuscript was edited by Judy L. Conmy.

RFF editors: Mark Reinsberg, Joan R. Tron, Ruth B. Haas,
Jo Hinkel

Copyright © 1975 by The Johns Hopkins University Press
All rights reserved
Manufactured in the United States of America

Library of Congress Catalog Card Number 74–24402
ISBN 0–8018–1701–3
Library of Congress Cataloging in Publication data will be
found on the last printed page of this book.

CONTENTS

TABLES

FIGURES

GLOSSARY

The values used in the text of this study are in 1969 U.S. dollar equivalents. Table A.1 in the Appendix indicates the approximate parity rates between the U.S. dollar and Argentine peso from 1960 to 1972.

All weights and measures are in metric units. The following table identifies symbols used and their approximate equivalents:

$$m = 1 \text{ meter} = 39.37 \text{ inches}$$
$$km = 1 \text{ kilometer} = 0.62 \text{ mile}$$
$$ha = 1 \text{ hectare} = 2.47 \text{ acres}$$
$$km^2 = 1 \text{ square kilometer} = 0.386 \text{ square mile}$$
$$m^3 = 1 \text{ cubic meter} = 35.3 \text{ cubic feet}$$
$$hm^3 = 1 \text{ cubic hectare} = 1,000,000 \text{ m}^3 = 809.7 \text{ acre feet}$$
$$kg = 1 \text{ kilogram} = 2.2 \text{ pounds}$$
$$kW = 1 \text{ kilowatt}$$
$$kWh = 1 \text{ kilowatt hour}$$
$$MT = 1 \text{ metric ton} = 2,200 \text{ pounds}$$
$$MW = 1,000,000 \text{ watts}$$
$$GWh = 1 \text{ billion watt hours}$$

FOREWORD

Water is a scarce resource in the arid zones of Latin America and is sure to become more so. Population growth and rising income, coupled with rapid urbanization, assure continued steep increases in demand for water for irrigation and for industrial and municipal uses. In many parts of the region the rise in demand is already pressing hard against existing supplies, stimulating mounting interest in finding new sources of water. Usually, developing these sources requires large investments in dams, canals, and other infrastructure, resulting in relatively high per unit costs.

The foreseeable rise in costs of new sources of water suggests that policies and technologies to encourage more efficient use of already developed supplies may yield high returns in Latin America. The conditions for achieving increased efficiency are not well understood, however, primarily because the historical response to rising scarcity has been investment in new works. Thus, investigation of these conditions is a necessary step toward developing efficiency as an important policy alternative to new works. Kenneth Frederick has undertaken such an investigation in this study. The Cuyo region of Argentina, one of the world's major producers of wine grapes, is wholly dependent upon irrigation for development of its agriculture. Until the mid to late 1940s surface water was adequate for agricultural demand; since that period the rise in demand has been accommodated by pumping ground water and building infrastructure designed to increase the usable supply of surface water. At present there is evidence that the ground water tables are falling at rates such that the economic life of the region's principal aquifers could be seriously threatened by the end of the century. In this event the entire regional economy, dependent as it is upon irrigated agriculture, would be imperiled.

Present patterns of water use in the Cuyo region do not fully reflect the shift from water abundance to scarcity. Since the aquifer is a common property resource, its rate of exploitation does not reflect the true *social* scarcity of water in the region. Government policies fail to compensate for this excessive rate of exploitation; indeed, in response to pressure from farmers they reinforce it. Frederick's study explores the dimensions of the emerging water scarcity in Cuyo, examines the economic, political, and institutional conditions determining present patterns of water use, and discusses a range of policy options that would induce farmers to adopt patterns of use more appropriate to present and prospective conditions of water scarcity. We think it an important contribution to the development of a literature demonstrating the value of increased efficiency as an alternative to development of new sources of supply in meeting Latin America's future demands for water.

This study is one of several undertaken at RFF on problems of natural resource development in Latin America. Others previously published, or to be published, all by The Johns Hopkins University Press, are Nathaniel Wollman, *The Water Resources of Chile* (1968); Orris Herfindahl, *Natural Resource Information for Economic Development* (1969); Pierre Crosson, *Agricultural Development and Productivity: Lessons from the Chilean Experience* (1970); Joseph Grunwald and Philip Musgrove, *Natural Resources in Latin American Development* (1970); Ronald Cummings, *Water Resource Management in Northern Mexico* (1972), and *Interbasin Water Transfers: A Case Study in Mexico* (1974); Michael Nelson, *The Development of Tropical Lands: Policy Issues in Latin America* (1973); and Hans M. Gregersen and Arnoldo Contreras H., *U.S. Investment in the Forest-Based Sector in Latin America* (1975).

PIERRE R. CROSSON
Director, Latin American Program

FOREWORD

ACKNOWLEDGMENTS

This book is the product of research undertaken in the course of my residence in Mendoza, Argentina, from July 1971 to July 1973, as part of the Latin American program of Resources for the Future, Inc.

I am deeply indebted to many people for their assistance. Pierre R. Crosson, Director of Resources for the Future's Latin American program, provided valuable suggestions at many stages of the study as well as detailed comments on a draft of the entire study. Darrell F. Fienup, professor of agricultural economics at Michigan State University and former agricultural advisor for the Ford Foundation in Argentina, and Robert Healy and Lawrence Libby of Resources for the Future reviewed and offered many helpful suggestions on a draft of the entire study. Ronald G. Cummings, of the University of Rhode Island and formerly with Resources for the Future, assisted in identifying the nature of the water problems in the Cuyo region and provided many useful suggestions on an earlier draft of Chapter 5. Walther G. Lichem, former acting director of the UNDP Special Fund project with the Centro de

Economía, Legislación y Administración del Agua (CELA) in Mendoza, provided helpful comments on chapters 2, 3, and 4.

This study has benefited enormously from the cooperation and assistance of numerous Argentines. The account of people in the Universidad Nacional de Cuyo, provincial and federal government agencies, and private companies who have assisted me is too long to enumerate here. However, my debt to some of these people is much too great to go unmentioned. Miguel Martinez, former director of the Instituto de Economía, Universidad Nacional de Cuyo, and Julio Rodriguez Arias, former president of CELA, provided general logistical support, advice, and encouragement during my stay in Mendoza. Juan Antonio Zapata, Armando Bertranou, Aldo Biondolillo, and Armando Llop of the Universidad Nacional de Cuyo gave generously of their time and were invaluable sources of information on the region's agriculture, water problems, and data sources. Roberto Cortegoso, who served as a research assistant for about ten months during the initial stages of the study, gathered, collated, and analyzed much of the data essential to the analysis.

My wife Susan was the first reader of some rather rough drafts. The organization, clarity of the arguments, and grammar have benefited greatly from her comments. Gayle P. Underwood in Washington, D.C., and Geraldine Upton in Mendoza, Argentina, typed the final draft. Penelope Harpold improved the presentation of the many tables; Judy Conmy edited the manuscript. To all of these people I wish to express my sincere gratitude.

A special thanks is also due to the Ford Foundation, which funded Resources for the Future's Latin American program and provided me essential logistical support during my stay in Argentina. In particular, the assistance of David Gunn, the Foundation's executive officer in Buenos Aires, did much to make the two years spent in Argentina very enjoyable ones for me and my family.

ACKNOWLEDGMENTS

Water
Management
& Agricultural
Development

introduction 1

The limits to growth imposed by limited supplies of natural resources and the economic implications of approaching these limits have long been of interest to economists. Well over a century ago Ricardo and Malthus predicted that fixed supplies of natural resources would prevent any substantial long-run improvement of income levels and severely limit population expansion. Technological change, however, has long since made their prognoses obsolete. Yet, in recent years the present and expected magnitude of population, production, and natural resource use have given rise to a group of neo-Malthusians. Indeed, when historical trends are projected several generations into the future, their implications for the environment and key natural resources are alarming. Such projections have led many to advocate drastic legal and institutional changes which would radically alter life styles and reduce or perhaps even reverse growth trends. Others argue that the neo-Malthusian predictions of today will be no more accurate than those of Malthus, since they underestimate our ability to develop new technologies and substitutes for scarce resources. Although basic differences in value judg-

1

ments regarding desirable life styles often prompt conflicting viewpoints, different expectations of society's ability to adjust to and the eventual outcome of such changes are also involved.

Changes in the relative availability, value, and cost of resources alter the optimal manner of utilizing such resources. A society's adjustment to changes in factor availability determines both the efficiency of resource use and the limits to economic growth. New technologies have provided suitable substitutes or new inexpensive sources of supply for many resources. However, the supply of other resources essential to certain production processes or living standards can be increased only at higher average costs, if they can be increased at all. Irrigation water in an arid environment, for example, cannot be completely displaced from the agricultural production process, and supply increases beyond some point already reached in many regions involve substantial rises in cost. While crop yields per unit of water can generally be increased through technology and greater use of complementary inputs and the usable supply of water can be enlarged through investment and improved water management practices, there are economic, if not physical, limitations to such changes. The adjustment process becomes more complicated and crucial to the economic viability of a region when an essential depletable resource such as ground water is involved.

It is by no means certain that a society will adjust readily and smoothly to changes in the relative availability of natural resources. One may cite numerous examples in which a society's perceptions of and responses to changing factor conditions were inadequate to avoid a deterioration in living conditions or the need for drastic responses to make up for a prior misuse of resources. The energy crisis is a recent example. Similarly, the full costs of industrialization and urbanization were not obvious until air pollution and congestion made some cities virtually unlivable for many. And free market forces have not provided reliable guides for an efficient exploitation of ground water stocks. The market underprices the full cost of present ground water use, encouraging a faster than efficient use of stocks. In some cases overuse has required costly "rescue" investments to avoid large income and investment losses.

Adjustment to changes in the relative supply and demand of an essential resource such as irrigation water can range from traumatic to smooth and well planned, depending on the role of market forces, government policies, laws, and regulatory institutions. These factors determine the incentives to develop and adopt new technologies and alter the relative factor use and product mix in response to changes in the availability and costs of production factors. This study examines an economy undergoing a major transition in the relative supply and demand for water, a resource essential to the economic survival and growth of the region, and provides suggestions for altering the current inefficient growth path, which runs a high risk of undermining the economic vitality and social stability of the region.

The Region

Cuyo is an arid to semiarid region on Argentina's western border, and comprises the provinces of Mendoza and San Juan (see Figure 1). The provinces cover some 237,000 square kilometers inhabited by 1.5 million people; the region represents 8.4 percent of the land and 5.8 percent of the people in Argentina. Mendoza accounts for 64 percent of Cuyo's area, 72 percent of the region's population, and 78 percent of its economic activity.

Cuyo's economy is based on the production and processing of agricultural products. The region's agricultural production and processing are in turn dominated by grapes and wine. There are currently nearly 500,000 hectares under cultivation in the region; grapes occupy almost 60 percent of the cultivated land and account for 75 percent of the value of agricultural production. More than 90 percent of the grape crop is processed into wine, and in recent years the grape-wine industry has accounted for 22 to 29 percent of Mendoza's and 38 to 45 percent of San Juan's total gross product.[1] The region produces about 92 percent of Argentina's grapes and wine. Cuyo's wine production from 1965 to 1970 was more than 2.3 times the production of the United States and was surpassed by the output of only four countries excluding Argentina.[2]

The primary resources, land and water, were not factors limiting the region's agricultural growth until recently. In fact, land with good natural and potential fertility capable of producing high yields when well irrigated is still abundant and poses no limitation on the region's future growth. However, with annual rainfall averaging only 8 inches in Mendoza and half that in San Juan, irrigation water is essential to the region's agriculture. Lacking irrigation water, rural land has little market value.

The past three decades have brought a fundamental change in the value of water in Cuyo. Until the mid-1940s river water in Cuyo had been abundant in relation to demand, and irrigation requirements had been supplied almost exclusively by the region's rivers and streams, fed

---

[1] Aldo L. Biondolillo, "Social Cost of Production Instability in the Grape-Wine Industry: Argentina" (Ph.D. dissertation, University of Minnesota, 1972), p. 2.
[2] Argentina, Instituto Nacional de Vitivinicultura, *Estadística vitivinícola 1970–71*, 1971, pp. 9, 39, 48.

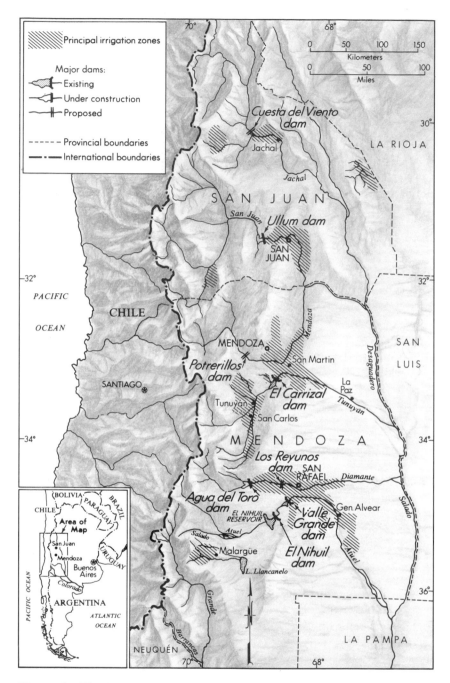

Figure 1 The Cuyo Region with Principal Irrigation Zones

4

primarily by snow melt in the Andes. Agricultural growth and declining river flows, however, eliminated the excess of readily available surface water. Since the early 1950s it has become increasingly expensive and difficult to satisfy the growing water demand. The supply of water has been augmented through large increases in the number of irrigation wells and investments designed to enhance the efficiency of surface water distribution. However, by the early 1960s ground water pumping from the region's major aquifers exceeded normal recharge; diminishing returns to water infrastructure investment have either set in or soon will. Moreover, the resulting increases in water distribution efficiency and irrigation wells were not sufficient to prevent substantial crop damage in the late 1960s when the region was hit by a series of five unusually dry years starting in 1967–68.

A doubling of the number of irrigation wells from 1967 to 1973 and the unusually plentiful rain and river flows during the 1972–73 agricultural year ended, at least temporarily, the short-run problem of insufficient water. However, an even more serious water problem is emerging and may have dire consequences only a few decades hence. The region is using water at levels that cannot be maintained without huge new investments in water infrastructure. Even proposed investments in dams and canals costing hundreds of millions of dollars may only postpone depletion of usable ground water stocks for an additional decade. Moreover, the long-run situation is being aggravated, first, by government policies which encourage new cultivation and irrigation wells and discourage on-farm investments to improve the efficiency of water use and, second, by the natural tendency of market forces to encourage a faster than optimal use of a common property resource such as ground water. In recent years from 30 to 50 percent of the region's irrigation water has come from the ground, and increases in cultivated areas and irrigation wells will raise this percentage. A continuation of recent rates of increase in water use could exhaust the usable ground water stock within about two decades.

The implications of a rather precipitous decline in the quantity and quality of water several decades hence are far reaching. Permanent crops currently account for over 75 percent of the cultivated land and about 87 percent of the value of agricultural production in Cuyo, and both these percentages have been increasing over time. Permanent crops represent a substantial fixed investment, roughly $2,000 per hectare for grapes, and generally have an expected economically productive life of at least thirty years. Only a small fraction of such an investment could be recovered if the source of good quality water dried up. In addition, there are currently more than 20,000 irrigation wells in the region, representing an average investment of about $10,000 per well, and the number of wells continues to grow rapidly. About half this cost is tied up in the drilling and encasing of the well, which would normally be amortized over about twenty years. These costs, however, could not be recovered if either the well went dry or the water quality fell to unusable levels. Moreover, substantial urban complexes centered around the cities of Mendoza, San Juan, and San Rafael have emerged and continue to grow largely on the expectation of continued agricultural prosperity and growth. Many of the investments currently being made and contemplated in permanent crops, irrigation wells, and urban construction may never be fully recovered if market forces and government policies continue to encourage a water-intensive agricultural growth in Cuyo.

Objectives and Scope of the Study

Principal objectives of this study are to increase the understanding of the interrelationships between Cuyo's agricultural development and resource base and to indicate and evaluate the impact of market forces and alternative government policies on the rate and efficiency of agricultural development and water use. It is hoped that this study might play a positive role in effecting changes which could greatly improve the efficiency of water use and the long-run economic development of Cuyo and avert the substantial investment losses and economic and social disruptions likely to emerge from current growth patterns and policies.

While the data and analysis of this study focus on the Cuyo region, the problems examined are unfortunately repeated in many areas. Ground water mining and the efficient use of water stocks are already important issues in such areas as northwestern Mexico and the southwestern United States; the tremendous increase in ground water use in developing areas associated with the "Green Revolution" suggests that the problems will become much more widespread in the near future. Moreover, the problems associated with the optimal, intertemporal use of a common property resource such as ground water have parallels in the exploitation of other important resources such as marine fisheries and oil fields. Other problems and issues of general interest examined here include how growth can alter the value and efficient use of basic natural resources, the impact of institutional and policy rigidities and high rates of inflation on intertemporal resource use efficiency, the relative advantages of direct and indirect controls to influence both the use of common property resources and the conjunctive use of ground and surface water, and the implications of alternative water management schemes on income distribution and on the long-run efficiency and viability of regional development.

In addition to its obvious interest to people concerned with Argentina's development, this book should provide a useful case study for researchers or policy makers interested in any of these broader issues. However, in order to support the policy conclusions relevant to the Cuyo area, this study contains detailed data, analysis, and description of limited value to the reader lacking a specific interest in Argentina. The reader with an interest in only the general issues and conclusions should proceed to the concluding sections of chapters 2 through 7 and then to the final chapter; the table of contents should enable such a reader to locate readily any data, analysis, and description of specific interest.

This study is primarily an economic analysis of the region and relevant policies. Political and social developments within Cuyo have obviously influenced the region's development, institutions, laws, and water use patterns and are of continuing importance in determining the possibilities for change. However, a detailed examination of the role of political and social factors on the region's development is beyond both the scope of this study and the expertise of the author. Nevertheless, this study does examine the impact of current and alternative policies on the distribution as well as the growth and level of income. Moreover, the recommendations of this study are not tied to any single social or political view. The author does conclude, however, that water use efficiency in Cuyo would best be improved by increasing the marketability of water.

historical growth

2 of agriculture and water use

AGRICULTURAL GROWTH

General Economic Trends

Completion of the railroad between Buenos Aires and Mendoza in the mid-1880s ended over a century of virtual economic stagnation within Cuyo. The railroad made the large and rapidly expanding coastal market available to Cuyo's farmers and brought an influx of immigrants, who provided much of the labor for agricultural expansion. This agricultural expansion has continued, with only brief pauses, until the present.

Though the Andes separate Cuyo from the west, the region's initial political and commercial links were with the Pacific rather than the Atlantic coast. Spaniards crossing the Andes from Chile established the first European settlements in Mendoza and San Juan. The region became a supplier of agricultural products, primarily grapes and wheat, for the Spaniards' mining and commercial economy in western South America. Consequently, Cuyo's early development paralleled that of the

Spanish empire in South America. The economic plight of Cuyo after the decline of Spanish influence until the completion of the railroad to Buenos Aires is described by Scobie:

> The collapse of the silver-mining economy and of the Spanish commercial system contributed to Cuyo's decline in the nineteenth century. The link with Chile grew weaker. Administrative changes late in the colonial period had brought the provinces of Cuyo under the control of Buenos Aires. After the nations became independent, the Argentine and Chilean economies drew even further apart. With the exception of cattle, products on the two sides of the Andes became increasingly competitive, and Mendoza lost much of its vitality as a commercial center. The promise of wealth from copper, silver, and lead deposits proved largely illusory. Even the vineyards fell on hard times. The formerly prosperous outlets in the northwest had dried up, and costs of oxcart freight made it cheaper for the coast [Buenos Aires] to secure its wines from France, Spain, or Italy than from Cuyo.[1]

Since the 1880s grapes have dominated agricultural expansion; this crop currently occupies nearly three-fifths of the cultivated land and accounts for almost three-fourths of the value of agricultural production in the region. The land planted to grapes in Mendoza rose from less than 5,000 hectares in 1887 to nearly 20,000 hectares by 1900.[2] Then for the following thirty-six years vineyards grew at an average geometric rate of 4.6 percent per year before peaking temporarily at about 100,000 hectares. This growth trend in grapes halted temporarily in 1936 when the government prohibited new plantings and initiated an eradication program to eliminate production surpluses and raise growers' prices. Total acreage planted to grapes in Mendoza declined more than 15 percent from 1936 to 1938.

Grape planting started again in Mendoza in 1939, and during the next twenty-nine years vineyards grew at an average geometric rate of 3.1 percent per year. In San Juan land devoted to grapes increased at an average geometric rate of 2.1 percent from 1945 to 1968. By 1967 there were over 260,000 hectares planted to grapes in Cuyo, about

[1] James R. Scobie, *Argentina: A City and a Nation*, 2nd ed. (New York: University Press, 1971), p. 18.

[2] With the exception of grapes and wine, reasonably reliable data on production and land cultivated are virtually nonexistent prior to 1940. For reasons detailed in the appendix, even the data for grapes and wine should be treated with some skepticism. The data for grapes up to 1960 are from Argentina, Gobierno de Mendoza, Asesoría de Desarrollo, *Series estadísticas* (Sector Agricultura, Vol. 5), 1970.

80 percent of which were in Mendoza. Severe water shortages, combined with low grape prices and government restrictions on the varieties of grapes planted, brought a second brief halt to the expansion of vineyards. Total land under grapes in the region actually declined by several thousand hectares between 1968–69 and 1969–70 as some growers lost their vineyards and lack of water discouraged new plantings. In the last several years higher grape prices and an increased capacity to pump ground water have renewed substantial grape planting in the region.

Annual fluctuations in grape production have been one of the greatest sources of instability in the region's economy. Since grapes are a permanent crop and represent a substantial long-term investment, short-run fluctuations come primarily from changes in yields rather than changes in the amount of land planted to grapes in the productive stage. On the other hand, since average grape yields have fluctuated around a zero long-run trend for at least the last sixty years, long-run changes in grape production have directly reflected the quantity of land devoted to grapes. The three most severe situations of instability in the grape and wine markets were in 1917, when 75 million liters of wine were poured into the irrigation canals of Mendoza and San Juan in an effort to support prices; in the mid-1930s, when the extremely depressed market led to government intervention in support of grape prices; and in the several years following the record 1967 grape harvest.

Methodology for Analyzing Recent Growth

A much more detailed examination of agricultural growth is required to illuminate the interrelations between agricultural growth and the supply and demand for irrigation water. The minimum data desirable for such a detailed growth analysis are crop water requirements and time series data on the land planted to and production of each crop in the region. The data are sufficient to warrant such an analysis for only the last twenty to twenty-five years. While the examination of longer periods would be desirable, the last two decades cover the most important period for studying the relations beween water use and agricultural growth in Cuyo. This section explains the methodology and data underlying the analysis of agricultural growth in Mendoza and San Juan during the last several decades; the three sections after this describe and explain this growth. Later sections of this and the following chapter examine the institutional, legal, and cost factors affecting the supply of irrigation water and the relations between agricultural growth and water.

Although short-run production variations resulting from changes in water receipts are of interest, the data do not enable one to separate adequately the influence of short-run variations in water receipts on yields and annual plantings from the influence of such other factors as weather and crop prices. Moreover, primary interest here is not in the interannual changes in water use and agricultural production but in the longer-run sources of growth and their implications for water use. Consequently, the analysis attempts to explain the change between estimated values of agricultural production in initial and terminal years with short-run yield and price variations eliminated.[3]

The estimated provincial production values for each crop in the initial and terminal years were calculated by multiplying the number of hectares planted to each crop by the estimated yields (in value terms) in the respective years.[4] Physical crop yields were calculated from time series data on physical production and area planted, collected for as many years as possible. Physical yields in the initial and terminal years were estimated from a least-squares regression of yields over the entire period to eliminate the impact of short-run fluctuations. The physical production figures were converted into value units using constant growers' prices.[5]

The primary periods examined are 1947–48 to 1969–70 in Mendoza and 1954–55 to 1971–72 in San Juan. To achieve greater comparability, it would have been highly desirable to use similar periods for each province. Unfortunately, comparable periods could not be used without either making numerous additional assumptions to compensate for missing data or greatly reducing the time periods examined. For example, in San Juan the data available prior to 1954–55 are much less complete, while in Mendoza there are no data on the number of fruit and olive trees during the mid-1950s or after 1969–70.

Several methods are used to examine the sources of agricultural growth in Mendoza and San Juan between these periods. The crops are divided into five major groups; grapes, other fruits, vegetables, cereals and forage, and olives. Table 2.1 presents the annual geometric growth rates of the estimated value of agricultural production, the land planted,

[3] Items excluded because of insufficient data include forestry, livestock, and a few vegetables of minor importance. The omissions probably do not amount to more than 1 to 2 percent of the value of crop production in San Juan and about 2 to 3 times that percentage in Mendoza. The effect of the omissions on the calculated growth rates and sources of growth over the periods considered are probably minor; there is no reason to expect that they would significantly alter the conclusions. There is no attempt in the text to allow for the items omitted. Additional limitations of these data are discussed in the appendix.

[4] In an attempt to reduce the impact of short-run fluctuations in the acreage of annual crops, three-year averages are used when the data permit. The estimated 1971–72 figures for annual crops in San Juan are an average of 1970–71 and 1971–72 actual data; most of the other acreage figures for annual crops are a three-year average centered on the indicated year.

[5] The constant growers' prices are an unweighted average of growers' prices from 1960 to 1962 deflated to 1960 pesos.

Table 2.1 Average Annual Geometric Growth Rates of Agricultural Production

(in percentages)

Crop	Mendoza, 1947–48 to 1969–70			San Juan, 1954–55 to 1971–72		
	Estimated value of production[a]	Land planted	Yield	Estimated value of production[a]	Land planted	Yield
Grapes	3.0	3.0	0.0	1.9	1.6	0.2
Other fruits	2.0	1.8	0.2	0.8	1.1	−0.3
Vegetables	2.0	−1.8	3.8	−0.8	−0.9	0.1
Cereals and forage	−2.3	−1.8	−0.5	−2.6	−4.2	1.7
Olives	4.8	−0.3	5.2	2.1	−0.1	2.2
All crops	2.4	1.0	1.3	1.4	0.0	1.4

Source: Calculated from data presented in the appendix.

[a] The production values are based on an average of growers' prices from 1960 to 1962 deflated to 1960 pesos.

and the yield of each crop group in both Mendoza and San Juan. Table 2.2 separates the change in the value of agricultural production of each crop group into three growth components: that due to the change in land planted with yields held constant, that due to the change in yields on the land planted in the base period, and that due to changes in yields on changes in cultivated land.[6] This last term is referred to as the residual effect. Table 2.2 presents the change in the value of production of each crop group and the contribution of the three growth components to this change as a percentage of total agricultural growth in each province. Table 2.3 shows the land planted to each crop group and the value of agricultural production from each crop group in the initial and terminal years as a percentage of the provincial totals. And Table 2.4 presents aggregate agricultural growth factors for Mendoza and San Juan both as a percentage of production in the initial year and as a percentage of the growth during the periods examined.

Table 2.4, having four growth factors instead of the three in Table 2.2, needs further explanation. The fourth factor emerges since a change in the aggregate yield per hectare can result from a change in

[6] The sum of these three components is equivalent to the total change in agricultural production. This can be demonstrated by starting with the following definition:

$$V_t^i \equiv T_t^i \cdot Y_t^i$$

where V_t^i is the value of production of the ith crop group in year t; T_t^i is the land planted (in hectares) to the ith crop group in the year t; and Y_t^i is the average value per hectare of the ith crop group in year t. If Δ indicates the change between some base year 0 and terminal year t, then $\Delta V^i \equiv V_t^i - V_0^i = \Delta T^i \cdot Y_0^i + \Delta Y^i \cdot T_0^i + \Delta T^i \cdot \Delta Y^i$. Thus, the change in the value of agricultural production equals the sum of the three growth components represented on the right-hand side of the equation.

Table 2.2 Sources of Agricultural Growth, by Crop Group and Growth Component
(in percentages of total agricultural growth)

Crop	Δ Value of production $\dfrac{\Delta V^i}{\Sigma \Delta V} \cdot 100$	Δ Land planted $\dfrac{\Delta T^i Y_0^i}{\Sigma \Delta V} \cdot 100$	Δ Yield $\dfrac{\Delta Y^i \cdot T_0^i}{\Sigma \Delta V} \cdot 100$	Residual effect $\dfrac{\Delta T^i \cdot \Delta Y^i}{\Sigma \Delta V} \cdot 100$
Mendoza, 1947–48 to 1969–70				
Grapes	89.5	90.0	−0.3	−0.3
Other fruits	7.3	6.4	0.6	0.3
Vegetables	8.6	−5.1	20.5	−6.8
Cereals and forage	−7.9	−6.4	−2.2	0.7
Olives	2.6	−0.1	2.9	−0.2
All crops	100.0	37.5	49.8	12.7
San Juan, 1954–55 to 1971–72				
Grapes	106.6	91.8	11.3	3.6
Other fruits	1.4	2.0	−0.5	−0.1
Vegetables	−5.8	−6.6	0.9	−0.1
Cereals and forage	−5.9	−8.7	5.6	−2.9
Olives	3.7	−0.1	3.8	0
All crops	100.0	1.0	98.6	0.3

Source: Calculated from data presented in the appendix.

Note: The symbols used to identify the columns are consistent with those defined in note 6, p. 12; $\Sigma \Delta V$ is the total increase in the estimated value of agricultural production for the province.

the yield of one or more of the individual crops as well as from a change in the product mix, e.g., a change from crops with a low value to crops with a high value per hectare. These two factors represent responses to very different forces—the former representing technological change or perhaps a change in the average natural fertility of the land and the latter probably representing a response to changes in relative crop and input prices. The first column in Table 2.4, change in land cultivated, indicates the growth resulting from increasing the total quantity of land cultivated with no change in the average return per hectare. Thus, it assumes both constant yields for every crop and no change in the proportion of land planted to any crop. The second column shows the combined impact of changes in the yields of individual crop groups when the land planted to each group is held constant at initial year levels. The third column measures the residual effect of a change in the yield on the change in the land planted to each crop group. And the fourth column, the change in the product mix, indicates the importance to overall growth of the relative shift in land planted to crop groups with different average returns per hectare.[7] The combination of columns two, three, and four explains changes in aggregate yields, the second

[7] Column 4 is calculated as the difference between the total change in the value of agricultural production and the sum of the other three sources of this change.

Table 2.3 Percentage Distribution of Cultivated Land and Value of Agricultural Production by Crop Group

| | Mendoza | | | | San Juan | | | |
| | Land cultivated | | Value of production[a] | | Land cultivated | | Value of production[a] | |
Crop	1947–48	1969–70	1947–48	1969–70	1954–55	1971–72	1954–55	1971–72
Grapes	37.0	57.1	65.6	75.3	49.2	64.7	77.8	83.9
Other fruits	12.1	14.2	9.2	8.4	3.9	4.6	2.8	2.5
Vegetables	11.0	5.9	10.6	9.7	8.5	7.3	12.5	8.6
Cereals and forage	33.6	18.2	13.7	4.9	29.0	14.1	4.6	2.3
Olives	6.3	4.6	1.0	1.6	9.4	9.3	2.3	2.6
Provincial total	100.0	100.0	100.0	100.0	100.0	100.0	100.0	100.0

Source: Calculated from data presented in the appendix.
[a] The production values are based on an average of growers' prices from 1960 to 1962 deflated to 1960 pesos.

Table 2.4 Components of Total Agricultural Growth for Selected Years

	Δ Land cultivated	Δ Yield	Residual effect	Δ Product mix	Total growth
Mendoza, 1947–48[a] *to 1969–70*					
Percentage of 1947–48 production	25.5	14.6	−4.3	32.3	68.1
Percentage of growth, 1947–48 to 1969–70	37.5	21.5	−6.3	47.3	100.0
San Juan, 1954–55[a] *to 1971–72*					
Percentage of 1954–55 production	0.3	5.7	0.1	20.9	27.0
Percentage of growth, 1954–55 to 1971–72	1.0	21.2	0.4	77.4	100.0

Source: Calculated from data presented in the appendix.
[a] Base years.

column representing the contribution of technological change, the fourth column representing the contribution of a change in the composition of crops, and the third column, by measuring the impact of a change on a change, combining elements of both.[8]

Agricultural Growth in Mendoza: 1947–48 to 1969–70

The value of agricultural production rose 68 percent during this twenty-two-year period for an annual growth of 2.4 percent. Almost 90 percent of this growth can be attributed to grapes, the value of which rose nearly 93 percent or 3 percent per annum. Grapes increased from 65.6 to 75.3 percent of the value of agricultural production and from 37.0 to 57.1 percent of the cultivated land in the province. Grape yields actually declined about 0.3 percent during this period.

Permanent crops, which include grapes, other fruits, and olives, accounted for 99.3 percent of the total growth in the value of agricultural production. The land devoted to permanent crops increased more than 116,500 hectares and from 55.4 to 75.9 percent of cultivated land. In contrast, the area planted to annual crops declined by 42,000 hectares. Cereals and forages, which accounted for three-fourths of this decline, experienced a 31.8 percent decline in acreage, a 10.8 percent decline in

[8] Since there has been no attempt to separate the influence of the change in product mix and higher yields per hectare of the individual crops within a crop group containing more than one crop, there is probably some overestimation of the importance of technological change and a corresponding underestimation of the importance of the change in the product mix. The bias could actually be in the opposite direction if the relative shift within a crop group was from crops with relatively high returns per hectare to crops with lower returns per hectare. The net bias is probably not important since, in general, there are not wide differences in the value per hectare of crops within the same crop group nor have there been major changes in the relative importance of crops within the crop groups.

value per hectare, and a 39 percent decline in value of production. While vegetable acreage declined 33 percent over this period, a 132 percent increase in their average value per hectare brought a 55 percent increase in the total value of vegetable production.

The change in the relative product mix, which reflects primarily a shift from cereals and forages to grapes, accounted for 47.3 percent of total agricultural growth, while the increase in the amount of land cultivated accounted for 37.5 percent, and the increase in yields per hectare of the individual crop groups accounted for 21.5 percent. The residual actually caused a 6.3 percent drop in the aggregate value of agricultural production in Mendoza due largely to the simultaneous rise in yields and decline in plantings of vegetables.

Agricultural Growth in San Juan: 1954–55 to 1971–72

The value of agricultural production in San Juan rose 27.0 percent during this seventeen-year period for an average annual increase of 1.4 percent. Grapes were even more important to overall agricultural growth in San Juan than in Mendoza. Grape production in San Juan grew at an annual rate of 1.9 percent and accounted for 106.6 percent of the total increase in the value of agricultural production. Vineyards increased from 49.2 to 64.7 percent of the cultivated land, and grape production increased from 77.8 to 83.9 percent of the value of agricultural production in San Juan.

Permanent crops accounted for 111.7 percent of the rise in the value of agricultural production. The land planted to permanent crops rose nearly 12,900 hectares and from 62.5 to 78.6 percent of cultivated land. In contrast, the land planted to annual crops declined nearly 12,700 hectares. The cereals and forages, which alone accounted for 92 percent of this decline, fell from 29.0 to 14.1 percent of all cultivated land and from 4.6 to 2.3 percent of agricultural production. All annual crops fell from 17.1 to 10.9 percent of the value of total agricultural production.

The change in the relative product mix accounted for 77.4 percent and the increase in yields per hectare of the individual crop groups accounted for 21.2 percent of total agricultural growth. The total amount of land cultivated increased only 0.3 percent and accounted for only 1.0 percent of total agricultural growth. The residual term had a negligible impact on growth.

Comparison of the Growth Experiences in Mendoza and San Juan

The difference between the annual growth rates of total agricultural production (2.39 percent in Mendoza and 1.41 percent in San Juan) is fully accounted for by the difference in annual growth rates of total land cultivated (1.04 percent in Mendoza and 0.02 percent in San Juan). Consequently, the average value per hectare increased at virtually the same annual rates in the two provinces, 1.34 percent in Mendoza versus 1.40 percent in San Juan. For both provinces the change in the product mix accounted for more than three-fourths of the increased value per hectare. On an annual basis, the increase in the percentage of land devoted to grapes was virtually the same in both provinces, 20.1 percent over twenty-two years in Mendoza and 15.5 percent over seventeen years in San Juan. Technological change, measured as the change in the yield of individual crop groups, increased the value of agricultural production only 0.5 percent per annum in Mendoza and 0.3 percent in San Juan.

Differences in the growth experiences of San Juan and Mendoza are in part due to the different periods considered. An idea of the importance of the different time intervals on the growth trends can be obtained from available production and acreage data. Using three-year averages centered on 1947–48, 1954–55, and 1969–70, the actual value (as opposed to the estimated values used above) of San Juan's agricultural production in constant prices grew at annual rates of 3.7 percent from 1947–48 to 1954–55 and only 0.4 percent during the following fifteen years. In Mendoza land planted to grapes increased at average annual rates of 4.5 percent from 1947–48 to 1954–55 compared to 2.4 percent during the following fifteen years. Although the available data do not permit more precise comparisons, they indicate that growth was higher in Mendoza during both periods and higher in the period prior to 1954–55 in both provinces.

The most important factor for explaining both the interprovincial and intertemporal differences in agricultural growth rates is the availability of water. To support this statement, we must examine the water supply conditions and the impact of these conditions on agricultural growth in the two provinces. But before leaving the description of historical agricultural growth trends, it is instructive to focus on the growth experience during the more immediate past. This is particularly useful for the subsequent examination of underlying growth factors since this period includes a four-year period of acute water scarcity within Cuyo.

Agricultural Growth Since 1960–61

The eleven years starting with 1960–61 comprise two fairly distinct growth periods: 1960–61 to 1966–67, a period of general growth, and 1967–68 to 1970–71, a period of overall agricultural stagnation. Al-

Table 2.5 Percentage Changes in Agricultural Production and Land
Cultivated in Selected Years

	Land cultivated		Value of production	
	1960–61 to 1966–67	1966–67 to 1970–71	1960–61 to 1966–67	1966–67 to 1970–71
Mendoza				
Grapes	18.6	5.0	69.8	−18.0
Other permanent crops	a	a	20.0	40.1
Annual crops	1.1	−5.6	15.8	−3.4
Total	12.4[b]	1.6[b]	55.5	−11.4
San Juan				
Grapes	15.0	−0.2	61.1	−37.1
Other permanent crops	−5.5	−2.7	93.8	−16.0
Annual crops	−3.0	−34.4	−10.1	−13.2
Total	6.5	−10.1	52.2	−33.9
Cuyo Region				
Grapes	17.8	3.9	67.2	−23.6
Other permanent crops	a	a	28.9	29.2
Annual crops	0.2	−11.6	9.1	−5.5
Total	11.6[b]	−1.0[b]	54.5	−17.6

Source: Calculated from data presented in the appendix.
[a] Data are not available.
[b] Figures include only grapes and annual crops.

though the data are preliminary and incomplete, 1971–72 appears to
have brought minor increases in agricultural production and total plantings, while 1972–73 seems to have resulted in major increases in the
total cultivated area within Cuyo. Cuyo appears to have embarked on
a new period of agricultural expansion.

The data in Table 2.5 indicate the contrasting agricultural growth
records of the first two periods. This table presents the percentage
changes in land cultivated and value of production (in constant prices)
by crop group for the periods 1960–61 to 1966–67 and 1966–67 to
1970–71.[9] The magnitudes of the changes in the values of production
presented in Table 2.5 are especially high as 1966–67 was an unusually
good agricultural year in the Cuyo region. The direction of the changes,

[9] The calculations are based on actual production and acreage figures. Since the
periods under consideration are relatively short and since a major purpose is to
focus on changes resulting in part from relatively short-run changes in water availability, the production values are not estimated from trends in yields and average
hectares planted to annual crops for several years. Consequently, the changes in
the value of production indicated in Table 2.5 are subject to short-run fluctuations
in yields which were eliminated in the prior analysis of agricultural growth in
Mendoza from 1947–48 to 1969–70 and San Juan from 1954–55 to 1971–72.

however, are not dependent on the selection of this year: the period before 1966–67 was generally one of rising production and total cultivated land; the reverse was true of the subsequent period. Changes in acreage deserve greater emphasis since the acreage data are susceptible to changes in water availability but less susceptible to other random factors which have an important effect on agricultural production in Cuyo, such as frost and hail damage.

The differences between the agricultural changes from 1960–61 to 1966–67 and 1966–67 to 1970–71 are striking. In the region as a whole the land cultivated increased about 11 percent from 1960–61 to 1966–67 and declined 1 percent from 1966–67 to 1970–71; the value of agricultural production rose 55 percent in the earlier period and declined 18 percent in the later period. In Mendoza from 1960–61 to 1966–67 vineyards increased 2.9 percent per annum, and the total land planted to grapes and annual crops grew at 2.0 percent per annum. During the following four years net grape plantings fell to less than half the prior average annual rate, and the area planted to annual crops declined 5.6 percent. In San Juan vineyards increased 2.4 percent per annum and total cultivated land grew 1.1 percent per annum from 1960–61 to 1966–67. Over the following four years grape land declined slightly, and total cultivated land fell 10.1 percent. The implied annual growth rates from 1960–61 to 1966–67 were generally higher and the rates from 1966–67 to 1970–71 much lower than the rates for the longer periods discussed earlier—1947–48 to 1969–70 in Mendoza and 1954–55 to 1971–72 in San Juan.

Two factors, water availability and grape prices, played a dominant role in the agricultural growth patterns in Cuyo after 1960–61. The impact of these factors on agricultural growth is considered after an examination of water availability and use within the region.

WATER SUPPLY AND USE

Historical River Flows

The growth of cultivated land in Cuyo has been in sharp contrast to the trend in the flow of the region's rivers during the last thirty to forty years. Table 2.6 lists the average annual flows for ten-year intervals starting with 1909–10 and for the three years from 1969–70 to 1971–72 of the rivers supplying most of the surface irrigation water to the region. Since complete data are available for only the Mendoza and San Juan rivers, the number of years included in the calculation of each average are indicated in the table. The averages based on only a few

Table 2.6 Average Annual River Flows, by Decade

(in millions of cubic meters)

River	1909–10 to 1918–19	1919–20 to 1928–29	1929–30 to 1938–39	1939–40 to 1948–49	1949–50 to 1958–59	1959–60 to 1968–69	1969–70 to 1971–72
Mendoza Province							
Mendoza	1753	1838	1850	1659	1342	1226	1080 (3)[a]
Upper Tunuyán			1199 (3)	983 (7)	761	860	790 (3)
Lower Tunuyán			1062 (8)	995 (6)	1105	901	
Diamante				1178	1323 (9)	1056	750 (3)
Atuel				947 (1)	904	960	795 (3)
San Juan Province							
San Juan	1905	2552	1917	1926	1445	1327	633 (3)
Jachal	281 (2)	491 (5)	202 (2)	371 (7)	256	202	135 (3)

Source: Annual river flow data are from Departamento General de Irrigación, Mendoza, for Mendoza's rivers and Departamento de Hidráulica, San Juan, for San Juan's rivers. The flows are measured above the principal irrigated areas.

[a] All figures in parentheses indicate the number of years included in the calculation in periods with fewer than ten observations.

observations are more susceptible to the vagaries of the substantial interannual fluctuations.

If we focus on the Mendoza and San Juan rivers, which are the most important, it is obvious that water flows during the last twenty years have been well below the flows of earlier recorded periods. For example, the average annual flows of the Mendoza River were 72.5 percent during the 1950s and 66.3 percent during the 1960s of the average during the 1930s. The comparable percentages for the San Juan River were 75.4 and 69.2. Water receipts were particularly low from 1967–68 to 1971–72, when the average flow of the Mendoza River was only 54.8 percent and the San Juan River only 34.4 percent of their averages during the 1930s.

Water has played an increasingly important role in the development of Cuyo's agriculture during the past twenty years or so. About the mid-1940s agricultural water requirements, which had been rising over time, and river flows, which had been declining for several decades, converged to the point where river water flows became insufficient for agricultural needs. The following section examines in some detail the changes in the relative supply and demand for irrigation water and its effects on the sources of irrigation water; later sections consider the impact of these changes on water costs and agricultural development.

Changes in the Demand for and Sources of Irrigation Water Since the 1940s

Of the various sources of agricultural growth measured in Table 2.4, the only one which clearly increased the demand for irrigation water was the increase in the total land cultivated. The technological change component of growth probably slightly increased the average water requirements per hectare for some crops.[10] But since there is no way to estimate this change nor reason to believe it is quantitatively significant, it is assumed that there was no change in the per hectare water requirements of individual crops. The change in the product mix clearly decreased the average water requirements per hectare planted, the result of a decline in land planted to alfalfa, which has a very high water requirement per hectare.

A rough calculation of the net change in the total water requirements of the plants indicates an increase of 450.8 cubic hectometers (hm^3) or 19.2 percent in Mendoza from 1947–48 to 1969–70 and a decrease of 50.9 hm^3 or 6.0 percent in San Juan from 1954–55 to 1971–72.[11] With a project efficiency rate of 60 percent, the demand for irrigation

[10] While some measures such as pesticide application may increase yields per hectare without increasing water requirements, the adoption of fertilizer and high-yielding seeds frequently requires more water per hectare to be effective. Increases in yields per hectare have resulted from a combination of these and other factors with similar effects on water use. Consequently, aggregate yield increases have probably been accompanied by some increase in average water requirements per hectare.

[11] The calculations are based on estimates of the annual quantity of water that should be delivered to the plant to maximize the harvest. The water requirements for each crop group in each province are estimated from data on the water requirements of individual crops and the number of hectares planted to each crop. Water requirement data were not available for all crops. The average water requirements per hectare for each crop group are multiplied by the number of hectares planted to each crop group in the initial and terminal years. Alfalfa is treated as a separate crop group because of its much higher water requirements and the importance of the change in the land planted to alfalfa. The assumed water requirements in m^3 per hectare for Mendoza and San Juan respectively are grapes, 7,230 and 9,400; other fruits, 6,615 and 9,200; vegetables, 6,866 and 8,750; olives, 9,726 and 11,000; alfalfa, 10,770 and 15,000; and other cereals and forage, 6,000 and 6,900. The higher water requirements in San Juan are due to differences in atmospheric conditions between the two provinces. Data on the annual crop water requirements were obtained from the following sources: field experiment data provided by Ing. Castro of the INTA station in San Juan; calculations by Ing. Agr. Jorge Chambouleyron of CIMALCO based on the Blaney-Criddle equation; and "Projecto quebrada de Ullum, Estudio de factibilidad," Vol. 2, a study by Edison-Harza for the government of San Juan, 1969, Appendix I, pp. 10–23.

water rose about 750 hm³ in Mendoza and declined about 85 hm³ in San Juan.[12]

The table below focuses on the changes in river water receipts over approximately the same time intervals used in the prior agricultural growth analysis. This table indicates the average annual water receipts of the region's principal rivers for the past five years and for the five-year periods centered on 1947–48 in Mendoza and 1954–55 in San Juan, the initial years used for their respective growth analyses. The

---

[12] References to water use efficiency in this study conform to the three concepts of efficiency presented in Charles W. Howe and K. William Easter, *Interbasin Transfers of Water: Economic Issues and Impacts* (Baltimore: The Johns Hopkins Press, 1971), pp. 112–113. Their general definition of efficiency is

$$e = \frac{C}{G - \rho R}$$

"where C is the amount of water usefully stored in the root zone during one application, G is the gross amount withdrawn from the source, R is the return flow of water finding its way back to some surface or ground watercourse, and ρ is the percentage of the return flow that is useful for the other applications, account being taken of the quality and timing of the return flow." The three concepts of efficiency depend on where G is measured. "If (G) is measured at the point of diversion . . . , the above measure is called project efficiency; if G is measured at the farm head gate, then e is the farm efficiency; and if G refers to the amount delivered to the field, e is called field efficiency."

This study of Cuyo assumes an average project efficiency rate of 60 percent for the use of surface water in the region. This is intended to be a high estimate of efficiency with ditch irrigation, the method generally used in the region. One study estimates that only 40.5 percent of the irrigation water in Cuyo is used by the plants. (See Consejo Nacional de Desarrollo, Oficina Regional de Desarrollo Cuyo, *Análisis y diagnóstico regional*, Mendoza, 1969, Vol. 1, p. 31). Some of these losses, however, serve to recharge the aquifers. For example, about 22 percent of the average annual river flows (measured above the irrigated zone) in northern Mendoza from 1963 to 1969 infiltrated to the usable aquifers through the riverbeds, canals, and irrigated lands. The comparable percentage was also 22 for the principal irrigated zone in San Juan (calculated from data in Programa de las Naciones Unidas para el Desarrollo, *Investigación de las aguas subterraneas en el noroeste Argentina*, New York, 1972, Summary Volume, tables 1–7). However, the impact of this infiltration on the usable stock of ground water is reduced somewhat by the resulting increase in salinity of the ground water. Ground water salinity, which is becoming a major problem in many areas of Cuyo, is being studied at the Facultad Ciencias Económicas, Universidad Nacional de Cuyo. Ground water efficiency rates should be somewhat higher since pumping is usually done at the farm eliminating distribution losses to the farm. For ground water pumping on the farm, project and farm efficiency are equivalent. It is assumed that the farm efficiency of ground water is 70 percent with ditch irrigation. This is again intended to be a high estimate. Howe and Easter (*Interbasin Transfers*, p. 113, Table 38) indicate that farm irrigation efficiency typically ranges from 45 to 65 percent depending on the type of soil. The overall project efficiency of water use in the region would be the weighted average of the efficiencies of ground and surface water. In view of the greater importance of surface water use and the high nature of the efficiency rates used for both ground and surface water, 60 percent is also used for overall project efficiency.

decline in the average annual river flows over the respective periods totaled 710 hm^3 for Mendoza's four rivers and 1,209 hm^3 for San Juan's two rivers.

Mendoza Province	1945–46 to 1949–50	1967–68 to 1971–72
Mendoza	1,345	1,013
Upper Tunuyán	833	708
Atuel	915*	775
Diamante	828	715
Province total	3,921	3,211

San Juan Province	1952–53 to 1956–57	1967–68 to 1971–72
San Juan	1,729	659
Jachal	282	143
Province total	2,011	802

* Data available for only 1948–49 and 1949–50.
Source: Table 2.6 indicates the source of annual river flow data. Figures are in millions of cubic meters.

The combined effect of the declining surface water flows and changing agricultural water requirements has been substantial. With a surface water use efficiency rate of 60 percent, the difference between annual agricultural water requirements and river flows increased by 1,460 hm^3 from about 1947–48 to 1969–70 in Mendoza and by 1,124 hm^3 from 1954–55 to 1971–72 in San Juan.

Mendoza in 1947–48 was reaching the point where the water from the four major rivers was being fully utilized at the existing efficiency rates for the distribution and utilization of water.[13] Thus, additional irrigation requirements and declines in surface water flows had to be met by greater irrigation efficiency, investment in infrastructure to increase the percentage of water available to the farm, or from ground water. The alternatives were the same in San Juan; however, by 1954–55 San Juan had already started to rely partly on ground water.

[13] The degree of utilization of the major rivers supplying Cuyo's irrigated areas is reflected in the flows of the Desaguadero River, which flows along the eastern border of the region and is fed by the rivers supplying most of the region's irrigation water. The average annual flow of the Desaguadero River at Arco del Desaguadero on Mendoza's eastern border fell from an average of 734 hm^3 from 1940–41 to 1946–47 to zero from 1947–48 to 1950–51, when measurements were suspended. The flow of the Desaguadero River at Paso Las Tunitas on the border of Mendoza and San Juan provinces where the Mendoza and San Juan rivers converge dropped to zero in 1947–48. The flow in the following year recovered to 81 hm^3, about 9 percent of the average flow from 1940–41 to 1946–47, before the observations were suspended. These data are from the files of the Departamento General de Irrigación in Mendoza.

Table 2.7 Registered Irrigation Wells in Mendoza

Year	Annual increase	Cumulative totals as of 12/31
1959	—	4,874
1960	257	5,131
1961	362	5,493
1962	279	5,772
1963	366	6,138
1964	351	6,489
1965	389	6,878
1966	515	7,393
1967	464	7,857
1968	495	8,352
1969	861	9,213
1970	1,489	10,702
1971	2,069	12,771
1972[a]	(978)	13,749
1973[a]	(1,669)	15,418

Source: Departamento General de Irrigación, Mendoza.

[a] The 1972 figure is an estimate as of June 1972; the 1973 figure is the number of wells registered with the Departamento General de Irrigación as of May 24, 1973.

The net increases in irrigation requirements in relation to surface water flows over the past several decades have been met largely by ground water in both provinces, making a substantial portion of the agriculture in both provinces dependent on ground water. While there are no data available on the quantity of ground water pumped for agriculture, very rough estimates indicate that ground water supplied as much as 40 percent of Mendoza's and 60 percent of San Juan's crop water requirements during some recent years of unusually low surface water receipts.[14]

These estimates imply ground water use levels that are well within the known pumping capacity of the two provinces. Table 2.7 indicates the number of irrigation wells registered in Mendoza from 1959 to 1973. The number of wells rose 3.2-fold during this period to 15,418 wells in May 1973. From the end of 1966 to the end of 1971, a period of particularly low surface water receipts, the number of irrigation wells increased by 5,378. Official registrations in San Juan do not provide a reliable indication of the number of wells. As of May 11, 1972, there were only 2,462 wells registered with the Departamento de Hidráulica

[14] These estimates are based on rough calculations of crop water requirements, other water use, total surface water availability and irrigation efficiency rates of 60 percent for surface water. In comparison, an official of the national agricultural research and extension agency in San Juan indicated that during the last three years approximately two-thirds of San Juan's irrigation water came from the ground.

in San Juan, yet officials of this department estimated the actual number of irrigation wells in the province at about 7,000.

MAJOR FACTORS INFLUENCING RECENT AGRICULTURAL GROWTH

The combination of the increased demand for water, declining river flows, and increased reliance on ground water during the past decade or two have altered the costs of water to many farmers as well as the reliability of receiving the necessary quantity at the proper time. The quantity of river water received by farmers has been highly erratic and generally declining over the past twenty years. To eliminate this new risk element many farmers have drilled wells to tap the ground water. This alternative, however, substantially increases water costs. The next section examines the costs of surface and ground water in Mendoza. The effects of the changing sources of water on the demand for water and agricultural growth are examined in the following sections.

Water Costs: Surface versus Ground Water

There are wide variations in the private costs of both surface and ground water within Cuyo. While these variations complicate a cost comparison of the two sources, the cost variations within each water source are not so large as to blur the substantial cost differences between surface and ground water.[15]

Farmers possessing land with surface water rights pay an annual fee, based on the number and location of the hectares possessing rights but independent of the quantity of water received per hectare. While the administrative costs of the irrigation agency are divided among all lands with water rights, the charges for amortizing and maintaining the infrastructure are set such that a farmer pays only for the costs of dams and canals serving his land. The per hectare charge for a water right in Mendoza in 1971 varied from as little as 8.08 pesos in Uspallata to 98.54 pesos for some land benefiting from the recently constructed El Carrizal dam. This is a range of about 3.4 to 25.9 dollars per hectare.

A major problem in determining a farmer's per unit cost of surface water is that the cost is independent of the quantity of water received, and the quantity of water varies tremendously from year to year, from river to river, and even from canal to canal. A water right supposedly

---

[15] This section considers only the cost of water to the farmer. Social water costs are considered in chapters 5 and 6.

entitles a hectare to the amount of water required for the particular crop and soil in Mendoza and to 1.3 liters per second per hectare in San Juan. If these legal claims ever had any practical significance, it has certainly disappeared with the recent water shortages; some lands with so-called permanent water rights have gone long periods without receiving any water at all. Farmers have been forced to reduce the area under cultivation or to supplement their surface water with ground water.

Ground water provides a farmer much greater control, at least in the short run, over the quantity of water. The cost, however, is invariably high compared to surface water charges and is prohibitive for many farmers. Ground water costs are affected by many factors, such as drilling and pumping depths, farm size, availability of power, and the ability of a farmer to take advantage of government subsidies. Consequently, the costs differ widely among farms. This section focuses on the costs of ground water in the absence of government incentives; the impact of the government on ground water use is examined in the following chapter.

Table 2.8 presents estimates of the total and per hectare annual water costs on a 20-hectare farm pumping 10,330 m³ per year per hectare.[16] The water requirements are based on the annual and monthly requirements for grapes in Mendoza, as estimated by CIMALCO, with the assumption of a 70 percent farm irrigation efficiency. The estimates in Table 2.8 also assume a 30-meter pumping depth, a 10 percent discount rate, and a number of other assumptions detailed in the notes to the table. The table provides cost estimates under two alternative situations: nonpeak pumping into a storage pool and day pumping without a storage pool. When the existence of a storage pool is assumed, its cost is annualized and included in total water costs. Power rates for pumping from 11:30 P.M. to 7:30 A.M., 11:30 A.M. to 2:30 P.M., and all day on Sundays, which are referred to as nonpeak rates, are considerably less than rates during other hours, referred to as daytime rates. It is assumed that a month's water requirements can be satisfied at any time during that month. Thus, when nonpeak pumping is assumed, the lower rates are used to satisfy as much of a month's water requirements as possible with the assumed pump size. The alternative of no storage pool and nonpeak pumping would involve night irrigation and, therefore, higher labor costs. Since this alternative is seldom encountered in practice on a 20-hectare farm, it has not been included in Table 2.8.

Estimates of annual ground water costs in Table 2.8 range from $122 to $129 per hectare, levels more than 4.7 times the highest cost for

---

[16] While a smaller farm would be more representative of the average farm in the region, the 20-hectare farm is more representative of farms with irrigation wells, since there are substantial economies of scale with ground water use.

Table 2.8 Estimated Annual Ground Water Costs

(in 1969 dollars)[a]

	Cost for 20 hectares	Cost per hectare
Storage pool and nonpeak pumping		
Capital costs[b]	2,272	114
Energy costs[c]	296	15
Total costs	2,568	129
No storage and day pumping		
Capital costs[b]	1,771	89
Energy costs[c]	659	33
Total costs	2,430	122

Sources: The data for this table were collected by Roberto Cortegoso from the following sources:
Cost of drilling, pump, and legal work from Sanmartino ICFSA.
Cost of an electric motor from Siemens.
Cost of electric power installation from Ingeniera Constructora, Ing. Jorge Von Sprecher.

Note: Assumes farm with 20 cultivated hectares; 25-hp electric motor; 30-meter pumping depth; annual pumping requirements of 10,330 m³, drilling a 6-inch diameter well 220 meters deep. The water requirement is calculated to irrigate grapes in Mendoza with a 70 percent farm water use efficiency. While water is generally encountered long before 220 meters, a major drilling company in Mendoza feels the greater depth is frequently necessary to ensure good water quality.

[a] Prices are based on quotes obtained in Mendoza early in 1972. The 1972 peso costs were converted to 1969 dollars at the rate of 6.3 pesos to one dollar.

[b] Capital costs are broken down as follows: drilling and encasing a 220-meter well, $7,675; power installation, $2,779; a 1,000 m³ storage pool, $4,286; legal costs, $63. These items are amortized over twenty years at 10 percent for an annual cost of $1,732. The pump and a 25-hp electric motor cost $3,312. They are amortized over ten years for an annual cost of $540.

[c] Energy costs: The number of pumping hours required each month are calculated assuming a water flow of 80 m³ per hour. With a power consumption of 11 kw per hour, total power costs are calculated from the official table of power rates for Mendoza effective as of January 1972. The agricultural rates are fairly complex. There is a fixed monthly charge which depends on the power of the motor installed and charges per kilowatt consumed which are lower in the off-peak hours and decrease as the monthly consumption rises during peak hours.

surface water rights in 1971. A cost comparison per unit of water, however, is complicated by the unreliability of surface water receipts and surface water charges unrelated to the quantity of water received. Although some lands with water rights have received no water in recent years, most lands with surface water rights have some minimum quantity of water which normally arrives at the required irrigation times. While this amount of water is now seldom sufficient for irrigating all the land with water rights, if it is sufficient for 50 or even 25 percent of the land with water rights, the farmer's cost for this water is still substantially below the cost of ground water.

Tables 2.9 and 2.10 indicate the estimated impact of pumping depth

Table 2.9 Estimated Annual Water Costs as a Function of Pumping Depth[a]

	Pumping depth (meters)	Total water cost (1969 dollars)		Costs as % of costs at 30 meters		
		20 ha	per ha	Capital	Energy	Total
Small motor[b] *and well*	30	2,568	128	100.0	100.0	100.0
	50	2,970	149	112.5	139.9	115.6
	70	4,082	204	126.2	274.6	158.9
Large motor[c] *and well*	30	3,254	163	100.0	100.0	100.0
	50	3,683	184	110.1	134.3	113.2
	70	4,110	206	118.1	182.2	126.3
	90	4,562	228	128.2	222.2	140.2
	110	4,989	249	137.2	263.4	157.3

Sources: See Table 2.8.

[a] This table probably slightly underestimates the change in the cost as pumping distances change since amortization is not considered to vary as use intensity changes.

[b] Assumptions are identical to those in Table 2.8 for the alternative which includes a storage pool and nonpeak pumping except for changes due to variations in pumping depths. These changes include higher capital costs for more pipe and changes in hourly water flows and energy use. The hourly pumping flows are 80 and 51 m^3 for depths of 50 and 70 meters respectively, and the hourly power uses are 18 and 18.4 kilowatts for depths of 50 and 70 meters respectively.

[c] At the greater pumping depths a larger motor is required. The cost estimates for the section entitled "large motor and well" are based on a 60-hp electric motor and a well 10 inches in diameter for the first 60 meters and then 8 inches in diameter. As pumping depths increase by 20 meters from 30 to 110 meters, the water flows are 280, 204, 122, 91, and 75 m^3 per hour respectively, and power uses are 33.5, 44, 44.2, 44.2, and 44.2 kilowatts per hour respectively. All other assumptions are identical to those in the first part of the table.

and farm size on ground water costs. In comparison to the costs of irrigating 20 hectares with a pumping depth of 30 meters, the annual water costs are 16 percent higher at 50 meters and 60 percent higher at 70 meters. The per hectare costs of ground water are even more sensitive to farm size than to pumping depth. As a percentage of the costs on a 20-hectare farm, the per hectare ground water costs are from 300 to 378 percent on a 5-hectare farm and only 63 percent on a 36-hectare farm. Yet, in spite of these substantial economies of scale, the per hectare water cost of the 36-hectare farm using ground water would still be about four times the maximum cost of a surface water right in Mendoza. The importance of economies of scale has led to the emergence of ground water consortia. While these arrangements have enabled many smaller farmers to obtain ground water at attractive prices, a farmer can only participate in a consortium if the water can be distributed economically to his land.

Other things being equal, a larger well and motor become more attractive economically, if not essential, as the pumping depth and farm size

Table 2.10   Estimated Annual Water Costs as a Function of Farm Size[a]

Farm size (hectares cultivated)	Costs per hectare (1969 dollars)				% of per hectare costs on a 20-hectare farm			
			Energy				Energy	
	Capital	Fixed	Variable	Total	Capital	Fixed	Variable	Total
5	⎰354 ⎱454	22	9	⎰385 ⎱485	⎰312 ⎱400	400	100	⎰300 ⎱378
10	⎰177 ⎱227	11	9	⎰197 ⎱247	⎰156 ⎱200	200	100	⎰154 ⎱193
15	⎰118 ⎱151	7	9	⎰134 ⎱167	⎰104 ⎱133	133	100	⎰105 ⎱131
20	114	6	9	129	100	100	100	100
30	76	4	13	93	67	67	140	72
36	63	3	15	81	56	56	164	63

[a] The largest farm size considered, 36 hectares, is the maximum that can be supplied the assumed quantity of water with the 25-hp electric motor. The costs for the farms of 20 hectares and over assume the use of a storage pool and nonpeak pumping when possible. For the farms of 5, 10, and 15 hectares nonpeak pumping is assumed, and two estimates of capital and total costs are given. The first estimate assumes no storage pool while the second assumes the same size storage pool found on the larger farms. The higher cost estimates undoubtedly overstate economies of scale since amortization is not considered to vary with intensity of use and a single pool size, based on the requirements of 20 hectares, is used for all farm sizes. The lower estimates may understate the economies of scale since there is no allowance for the higher labor costs or inconvenience of irrigating just during the periods of low energy rates. All other assumptions and the sources of the basic data are the same as in Table 2.8.

increase. With a small well and motor and a pumping depth of 30 meters, 36 hectares is the maximum area that can be irrigated with a 70 percent farm water use efficiency. However, with a larger well and motor and pumping depths of about 30 meters, the minimum per hectare ground water costs are probably not reached until a well is irrigating 50 to 60 hectares.[17] If the pumping depth exceeds 70 meters, the larger well and motor are required for irrigating 20 hectares.

If a farm dependent on ground water is not fully utilizing its pump capacity, the marginal cost of pumping more water is relatively small. For example, if we alter the irrigation efficiency of the hypothetical farm considered in Table 2.8 from 70 to 40 percent, the total cost of the water to the farm would rise only 13.1 percent. In other words, 75 per-

[17] On-farm water distribution losses are an important limiting factor to the extent of economies of scale. These losses can vary substantially from farm to farm depending on the gradient of the land, type of canals, and soil. The estimate that a single well could efficiently irrigate as much as 50 to 60 hectares assumes that the land has been leveled, and is based on the actual investment project of a company planning to plant and irrigate about 350 hectares in Mendoza with ground water.

cent more water could be obtained with an increase in annual water costs of about 13 percent.

Marginal Water Costs and Ground Water Use

To maximize profits a farmer should use ground water to the point where his marginal costs for the water are equal to his marginal revenue from the water.[18] The relevant marginal costs and revenues vary substantially depending upon whether a farmer already has land cleared and planted to permanent crops and an irrigation well with excess pumping capacity. Consequently, an individual's and a region's aggregate derived demand for ground water will vary tremendously depending upon initial conditions. It is useful to distinguish among at least three important ground water demand situations which we might refer to as the "long-run" situation in which all costs are variable, the "rescue" demand when ground water becomes essential for preventing the loss of a permanent crop, and the "short-run" demand for ground water once the well, pump, and motor have been fully installed.

The long-run situation refers to the farmer considering the cultivation of land which would require the drilling of a well. In this case all costs are variable and relevant for the derivation of the farmer's derived demand for ground water. Thus, the costs of land clearing and leveling, crop planting and cultivating, as well as the costs of the well, pump, motor, and energy, should be taken into account and balanced against the expected revenues from the investment. As was noted above the investment required to pump ground water is substantial and greatly increases water costs as compared to the cost of surface water. However, when these costs are annualized over their productive lives and treated as part of total farming costs, which is relevant for the long-run situation, ground water costs are not necessarily one of the most important cost components. For instance, the annualized cost of ground water on a 20-hectare farm (see Table 2.8) amounts to only about 5 percent of the costs incurred in planting and cultivating grapes for three years (see Table 6.1), the gestation period for significant production. The expected price for grapes and the availability of credit are likely to be more important factors in the investment decision on such a farm than the cost increase resulting from a dependence on ground water. However, because of the economies of scale in ground water use, annualized ground water costs are likely to exceed 15 percent of total crop costs for a 5-hectare vineyard. On the smaller farm the higher ground water

[18] The second and third order conditions for a maximum are ignored in the following discussion.

costs are likely to become a major, if not decisive, factor in the investment decision.

The "rescue" demand for ground water emerges when ground water means the difference between saving or losing permanent crops. In this case all the planting and prior cultivation costs are sunk and, therefore, irrelevant for the decision to install a well. The ground water investment should depend on a comparison of the present value of costs associated with the rescue, i.e., water costs plus the additional cultivation and harvest costs associated with continued production, and the present value of the expected gross revenue from the crops that could be saved by the ground water. Even for a 5-hectare farm the annualized ground water costs probably amount to less than 20 percent of the initial cost and only about 40 percent of the average annual revenue of a productive vineyard. Unless a vineyard is nearing the end of its productive life, it is unlikely that expected product prices would fall to such low levels as to make the "rescue" irrigation well uneconomic for a vineyard that would otherwise lose 5 hectares or more.[19] Consequently, in such a case the crucial factor in the investment decision is not the expected economic return from the investment but the availability of credit.

The "short-run" demand situation emerges when a farmer has a well, pump, and motor with excess capacity above that needed to reduce the risk of low surface water flows. In this case the marginal water cost is just the cost of the additional power required to pump one more unit of water. On land that is already cultivated such a farmer should apply water to the crops up to the point where the marginal water cost equals the marginal revenue from the last unit of water. If a farmer is considering expanding his cultivated land, the relevant water cost to include in the investment decision is the energy costs of pumping longer hours and the increased risk of reducing the reserve capacity of the pump. In this case planting and cultivation costs are marginal and, therefore, relevant for the decision to plant more land.

When a pump is being operated at capacity there is a discontinuity in the water cost function. The relevant marginal water cost should take into account the cost of either a new well or a conversion to a larger well, pump, and motor. Depending on the circumstances, the decision criteria in this situation are similar to the "long-run" or "rescue" demands for ground water discussed above.

The "long-run" and "rescue" demand situations affect the number of irrigation wells, while the "short-run" demand situation affects the quantity of water pumped from each well. In the "short-run" case, which assumes that the number of wells is fixed, individual ground water

[19] See Chapter 6, p. 115.

demand curves have been statistically estimated.[20] The short-run aggregate derived demand would be the summation over all price levels of each individual demand for ground water. A long-run aggregate demand for ground water must allow for new investment. In general the expected return from an irrigation well will be higher and, therefore, the investment more likely to be undertaken, the greater the relative strength of the "rescue" component in justifying the well. But in terms of actual ground water use, wells which are viewed primarily as protection against low surface water receipts will have a lower utilization rate during years of average or above average surface water receipts. This is true for two reasons: the "rescue" demand is more likely to result in wells on smaller farms where excess pumping capacity is likely even in dry years; and since these wells supplement surface water, farmers will want excess pumping capacity in average years to be able to compensate for the years with low surface water receipts.

Decisions to invest in ground water irrigation have frequently been based on a mixture of the "long-run" motivation to expand cultivated land and as a hedge for existing crops against the risk of low surface water receipts. The importance of the "rescue" demand in ground water investment increased steadily from about 1950 to 1967, when its importance rose sharply with the fall in surface water flows. It was the strength of the "rescue" demand for ground water which accounted for the rapid rise in ground water investment from 1969 to 1971 despite relatively low grape prices. The importance of the "rescue" demand in the drilling of irrigation wells during this period was evident from both the rapid increase in the number of wells in the late 1960s, when total cultivated land changed very little, and the substantial reduction in pumping following the unusually high surface water flows during the 1972–73 agricultural year. The influence of the very favorable grape and wine prices on the long-run demand for water was evident in the continuation of high rates of investment in irrigation wells despite the existence of excess pumping capacity.

Water and Agricultural Growth

As we might expect, changes in the costs and certainty of water receipts have been reflected in the overall rate of agricultural growth and in the overall crop composition. This section examines the relation between agricultural development and water scarcity where an increase in water scarcity refers to the combination of an increase in the demand for water relative to the supply of surface water, an increase in the uncer-

---

[20] See the discussion in Chapter 6, p. 120.

tainty of receiving adequate surface water, and higher average water costs associated with an increase in relative ground water use.

Land planted to grapes from 1900 to 1936, a period when surface water was generally more than sufficient for the region's requirements, increased at an average geometric rate of 4.6 percent per year in Mendoza compared to the 3.0 percent annual increase since 1947–48. Differences in the respective growth rates of total cultivated land were probably much greater since in recent years much of the increase in the land planted to grapes has been at the expense of the grains, while during the first third of this century the increase in grapes was complementary to and not largely a substitute for other crops.

The cropping patterns two decades ago in both Mendoza and San Juan reflected situations in which farmers viewed water as not especially scarce or expensive. This is particularly evident in the amount of land devoted to alfalfa in both provinces. During the 1947–48 crop year about 21 percent of Mendoza's cultivated land was planted to alfalfa, which requires nearly 50 percent more water per hectare than grapes and has an average gross monetary return less than one-fourth the per hectare return to grapes.[21] Consequently, alfalfa's gross return per unit of water is less than 15 percent of the comparable return to grapes in Mendoza. In 1954–55 San Juan had about 24 percent of its cultivated land under alfalfa, which has an average gross monetary return per unit of water of less than 8 percent of the return to grapes in the province.

Agricultural growth in both provinces during the past twenty years or so has clearly reflected an increase in the scarcity of water. Not only has the entire increase in land been in permanent crops with a relatively high return to water, but there has been a major shift out of grains and into grapes. On an aggregate basis the impact of water scarcity on recent growth is evident from the fact that agricultural production grew at much more rapid rates than did water use. In Mendoza from 1947–48 to 1969–70 the estimated value of agricultural production rose about 68 percent, while estimated irrigation water use rose only 19 percent. In San Juan from 1954–55 to 1971–72 estimated irrigation water use actually declined 6 percent, while the estimated value of agricultural production rose 27 percent. Yet despite these trends, current cropping patterns reveal that many farmers still view water as a

---

[21] These returns to alfalfa are based on growers' sale prices. These prices, however, may not adequately reflect the value of alfalfa to many farmers. Alfalfa is sometimes planted in Cuyo because of its value for preparing the land for other crops or as an input for the dairy industry. For example, before planting grapes in many areas, it is useful to plant alfalfa for about three years in order to add nitrogen to and clean out salts from the soils. Nevertheless, this is an economical means of improving soil productivity only if water is cheap.

Table 2.11   Average Annual River Flows
(1960–61 to 1966–67 average = 100)

River	1967–68 to 1970–71	1971–72
Mendoza	76.9	83.7
Upper Tunuyán	72.2	94.3
Atuel	75.0	92.7
Diamante	59.0	72.1
San Juan	43.5	39.7
Jachal	66.4	65.1
Total[a]	63.7	72.8

Source: Table 2.6 indicates the source of the annual river flow data.

[a] This row is based on the aggregate flow of the six rivers.

relatively inexpensive input. This is evidenced by the 52,700 hectares planted to alfalfa in the region in 1970–71.

An earlier section of this chapter[22] indicated that agricultural growth in Cuyo was considerably higher from 1960–61 to 1966–67 than in the following four years. These contrasting growth performances along with the revival of growth in 1971–72 and the expected continuation of the expansion during 1972–73 primarily reflect changes in total water availability.

The interruption in agricultural growth in Cuyo starting in 1967–68 was a forced adjustment to a very sharp decline in surface water receipts. Table 2.11 indicates that the annual flows of Cuyo's major rivers during the 1967–68 to 1970–71 period averaged from only 43.5 to 76.9 percent of the 1960–61 to 1966–67 average flows. The abruptness of this decline superimposed on an agriculture which was previously fully utilizing its surface water required some painful and costly readjustments. Investment which might have gone for an expansion of cultivated lands was channeled into irrigation wells, and the planting of annual crops was curtailed in order to save more water for permanent crops. Total cultivated land in Cuyo declined slightly from 1966–67 to 1970–71, and land planted to annual crops declined 5.6 percent in Mendoza and 34.3 percent in San Juan.[23] The percentage declines in both surface water flows and land cultivated were greater in San Juan than in Mendoza.

Because of the key role of grapes in Cuyo's agricultural growth and overall prosperity, the economic position of the grape growers was an important factor in the region's capacity to compensate for the water deficits in the late 1960s. High returns to grapes would have meant more capital for investment in ground water irrigation and more incen-

[22] See pp. 17–19.
[23] See Table 2.5.

tive to maintain and expand grape lands. The grape growers, however, were unusually hard pressed from 1968 to 1970, and their problems were only in part due to reduced production and surface water receipts. In Mendoza grape yields from 1968 to 1970 ranged from 92 to 98 percent of the levels estimated from a least-squares regression of yields from 1948 to 1971. In San Juan the water scarcity had a much more pronounced effect on grape production, and actual yields in 1968, 1969, and 1970 were only 91, 70, and 78 percent respectively of the levels estimated from a least-squares trend of actual yields from 1953 to 1971. While the relatively low yields are not unexpected in view of the magnitude of the water scarcity, it is surprising that growers were also confronted with unusually low grape prices from 1968 to 1970.[24] Average annual grape prices from 1968 to 1970 deflated by a cost of living index were almost 24 percent less than the average price from 1960 to 1967. The combined effect of the unusually low grape prices and production levels from 1968 to 1970 resulted in gross annual grape sales that were only 73 percent of the 1960 to 1967 average.

The accumulation of problems confronting grape growers after the 1967 harvest undoubtedly slowed the region's adjustment to surface water shortages. Nevertheless, there was a sharp rise in irrigation wells starting in 1969. The decision to drill was easily made when the alternative meant the loss of one's entire investment in permanent crops. In addition, government credit, tax, and energy pricing policies enabled many farmers to greatly reduce their costs of ground water.[25] In Mendoza the rate of investment in ground water equipment as measured by the number of wells rose 74 percent in 1969, an additional 73 percent in 1970, and another 39 percent in 1971. The annual increase in irrigation pumps averaged 383 from 1960 to 1967 and 1,473 from 1969 to 1971.[26]

[24] The positive relation between growers' prices and production is surprising in view of the monopolistic nature of Cuyo's grape-wine industry and the inelasticity of the country's demand for grapes. Cuyo produces over 90 percent of Argentina's grapes, and the country has been virtually isolated from foreign grape and wine markets. Thus, the demand for Cuyo's grapes should be fairly inelastic. However, in order to explain the simultaneous relatively low price and production levels from 1968 to 1970, prior production and stock levels and government policies must be taken into account. While Argentina's 1966 grape harvest was their highest to that date, their 1967 crop was nearly 33 percent higher. The provincial government of Mendoza maintains some control over the prices of grapes and wine by operating the world's largest winery, Giol, and by setting minimum prices for grapes. It was in part through the efforts of Giol that the 1967 crop was absorbed at fairly good average growers' prices. The resulting stock levels of wine, however, limited Giol's ability to support future grape prices and depressed grape prices during subsequent years.

[25] The impact of government policies on ground water costs are examined in the next chapter.

[26] The number of irrigation wells in Mendoza are presented in Table 2.7, p. 24.

Table 2.12 Estimated Irrigation Water Availability in Mendoza

(in cubic hectometers)

| Year | Surface Water | | Ground Water | | Total Water |
	River flows[a]	Potential deliveries to crops[b]	Potential pumping[c]	Potential deliveries to crops[d]	Potential deliveries to crops
1959–60	4,694	2,816	700	490	3,306
1960–61	4,083	2,450	737	516	2,966
1961–62	5,133	3,080	789	552	3,632
1962–63	3,500	2,100	829	580	2,680
1963–64	5,565	3,339	881	617	3,956
1964–65	3,133	1,880	932	652	2,532
1965–66	4,870	2,922	988	692	3,614
1966–67	4,268	2,561	1,062	743	3,304
1967–68	3,363	2,018	1,129	790	2,808
1968–69	2,450	1,470	1,200	840	2,310
1969–70	3,963	2,378	1,323	926	3,304
1970–71	2,573	1,544	1,537	1,076	2,620
1971–72	3,706	2,224	1,834	1,284	3,508

Sources: See Table 2.6 for the source of annual river flow data. The number of pumps are given in Table 2.7.

[a] These are the sums of the flows of the Mendoza, Upper Tunuyán, Diamante, and Atuel rivers. These flows are measured above the principal irrigation zones.

[b] This assumes that 60 percent of the river water arrives at the plant. During this period virtually all the river water was diverted for irrigation.

[c] This assumes that every 6.9 wells pump 1 hm³ per year. This was derived from the assumptions that the average pump produces 80 m³ per hour and is operated 12 hours per day for 150 days per year. Since many wells are to supplement surface water, the actual pumping per well would be inversely related to the quantity of surface water.

[d] This assumes that 70 percent of ground water pumped arrives at the plant.

In order to provide an idea of Mendoza's ability to adjust to the declining river flows, Table 2.12 estimates the relative changes in the combined availability of surface and ground irrigation water from 1959–60 to 1971–72. The table takes account of most, but not all, of the province's river flows and is necessarily dependent on several assumptions, explained in the table, regarding average water use efficiencies for ground and surface water and average water pumped per well. While the estimates neglect the important problems of the timing of the water availability and its distribution among the cultivated lands, they provide a rough idea of the relative changes in the overall availability of irrigation water in Mendoza. Making allowance for ground water, Mendoza's crops received an estimated 15 percent less water per year during the 1967–68 to 1970–71 agricultural years than from 1960–61 to 1966–67. In 1971–72, however, the estimated availability of irrigation water in Mendoza was 8 percent above the 1960–61 to 1966–67 average. The improved water situation combined with grape prices nearly 50 percent above the 1960 to 1967 average provided favorable conditions for a renewed agricultural expansion in Mendoza starting in 1971–72.

The declines in surface water starting in 1967–68 were much more pronounced and traumatic in San Juan than in Mendoza. Unfortunately the lack of reliable time series data on the number of irrigation wells prevent reasonable estimates of the relative changes in total irrigation water for San Juan. It is evident, however, that San Juan's adjustment required much greater changes in cropping patterns to reduce crop water requirements and an even greater reliance on ground water than in Mendoza. Nevertheless, in 1971–72 San Juan was able to reverse the four-year decline in total cultivated area despite the fact that the 1971–72 flows of San Juan's two major rivers were actually somewhat below the already depressed average levels of the preceding four years.

Conditions in both provinces were particularly favorable for an expansion of cultivated land at the start of the 1972–73 agricultural year. The snowfall in the Andes during the winter of 1972 promised plentiful surface water for the coming irrigation season, and the provincial governments in Mendoza and San Juan had demonstrated a strong determination to maintain relatively high grape and wine prices. The prospect of ample water and high grape prices stimulated record grape planting in both provinces. Preliminary data indicate the addition of more than 16,000 hectares to Cuyo's vineyards from January 1972 to January 1973.[27] This would represent the largest annual increase in Cuyo's history and an annual rise of 6 percent, well above historical growth rates.

By the end of the 1973 harvest, conditions were still favorable for continued agricultural expansion. Cuyo's 1972–73 river flows were the highest since 1953–54, and with strong assistance from the provincial governments in Cuyo, grapes were again marketed at very favorable prices. Even if river flows continue at the high 1972–73 levels, virtually all new plantings will use ground water. Moreover, in the absence of a sharp decline in surface water, future investment in new irrigation wells can be expected to be reflected in an expansion of cultivated land in both provinces and not just a recuperation of past water deficiencies.

SUMMARY

About the mid-1940s the combination of agricultural growth and declining river flows eliminated the surpluses which had long provided Cuyo's

[27] Preliminary data from the files of the Instituto Nacional de Vitivinicultura in Mendoza indicate an increase of nearly 13,500 hectares of grapes in Mendoza, and data from the office of Estimaciones Agropecuarias, Ministerio Agricultura Nacional in San Juan indicate an increase of about 2,700 hectares of grapes in San Juan.

farmers with ample water. Demands on the region's surface water have continued to grow relative to the available supply during the past three decades. Consequently, farmers have been confronted with the alternative of remaining dependent on an increasingly erratic and generally declining supply of surface water or, for those farmers able to afford it, making the costly investments required to use ground water.

These changes in the costs, certainty, and sources of water receipts have been reflected in the overall rate and sources of agricultural growth within the region. Data limitations prevent any in-depth analysis of the sources and rate of agricultural growth until the last several decades. It is apparent, however, that the expansion of land and water use during the five or six decades after the completion of the railroad between Cuyo and Buenos Aires in the mid-1880s was much faster than it has been since the disappearance of unutilized surface water in the middle to late 1940s. Total cultivated land in Cuyo grew at about 1 percent per annum from 1947–48 to 1969–70, which is probably about one-fourth of the growth rate over the previous fifty years.

The growth in the value of agricultural production was also reduced in recent decades although not as drastically as growth of cultivated land; the increased value of water induced changes which led to substantial increases in the value of agricultural output per unit of land and water. Value per hectare increased by 1.3 percent per annum in Mendoza from 1948 to 1970 and 1.4 percent per annum in San Juan from 1955 to 1972. However, only about one-fourth of these yield changes can be attributed to technological change. Changes in the relative crop composition accounted for about three-fourths of the change in the value of production per hectare and over 50 percent of the total growth in the region's value of agricultural production. The most striking aspect of the change in the relative product mix has been the relative increase in permanent crops, especially grapes. Grapes, fruit trees, and olives accounted for all of the growth in the value of agricultural production over these periods, and currently over three-fourths of the region's cultivated land is devoted to these crops.

The drought occurring between 1967 and 1970 brought agricultural expansion to a temporary halt in Cuyo. The abruptness of the decline in surface water receipts required some painful and costly adjustments of an agriculture which was previously fully utilizing its surface water. By 1972, however, the region had fully recovered and the combination of high grape prices, relatively large river flows, and a greatly expanded ground water pumping capacity provided very favorable conditions for a renewed, rapid expansion of cultivated land and agricultural water use.

the role of government 3

Until recently both the national and regional governments have played primarily passive roles in Cuyo's development. While the provincial governments have long regulated water use through legal restrictions and investments in the water distribution system, their role had been largely limited to those traditionally reserved for governments in *laissez-faire* economies—i.e., establishing order and bringing efficiency to an area where central management and ownership are essential to capture economies of scale.

The governments have assumed a much more active role in Cuyo's economy since water shortages have threatened the region's agricultural prosperity. Control of surface water assumed a new dimension and importance as legal claims and crop requirements greatly exceeded the available supply. Large-scale government investments to increase the efficiency of water distribution through dams or lined irrigation canals and projects to increase usable water sources, such as government irrigation wells and a proposed interbasin water transfer, assumed greater importance as rescue operations than they had had as growth stimulators. Such investments are greatly enlarging the financial outlays of the government as well as enhancing their ability to control inter- and intra-annual water flows. Moreover, within the last decade, credit, tax, and price policies have become very important tools in the official efforts to offset the existence and consequences of recent water shortages.

This chapter describes the direct government controls over water use and the policies which indirectly affect a farmer's incentive to make water extraction or water saving investments. The descriptions of government water regulations, credit, tax, and pricing policies are essential for evaluating the future implications of current growth trends and investment incentives in Chapter 4, the efficiency of water use patterns in Chapter 5, and the profitability of alternative on-farm investments in Chapter 6. The water infrastructure investments being undertaken and proposed are examined in Chapter 7.

REGULATION OF WATER USE [1]

Surface Water

Surface water, except in the unusual case in which its entire course lies within the land of a single owner, is public property and subject to government regulation. The regulation and use of an intraprovincial river or stream falls within the jurisdiction of provincial law, while a river or stream flowing through two or more provinces is also subject to national law. With the exception of the Grande River,[2] which is currently not used for any significant irrigation in Mendoza, the use of Cuyo's rivers is subject to provincial law.

[1] Much of the information in this section on water law and administration comes from Comisión Económica para la America Latina y Consejo Federal de Inversiones, *Los recursos hidráulicos de Argentina, Análisis y programación tentativa de su desarrollo*, 1969, Buenos Aires, (edición CFI), Vols. 6 and 7, and Guillermo J. Cano, *Reseña crítica de la legislación y administración de aguas de Mendoza* (Mendoza: n.p., 1967). As much more information is available for Mendoza, the discussion in this section focuses on that province.

[2] The Grande River originates in the southwest of the province of Mendoza and flows into the Colorado River, which passes through five provinces and is one of Argentina's major rivers. The use of the waters of the Colorado River has become a major national issue and is the subject of a major research project, authorized and financed by the Argentine government. Although Mendoza is currently making little use of its waters, there is considerable talk of an interbasin transfer from the Grande River into Mendoza's southern irrigated zone, and there is consternation in Mendoza that current downstream users will argue that they have a prior claim on the water because of current use patterns. Proposals for using water from the Grande River in Mendoza are examined in Chapter 7.

The legal use of public surface water in Cuyo requires a government concession. Water rights are attached to and inseparable from the land. The law carries this principal even to the unenforceable extreme that the landowner may not transfer the irrigation water from one part of his land to another.[3] These concessions have been the major means of controlling and, in recent years, rationing the use of surface water.

Mendoza's 1884 water law was the initial attempt to control agricultural water use. Under this law a landowner could register his land with the provincial irrigation agency and seek a permanent right to use river water. Between 1885 and 1887 a total of 209,018 hectares were granted water rights in Mendoza; as of 1886, 56,000 hectares possessed government water concessions in San Juan. Currently there are about 572,000 hectares in Mendoza and 167,000 hectares in San Juan with some legal rights to surface water for irrigation.

Cano describes two stages in Mendoza's water legislation after 1884.[4] Water legislation during the first stage, which ended in 1927, encouraged greater water use. In order to maintain control over and encourage the use of water, water concessions were granted subject to the condition that they would be utilized within a specified period, usually five years. In fact, however, water concessions were not revoked for lack of use, and the number of hectares with water concessions has generally exceeded the amount of land cultivated by a substantial margin. In Mendoza in 1929 the number of hectares with water rights exceeded by about 60 percent the number of hectares cultivated. Threats to void unutilized water rights were negated first by an extension of the time period for utilization and then by lack of enforcement. Even land taxes attaching a higher value to land with water rights have not prompted widespread renunciation of unutilized water concessions.

It seems likely that the initial water legislation was also motivated, at least in part, by a desire among the region's landowners to solidify their control over the region's basic agricultural resources before the start of a period of rapid immigration. The first extensive laws requiring water users to obtain government concessions coincided with the completion of the railroad which brought an influx of immigrants to the Cuyo region. Many of the immigrants came from the grape-growing regions of Italy and France, contributing much of the technical knowledge and labor for the first major growth of Cuyo's grape-wine industry. Initially, the immigrants planted and cared for the grapes of the Spanish descendants who owned the irrigable land and controlled the provincial

---

[3] The inseparability of water rights and land is included even in the Mendoza Constitution of 1916.

[4] Cano, *Reseña crítica*, pp. 20–21.

governments empowered to grant water rights in Cuyo. Only gradually were they able to obtain their own land with water rights.[5]

A 1927 Mendoza water law designed to stabilize and consolidate water rights ended government efforts to encourage greater water use and introduced what Cano calls the second stage in Mendoza's water legislation. The change in legislative emphasis was prompted by the uncertainties in the prerogatives attached to a water right that had been created by prior legislation and the impending water shortages.

The prerogatives attached to a water right became clouded with the emergence of various categories of concessions. The situation became particularly complex in Mendoza. Provisions that the initial water concessions were contingent on use led to uncertainty regarding the nature of the rights attached to many lands. The 1916 Mendoza Constitution stated that until the flow of the river had been measured, any additional water concessions were provisional and had to be approved by two-thirds of the legislature. After the flow of the river had been measured, the technical conditions of which were not specified, water concessions could be granted by a majority of the legislature. Presumably the status of any new water concessions would reflect the difference between the estimated safe yield of the river and prior claims on that water. Land with a provisional water right supposedly would receive water only after all the requirements of the permanent concessions had been fulfilled. Mendoza in 1917 instituted a complicated scale of water rights, whereby the claim on the available water varied according to the date of cultivation and location. This scale increased the uncertainty of the nature and permanence of the concession and, thus, created instability in the value of the land.

In an effort to stabilize land prices and consolidate water concessions, the 1927 Mendoza law ended the stipulation that the rights were dependent on use. Subsequent legislation and administrative rulings of the water agencies simplified further the differences among water concessions. There are currently two major types of concessions for farmers to use public surface water: permanent concessions called *definitivos* in Mendoza and *permanentes* in San Juan, and provisional concessions called *eventuales* in Mendoza and *accidentales* in San Juan. Legal dis-

[5] Luis Campoy has studied the change in land ownership in Mendoza between *criollos,* Spanish descendants born in Argentina, and *no-criollos,* other European and Asian immigrants and their descendants. Based on a random sample of 9 percent of the land with permanent water rights from the Mendoza River, Campoy found that in the nineteenth century 100 percent was owned by *criollos,* while in 1960 82 percent of the same land was owned by *no-criollos.* The average farm size over this period fell from 95 to 10.5 hectares. (Campoy, "Grupos culturales criollo y no-criollo, Disponibilidad para el cambio y niveles de movilización y desarrollo," Mendoza, mimeographed, 1971, UNC).

tinctions among concessions within these groups have been eliminated. Although the provisional concessions are legally entitled to water only after the permanent grants have been satisfied, in practice this distinction has been completely eliminated in San Juan and nearly so in Mendoza. In Mendoza the available river water is distributed among all the *definitivo* and *eventual* concessions such that a hectare with an *eventual* concession receives 80 percent of the water of a hectare with a *definitivo* concession.[6]

While there has been much less doubt regarding the priority of various water claims during the past two decades, an increase in the demand for surface water relative to its supply has generated doubts regarding the amount of water that will be received by each claimant. Provincial irrigation agencies presumably ration the available water such that each farmer receives water in proportion to the number of hectares with equivalent water rights. In Mendoza a water right was initially for a maximum of 1.5 liters per second per hectare, which over four months would be about 15,700 m³, more than twice the requirement of grapes. This quantity was seldom received or needed. In 1907 a Mendoza law put the quantity of the water right on a need basis. Land with water rights would supposedly receive the quantity of water necessary, taking into account the nature of the soil and crop. In San Juan a 1928 law set the quantity of the water right at 1.3 liters per second per hectare. Legal pronouncements regarding the quantity of water due concession holders in both provinces, however, have become meaningless in recent years since the river flows have not been sufficient to satisfy all users with legal claims to water. The irrigation agencies have not been able to alter significantly the temporal flow of water for irrigation purposes;[7] consequently, water receipts per hectare have fluctuated widely from year to year as well as from river to river. Moreover, there have also

[6] In Mendoza in 1966 there were 354,868 hectares with *definitivo* concessions and 168,396 hectares with *eventual* concessions. In addition there were 44,010 hectares with rights to drainage water, and 4,693 hectares with more tenuous claims to surface water. Drainage water is considered public property, and its use is supposedly controlled by provincial law. A Mendoza law requires farmers to install drainage; one-third the cost is paid by the farmer doing the draining and two-thirds by the farmer receiving the water. These laws, however, have never been well enforced. Public and nonagricultural water use concessions are also set in hectare equivalents. In 1966 in Mendoza public irrigation and potable water requirements had concessions for 13,712 hectares, and industrial users had concessions for 583 hectares. In San Juan as of 1968 126,879 hectares had *permanent* concessions and 40,108 *accidental*.

[7] Currently there are two dams for controlling the temporal flow of irrigation river water in the region: Valle Grande on the Atuel River and El Carrizal on the Tunuyán River. Construction has started on dams on the San Juan and Diamante rivers and plans exist for dams on the Mendoza and Jachal rivers. These projects are examined in Chapter 7.

been substantial variations within a year in the water receipts of land with equivalent concessions from the same river. For example, in recent years some farmers with *permanent* water rights have gone a year or more without receiving any water. The location of one's land within the water distribution system has become a more important determinant of the quantity of water received than whether the concessions are *permanentes* or *eventuales*.

Provincial control of surface water use has been weakened by illegal water use. While water concessions were initially granted free of charge, inconvenience or ignorance probably led many users to leave their land unregistered. Since surface water was originally abundant in relation to demand, many farmers may not have anticipated the conditions which now give the water concessions considerable value. In addition, land taxes and charges levied on registered water users by the provincial governments may have deterred farmers from seeking official concessions. Sanctions for illegal water use were gradually introduced, but enforcement was weak and fines were light. And when illegal water use was discovered, legislators generally legalized the use, especially if permanent crops were involved. In retrospect, one of the surest methods of obtaining water rights after the original grants were made has been to use the water illegally for permanent crops. At various times laws have been passed enabling such clandestine users to obtain water rights with the payment of only a nominal charge.

Control of water use became much tighter and penalties for illegal use much stiffer about 1950. The policy change roughly coincided with the date when surface water could no longer fully satisfy the requirements of farmers possessing water rights. The change in the relation between the supply and demand for water made government control a more urgent task.

Recent water shortages have revived questions regarding the status of unutilized lands with water rights. The number of hectares with water rights as a percentage of the amount of irrigated land was about 200 in San Juan in 1960 and about 160 in Mendoza during the 1960s. Since some of the irrigated land used ground water, the relation between the rights to and availability of surface water was substantially worse than indicated by these percentages. The existence of these so-called dormant water rights adds to the uncertainty regarding the amount of surface water a farmer can expect to receive and has created a sensitive political issue in recent years.

The impact of recent water shortages in Cuyo has been most acute in, but not limited to, the agricultural sector. Mendoza water law establishes priorities among water users; legally, all users within the higher priority categories receive water before any users in lower categories are satisfied. The categories in order of priority are: (1) domestic users, (2) railroads, (3) irrigation, (4) industry, and (5) swimming and other pools. Within each category the law grants preference first to the uses of greatest social value and second according to chronology of use. If the priorities were strictly followed, industrial and pool water would have been completely cut off from surface water in recent years since all the legal claims to irrigation water were not being fully satisfied. The law, however, was not strictly followed. Moreover, a strict compliance with the law would make only minor additions to irrigation water use since farmers currently consume about 95 percent of the region's water and many industrial uses are not totally consuming in that much water is reusable.

Economies of scale in water distribution have been achieved through government construction of irrigation infrastructure and laws preventing unnecessary duplication of canals. Water recipients pay the full costs of these works plus the administrative costs of the provincial irrigation agencies. The user costs are set in proportion to the size of a farmer's water concessions and the length of the canals leading to his land.

The maintenance and administration of all but the major irrigation canals are handled by the water users subject to the supervision and enforcement of the provincial water agencies. The farmers elect the authorities to control the secondary and smaller canals, and in 1960 there were 554 administrative canal units in Mendoza. This administrative decentralization is considered fundamental to the efficiency of Mendoza's water administration.[8]

Ground Water

In contrast to the extensive controls over surface water, ground water use is virtually unregulated. The only constraint on ground water use in Cuyo has been an individual's ability to undertake the substantial financial investments required to pump it.[9] This constraint has hardly deterred a rapid growth in ground water use from the early 1950s to recent withdrawal rates exceeding the average natural recharge to the aquifers.

While anyone may still withdraw ground water, a 1967 revision in the Civil Code made ground water part of the public domain. This legal revision foreshadows almost inevitable future controls on ground water use. Currently, before drilling a well for irrigation purposes in Mendoza, a farmer must, by law, describe the project publicly to give third parties

[8] Cano, *Reseña crítica,* p. 39.
[9] The impact of government policies on ground water costs is examined later in this chapter.

an opportunity to consider its effects and make objections; once the well is drilled the farmer is obliged to give details such as pump size, quantity of water extracted, and pumping depths to the authorities. In fact, however, there are no restrictions on drilling and pumping, and there is no enforcement of the requirement to inform the authorities annually of changes in pumping data. Pumps for potable water are subject to no regulation. Government controls over and knowledge of water use are even less in San Juan. This laxity is demonstrated by the fact that as of May 1972 only about 30 percent of the estimated number of irrigation wells were even registered with the relevant provincial agency. While a clandestine well can be closed down or the owner fined, there has been no attempt to do so. Currently there is a disincentive to register wells in San Juan since one pays a fine of 50 pesos (about 5 dollars) plus an annual charge for a registered well.

Water Planning

There is no overall plan for the development and use of water resources in either Mendoza or San Juan. The absence of such a plan is evident in the general lack of coordination among agencies using and controlling water in the region and in government policies and investment proposals which fail to consider their full ramifications and alternatives.[10] The immediate consequences of the lack of planning include weakened government control over and a relatively low efficiency level for water use. The longer-run consequences could include large investment losses and a serious disruption of the regional economy due to a substantial reduction in water availability.

Mendoza's irrigation department, Departamento General de Irrigación (DGI), has exclusive autonomy over surface water irrigation within the province. Their authority, however, does not extend to water in general. They have little control over ground water use other than the ability to drill their own wells and pump ground water to reinforce canal flows. Neither the irrigation department nor any other agency has the authority to coordinate the use of ground and surface irrigation water to reduce total irrigation costs. Moreover, there is little coordination among the various types of users receiving water from the same source. Two provincial agencies, DGI and the Dirección Provincial de Minas y Geología (DMG), have legal responsibilities over ground water use; yet there are no regular bonds between the two agencies, and neither agency exercises any real control over ground water use. Potable water use is

[10] The comments on the lack of coordination among various water users are based primarily on Cano, *Reseña crítica*, pp. 51–53, and CEPLA and CFI, *Los recursos hidráulicos de Argentina*, Vol. 7, pp. 612–613.

not closely coordinated with the irrigation department even though this use affects the availability of irrigation water. Although floods have caused substantial damage in the region, no agency had clear responsibility for flood control until a 1961 Mendoza law created a separate office for this purpose under the DGI. Industrial uses of water and forestation are still frequently not considered by any agency. Hydroelectric facilities are constructed and operated by the national power company, Agua y Energía Eléctrica (AEE). Although AEE maintains good working relations with the DGI and respects the DGI's authority over river control, the dams generally are operated to maximize the returns to either power or irrigation rather than total returns. Other potential benefits, including returns for recreation and flood control, are considered residual and do not enter into the planning or operation of water projects. Although the provincial agencies involved are different, the lack of coordination among water users and alternative water sources also characterizes San Juan.

INDIRECT CONTROLS

From the perspective of the farmer's investment decision and the efficient use of the region's ground water resources, the most important government measures are agricultural credit policies, tax incentives for private investment in arid lands, and electric power pricing. The cost and availability of water has become an increasingly important element in cropping decisions in Cuyo. And one of the most important factors in a farmer's water costs is his ability to take advantage of government credit and tax incentives. This section examines the impact of government policies on ground water costs; Chapter 6 examines the government impact on overall farm profitability.

Credit Policy

A farmer's access to official agricultural credit has a dual impact on the decision to invest in ground water. First, there are very few farmers in a financial position to invest in an irrigation well without credit, and there are few private sources of long- or medium-term agricultural credit. Thus, access to official credit is frequently a necessary condition for drilling private irrigation wells. Second, at recent rates of inflation and government rates of interest for agricultural lending, access to official credit can substantially reduce the real cost of ground water to a farmer.

The estimated annual ground water costs presented in Table 2.8

Table 3.1 Estimated Reductions in Ground Water Costs from the Credit
Subsidy under Alternative Assumptions

(in percentages)

Bank lending rate	Nominal discount rate	Effective cost reduction	
		Capital costs	Total costs
15	30	16.7	14.8
	40	24.5	21.7
	50	30.4	26.9
21	30	9.0	8.0
	40	17.7	15.7
	50	24.3	21.5

Notes: Assumptions for calculating the reduction in capital costs: financing is provided for 70 percent of capital costs with repayment of the principal in five equal, annual payments starting at the end of one year; interest is paid semiannually on the unpaid balance.

Additional assumptions for calculating the reduction in annualized total costs of ground water: the cost breakdown between capital and energy costs are those of Table 2.8 for the farm with a storage pool and night pumping.

assume a real discount rate of 10 percent. In recent years, however, official interest charges for agricultural credit have been substantially below inflation rates, implying negative real interest rates on such loans. For instance, the Banco de la Nación has financed 70 percent of the cost of a well, pump, motor, and low tension power line for up to five years at interest rates of 15 to 21 percent. The agricultural lending rate of the Banco de la Nación from March 1971 to March 1972 was 14 percent and prior to March 1971, 10 percent. In comparison, rates of inflation in Argentina, as measured by changes in the wholesale price index, were in excess of 70 percent during 1972, about 41 percent during 1971, and 27 percent during 1970.

Table 3.1 estimates reductions in the total and capital costs of ground water for nominal discount rates of 30, 40, and 50 percent. The relevant nominal discount rate must allow for both the expected rate of inflation and the investor's real opportunity cost of money. The table assumes lending conditions similar to those offered by the Banco de la Nación: 70 percent financing for five years, amortization in five equal annual payments, semiannual interest payments on the unpaid balance at alternative annual rates of 15 and 21 percent. At the 15 percent lending rate the effective level of the credit subsidy ranges from 17 to 30 percent of capital costs, depending on the nominal rate of discount used. As a percentage of the total annualized cost of ground water for the hypothetical 20-hectare farm using a storage pool and night pumping presented in Table 2.8, the reduction would range from 15 to 27 percent.

Table 3.2 Estimated Reductions in Ground Water Costs from the Investment Tax Credit

(in percentages)

Marginal tax rate	Nominal discount rate	Effective cost reduction	
		Capital costs	Total costs
33	30	25.4	22.5
	40	23.6	20.9
	50	22.0	19.5
46	30	35.4	31.3
	40	32.9	29.1
	50	30.7	27.2

Note: Assumes that the full capital cost of the well, pump, motor, and low tension electric power installation can be deducted from taxable income, the tax on which would have been paid one year after the investment. For calculating the reduction in annualized total costs of ground water, the cost breakdown between capital and energy costs are those of Table 2.8 for the farm with a storage pool and night pumping.

Tax Incentives

The national government is also providing a substantial incentive for investing in ground water use by enabling farmers to deduct twice the full cost of an irrigation well, pump, and motor from their taxable income.[11] Farmers are permitted to deduct 100 percent of these costs from their current taxable income in addition to amortizing the costs over the life of the investment and deducting them from future incomes. The laws are meant to encourage investment in arid lands, and for the purposes of this law all of Mendoza and San Juan are classified as arid. The incentive for ground water use and agricultural expansion provided by this legislation is actually much greater than just the potential reduction in ground water costs. The two-time reduction of taxable income applies to investment expenses for land clearing and leveling, installing irrigation canals, electrification, and planting and cultivating permanent crops until productive, as well as to the costs of the new irrigation well, pump, and motor.[12]

This tax investment incentive, of course, has meaning only for a person or corporation that would otherwise be paying income taxes. Many farmers within Cuyo, either because of low incomes or tax evasion, do not pay income taxes. The larger farmers and corporations, however, generally do pay income taxes. Moreover, there is no restriction on the source of the income from which these costs can be deducted. Consequently, the tax deductions make irrigated agriculture in Cuyo more attractive for other potential investors.

[11] The relevant laws are Ley 16883/66, article 24, and Ley 16882, article 62.
[12] Chapter 6 examines the impact of this incentive on farm profits.

Table 3.3 Estimated Increases in Ground Water Costs with Different Power Rates
(in percentages)

Electric rate schedule	Effective cost increase	
	Energy costs	Total costs
Storage pool and nonpeak pumping		
residential rates	231.9	26.8
commercial rates	342.0	39.5
industrial rates	207.8	24.0
No storage and day pumping		
residential rates	49.3	13.4
commercial rates	98.8	26.8
industrial rates	38.4	10.4

Note: All assumptions, with the exception of power rates, are identical to those in Table 2.8. The power rates for residential, commercial, and industrial users are the rates for the city of Mendoza and surrounding areas that went into effect in January 1972.

The extent of the incentive depends on the marginal tax rate of the individual investor. Table 3.2 indicates the percentage reduction in the capital and total annual costs of ground water on the hypothetical 20-hectare farm described in Table 2.8 with 33 and 46 percent marginal tax rates. The former rate is relevant for corporations while the latter is currently the highest personal marginal tax rate. It is assumed that the taxes saved by the reduction of taxable income would have been paid one year after the investment is made. Thus, the tax savings are discounted by a nominal discount rate. With a 33 percent marginal tax rate, the estimated reductions in total annualized ground water costs from this investment incentive are between 19.5 and 22.5 percent.

Electric Power Rates

The government also affects ground water costs through electric power rates. While an examination of the differences between private and social power costs is beyond the scope of this study, it is of interest to consider how ground water costs would differ if farmers paid the same power rates as other consumers.[13] Table 3.3 indicates the percentage increases in energy costs and total annualized ground water costs that would result on the hypothetical 20-hectare farm considered in Table 2.8 if farmers paid the same power rates as residential, commercial, or industrial users. The increases in the total annualized cost of ground water that would result from these alternative power rates range from

[13] Chapter 5, p. 84, provides some reasons why one might expect that the social costs of power, at least for peak-time consumption, are closer to the rates charged nonfarm users.

Table 3.4 Estimated Reduction in Total Ground Water Costs Resulting from Credit, Tax, and Power Pricing Policies

(in percentages)

Marginal tax rate	Bank lending rate	Nominal discount rate	Reduction in total costs[a]	
			Storage pool and offpeak pumping	No storage and day pumping
33	15	30	51.5	38.9
		40	54.7	42.8
		50	57.7	45.5
33	21	30	45.2	33.9
		40	50.0	38.3
		50	53.5	41.5
46	15	30	57.5	45.3
		40	61.2	48.8
		50	63.8	51.1
46	21	30	52.0	40.4
		40	56.5	44.3
		50	59.5	47.2

[a] The total "nonsubsidized" costs for irrigating 20 hectares are $3,256 for the alternative with the pool and offpeak pumping, and $2,754 for the alternative of day pumping with no storage pool. These costs are the same as the costs presented in Table 2.8 with the exception that residential power rates were used to calculate the energy costs. All other assumptions in this table correspond to the assumptions in tables 3.1 and 3.2.

24.0 to 39.5 percent for a farm pumping during nonpeak hours and 10.4 to 26.8 percent for a farm pumping during peak hours.[14]

Combined Impact of Credit, Tax, and Power Pricing Policies

For the investor able to take advantage of all government incentives, the subsidy on ground water is substantial.[15] Table 3.4 presents estimates of the percentage reductions in the total annualized cost of ground water that result from the government's tax, credit, and energy pricing policies. The so-called nonsubsidized costs assume residential power rates. Since the impact of the government policy varies substantially, depending upon whether a farmer initially uses nonpeak- or peak-time pumping, the estimated cost reductions for both pairs of assumptions are presented. For an investor with a marginal tax rate of 46 percent, borrowing rate of 15 percent, and nominal discount rate of 50 percent, the combined cost reductions are 63.8 percent compared to the nonsubsi-

[14] Agricultural power users are the only group to benefit from lower rates during nonpeak hours.

[15] Many farmers are too small and poor to pay taxes or obtain credit and will probably never be able to install their own irrigation pumps and benefit directly from these incentives. The implications of these policies and economies of scale in ground water use on optimal farm size are examined in Chapter 6.

dized off-peak pumping costs and 51.1 percent compared to the non-subsidized day-pumping costs. For a corporation borrowing at 15 percent, the cost reduction would amount to between 51.5 and 57.7 percent with a pool and off-peak pumping and between 38.9 and 45.5 percent with day pumping and no storage. The ranges for each alternative result from different assumptions regarding the nominal discount rate.

GOVERNMENT CONTROL OF THE GRAPE-WINE INDUSTRY

Recent increases in government participation in Cuyo's economy have also been evidenced in the grape-wine industry. Government interference in this industry is not new. Indeed, during the late 1930s buffer stocks and the forced eradication of 17,000 hectares of grapes were part of a six-year government program to reduce production. However, both before and for more than two decades after this interference, grape and wine prices and the incentives to invest in these areas were determined primarily by free market forces.[16] This tradition was altered with government efforts to market the 1967 record grape harvest, subsequent restrictions on the plantings of grapes, and more recent efforts to set grape and wine prices.

Prior to each grape harvest, Giol, which is owned and operated by the Mendoza government, now establishes prices at which it will purchase grapes. Since Giol has tremendous leverage on the market as the world's largest winery, its prices have generally served as minimum prices; other wineries must match or surpass Giol's prices if they expect to purchase sufficient grapes. Giol and C.A.V.I.C., a winery operated by the San Juan government, have been used in recent years to support the prices of both grapes and wine. In both 1972 and 1973 the efforts of the regional governments to increase grape and wine prices conflicted with the national government's efforts to curb inflation. Since wine is a significant item in the Argentine cost-of-living index, the national government attempted to establish maximum prices for common wines during the last two years. During both years, however, the national government acceded to the pressures of the producers and provincial governments in Mendoza and San Juan, and grape and wine prices were supported at levels very favorable to the producers. These successes have undoubtedly enhanced producers' expectations and local government resolve to actively support future grape and wine prices. Indeed, the regional wineries are rapidly expanding wine storage ca-

[16] Lucio Reca, "The Price and Production Duality Within Argentine Agriculture 1923–1965" (Ph.D. dissertation, University of Chicago, 1967), pp. 89–93.

pacity to gain greater control over and hopefully stabilize interannual grape and wine prices.

The implications of longer-run government intervention in the grape-wine industry are varied. Primary reliance on free market forces for marketing the production of and directing investment to a permanent crop such as grapes has frequently resulted in large annual price fluctuations and longer-run secular price and production cycles. On the other hand, government attempts to smooth out such price fluctuations have frequently failed because the long-run equilibrium price is unknown and there are strong pressures to support prices above the equilibrium level. Grape growers and wine producers, who have considerable political influence in Cuyo, tend to demand high prices and probably would not be content with any price fixed below the historical average. Yet, the stable long-run price that would equate supply and demand would be less than the average long-run price that would balance supply and demand in the absence of stability since price stability reduces risk, an important cost in agriculture. Cost reductions increase profitability which in turn increases production. Indeed, grape prices over the last two years have been supported at levels which have attracted large new investments to Cuyo's vineyards. Efforts to stabilize prices significantly above market equilibrium levels have generally resulted in either greater secular price and production swings than would emerge in the absence of government intervention or long-run government programs to support production surpluses.[17]

Historically, the agricultural areas within Argentina that have been most closely influenced by government policies have suffered as a result. Reca concludes that the contrasting agricultural performances in the Pampa and Cuyo regions of Argentina from 1945 to 1965 can be best explained by the contrasting roles of the Argentine government.[18] During this period agricultural production in the Pampas stagnated as a result of government price interference while production in Cuyo prospered under the influence of relatively free market forces. Moreover, Biondolillo states that the policies adopted in the later 1930s in response to the grape and wine surpluses and depressed prices were misguided and contributed to subsequent imbalances and price swings.[19]

---

[17] For example, government accumulation of coffee stocks in Brazil on at least two occasions and cocoa stocks in West Africa supported prices above long-run equilibrium levels. These price supports contributed to large additions in productive capacity which hit the market at about the time the storage facilities were overflowing. These experiences were followed by years of very depressed market prices and government attempts to eliminate excess productive capacity.

[18] Reca, "Price and Production Duality," pp. 89–97.

[19] Aldo Biondolillo, "Social Cost of Production Instability in the Grape-Wine Industry: Argentina" (Ph.D. dissertation, University of Minnesota, 1972), p. 7.

SUMMARY

Surface water is public property, and in Cuyo its use is regulated by the provincial governments. Historically granted water rights, which are attached to and inseparable from the land, provide the basis for the distribution of the river water. The number of hectares possessing water rights, however, far exceeds both the number of hectares under irrigation and the number of hectares that could ever be adequately irrigated with the available surface water. This situation has created much uncertainty regarding the quantity of water that will be received by each claimant, and during recent very dry years some lands possessing water rights received no water. The location of the land within the water distribution system has become an important determinant of the quantity of water received.

Neither Mendoza nor San Juan has an overall plan for developing and using its water resources. Moreover, there is little coordination among the numerous governmental agencies controlling water use, and some potential uses of water such as recreation and flood control are frequently omitted in the planning and operation of water projects. The only effective limits on ground water use have been the farmers' drilling and pumping costs. However, a 1967 revision in the Civil Code, which made ground water part of the public domain, is a likely precursor of future governmental controls of ground water use.

In recent years government credit, tax, and power pricing policies have played important roles in the use of water and the overall development of the region's agriculture. These policies have provided substantial subsidies to farmers drilling irrigation wells and pumping ground water with the subsidy component increasing with the rate of inflation and the marginal tax bracket of the investor. For some of the wealthier farmers, these policies have reduced total ground water costs by 50 percent or more during recent years.

The provincial governments in Mendoza and San Juan have recently become much more active in the operations of the grape-wine industry. The local governments were particularly successful in supporting high grape and wine prices in 1972 and 1973. However, the poor record of government interference in Argentina's agriculture and prior efforts to support and stabilize agricultural prices do not bode well for the longer-run impact of continued government intervention in the marketing of grapes and wine.

the past as prologue 4

While there are still farmers without an adequate and reliable supply of water, the region as a whole now has the short-run capacity to meet its agricultural water requirements even if surface water receipts return to recent low levels. However, as will be shown below, the adjustment has made the region's agriculture highly dependent on a level of ground water use that cannot be maintained indefinitely because pumping has exceeded natural recharge to the region's major aquifers. Moreover, government credit, tax, and energy pricing policies continue to encourage pumping and additional investments in irrigation wells and pumps. The prospect of diminishing ground water stocks assumes greater significance when it is realized that the region's agriculture is becoming increasingly dependent on permanent crops, representing substantial long-run investments which could not be fully recovered if there were a major decline in water availability. Currently about 85 percent of the value of the region's agricultural production comes from permanent crops, and the trend indicates even greater concentration in permanent crops in the future.

As a result of these changes in the region's basic water situation, the most important development issues now confronting the Cuyo region are the use of ground water stocks over time and the implications of current policies and trends on the future availability of ground water. This chapter examines the influence of recent trends, current government policies, and investment incentives on the growth of agriculture and ground water use, the implications of likely growth trends on the stock of ground water, and the proposition that water is the major constraint on Cuyo's growth.

FUTURE IMPLICATIONS OF HISTORICAL GROWTH SOURCES

The most important source of agricultural growth in Cuyo over the last two decades has been the change in the relative product mix, primarily a shift out of cereals and forages into grapes. This factor accounted for about 47 percent of Mendoza's estimated agricultural growth from 1947–48 to 1969–70 and about 77 percent of San Juan's estimated agricultural growth from 1954–55 to 1971–72.[1] This factor, however, cannot be a continual source of growth. With constant grape yields, increasingly larger shifts in land from relatively low value crops to grapes are necessary to maintain the same impact on the growth rate of the total value of agricultural production. Moreover, a limit would obviously be reached when 100 percent of the cultivated land were devoted to grapes. If the only future change were a continued shift to grapes, the estimated value of agricultural production would increase by less than 32 percent in Mendoza and by less than 30 percent in San Juan. Since 100 percent concentration in grapes is highly unlikely and undesirable, the future growth due solely to the shift to grapes should be considerably less than these percentages. Consequently, while the percentage of land devoted to grapes may continue to rise, the change in the product mix should play a greatly curtailed role in future agricultural growth.

The change in the product mix was the only source of growth in the value of agricultural production which clearly decreased water requirements.[2] Its importance in this regard is underlined by San Juan's experience from 1954–55 to 1971–72. San Juan's estimated water requirements declined 6 percent during this period while the change in the

[1] See Table 2.4. Although some vegetables now offer a higher return per unit of land and/or water than grapes, the trend has clearly been towards greater concentration in grapes.
[2] See the discussion in Chapter 2, p. 21.

product mix accounted for more than three-fourths of the 27 percent increase in the estimated value of the province's agricultural production. As the shift from crops with a low to a high value per hectare becomes a less important factor in Cuyo's agricultural growth, the water requirements associated with a given increase in the value of agricultural production will tend to rise.

The limited growth potential from a change in the product mix indicates that technological change is essential if the region's agriculture is to grow significantly without corresponding increases in water. Higher yields per unit of water could come from either a reduction in water losses between the water source and the plant or an improvement in yields per unit of water applied to the plant.

Government investments in lined canals and dams have improved water distribution in some areas and will probably continue to do so. Current proposals and projects under consideration indicate that the focus of such government investment in the next decade will probably be in the construction of large dams to regulate river flows for irrigation and hydroelectric purposes. A number of factors, however, suggest that the potential of these projects for expanding irrigated agriculture in the Cuyo region is very limited; e.g., although the timing may not now be optimal, virtually all surface water in the region, other than the Grande River, is currently used. Moreover, the storage of large quantities of water behind a dam will reduce the total quantity of water available due to substantial evaporation losses. The effects of the proposed dams on recharge to the ground water stocks are largely unknown.[3]

On-farm investments offer an important potential source of water savings. Such investments, however, have been and still are discouraged by the relatively low marginal water costs of most farmers. There is also potential for improving yields per unit of water applied to the plant. For example, measures to reduce crop losses from insects or frost would result in higher average yields per unit of water. Under current incentives, however, there is no reason to expect that higher yields per unit of water applied to a plant will become an important source of agricultural expansion in the near future.[4]

The measure of technological change employed here is the change in the average yield per unit of land within a crop group.[5] This factor accounted for about 21 percent of the growth in the estimated value of

---

[3] The major projects and their likely effects on irrigation are examined in Chapter 7.

[4] The various means for improving yields per unit of water, the potential water savings, and the policies that are likely to lead to their adoption are examined in Chapter 7.

[5] See Chapter 2, pp. 12–15.

agricultural production in Cuyo during the past several decades; on an annual basis it contributed an average of 0.6 percent in Mendoza and 0.3 percent in San Juan. As grapes increase in relative importance, the future impact of this growth factor becomes increasingly linked to grape yields. This is not a very encouraging prospect for future growth since grape yields have fluctuated around a zero long-run trend over the past seventy years in Mendoza. A continuation of this trend would reduce even further the future growth impetus from technological change. While the effect of this measure of technological change on water use is unknown, it probably increases both the average water required per hectare and the average yield per unit of water.[6] However, since there is no way to quantify the impact on water, estimates of water requirements in this study assume no change in the average water requirements per hectare for a given crop. While this assumption may somewhat underestimate changes in water requirements, the error is probably small.

In Mendoza, the second most important growth factor during the last several decades has been the expansion of total cultivated land. Cultivated land increased at an average annual rate of 1 percent from 1947–48 to 1969–70 and accounted for 37.5 percent of the province's total agricultural growth. While total land planted in San Juan hardly changed from 1954–55 to 1971–72, it grew at an average annual rate of over 1 percent from 1960–61 to 1966–67, a period of considerable growth. Increases in total cultivated land obviously increase overall water requirements. Historically, the 1 percent increase in total cultivated land more than offset the water-saving effects of the shift to crops with lower water requirements. For instance, total estimated water requirements rose about 19 percent between 1947–48 and 1969–70 in Mendoza and about 3 percent between 1960–61 and 1966–67 in San Juan. While percentage increases in total water requirements are not high, they assume greater significance when the increases are supplied entirely with ground water.

GROUND WATER USE: PROJECTIONS AND IMPLICATIONS

Future Ground Water Use

Government investment incentives, relatively high grape prices, and water availability make current conditions for increased planting as favorable as at any time during the past several decades. And since mar-

---

[6] Reasons for expecting an increase in the per hectare water requirements are given in Chapter 2, p. 21, note 10.

ginal water costs confronting most farmers are probably less than those of the early 1960s, there is no reason to expect farmers to adopt techniques that might lead to a less water-intensive growth. Consequently, conditions currently indicate the likelihood of a renewed water-intensive agricultural growth.

Statistical estimates of aggregate derived demand functions for ground water for anything but the short-run case would be exceedingly difficult to determine and of questionable value in view of the uncertainties regarding future water flows and product prices. However, some useful observations regarding the factors likely to affect ground water use in the not too distant future are possible.

First, the number of operational irrigation wells can be expected to continue to rise, although at a somewhat lower rate than during the 1969 to 1971 period when the "rescue" demand was particularly strong. In the absence of another sharp decline in surface water flows, the impact of the "rescue" demand should have been fairly well exhausted. This does not mean that all farmers needing irrigation water to prevent loss of permanent crops now have wells. However, farmers that did not obtain an alternative source of water have probably already lost at least part of their permanent crops, and the high expected surface water flows during the 1972–73 year should be sufficient for their surviving crops. On the other hand, favorable grape prices and substantial government agricultural investment incentives will undoubtedly encourage agricultural expansion requiring new wells. Drilling is also being encouraged by an expectation in both Mendoza and San Juan that the provincial government may soon either prohibit or impose strict controls on new irrigation wells. The combination of high grape prices and government investment incentives might be expected to bring a continued rapid increase in drilling if it were not for the considerable pump capacity that will go unutilized during the 1972–73 agricultural year. With excess pumping capacity, a higher percentage of agricultural investment should be directed into clearing new lands and new plantings than during recent very dry years.

Second, the total amount of water pumped in 1972–73 was less and the net reduction in the region's major aquifers substantially less than during recent years. The decline in the water tables was even temporarily reversed for some of the region's aquifers. The reasons for these changes are that the higher river flows both substantially reduced pumping from the wells that supplement river water and increased recharge in the aquifers. During 1972–73 these factors more than offset the additional pumping from the new wells.

Third, a continuation of current investment incentives will probably bring a rapid rise in cultivated land and total water use. Conditions, at least for the relatively large farmers and potential rural investor,[7] are currently favorable for agricultural expansion in Cuyo. Substantial excess ground water pumping capacity and at least a temporary improvement in surface water flows indicate that marginal water costs for many farmers are fairly low. The irrigation wells also provide their owners with at least a short-run degree of security and control over water receipts that existed only when average annual water flows far exceeded the region's agricultural requirements. This reduced risk should be particularly important for investment in permanent crops. Moreover, government credit, tax, and power pricing policies are substantially reducing the private cost of agricultural expansion and ground water use. On the negative side, there are the long-range concerns over declining water tables and renewed gluts in the grape market. Both these concerns, however, have been at least temporarily abated by the weather. Unusually heavy rains and snowfalls reduced concern over ground water tables; frost, which reduced the expected 1973 grape harvest in Mendoza by about 20 percent, dampened concerns over grape surpluses. In summary, both annual and permanent crops may be expected to increase substantially in the short run as farmers seek to utilize excess pumping capacity and regain some of the production lost during the very dry years. Permanent crops can be expected to continue their long-run growth. Consequently, even if river flows remain at their expected high 1972–73 levels, the use of ground water would rise sharply in subsequent years as total cultivated land rises.

Fourth, ground water pumping and aquifer depletion would substantially exceed any levels yet experienced if river flows return to the low levels experienced from 1967–68 to 1970–71. This would occur since both the capacity to pump and the amount of cultivated land, especially land under permanent crops, would be greater than in previous years. A sharp rise in ground water use would bring a sharp drop in the ground water tables which could make many pumps inoperative. A new "rescue" demand for ground water investment would appear on farms where deeper wells and larger motors became necessary to protect other agricultural investments. Although this new "rescue" demand might not significantly affect the number of operating wells, it would be a great incentive for investment to maintain pumping capacity as water tables fell.

Fifth, only direct government controls on ground water use, a substantial reversal in investment incentives, or the extremely unlikely

[7] Earlier discussions have mentioned how credit, economies of scale associated with ground water, and investment incentives tend to favor the larger farmers. The effects of changing agricultural conditions on optimal farm size are examined in more detail in Chapter 6.

situation of continually increasing surface water flows will prevent additional depletion of the region's aquifers in the coming decades. In the absence of one or more of these events, the important issues for the region are how fast the water tables may fall and the impact of these declines on agricultural growth. The following section examines the future interrelationships between ground water use and agricultural growth trends; Chapter 5 outlines how the region should be using its water over time.

Implications of the Growth in Ground Water Use

This section relates the growth in ground water use to the stocks of water stored in the region's principal aquifers. The figures used to project future ground water use are relatively conservative estimates of recent trends and current growth incentives. However, rather than predictions of what will occur, the estimates should be considered as arguments for altering current investment incentives to prevent the realization or approximation of these figures.

If the land planted to each crop group grew at the same geometric rate as the rates from 1947–48 to 1969–70 in Mendoza and 1960–61 to 1966–67 in San Juan, by 1985 annual plant water requirements would have increased by 768 hm³ or 28 percent in Mendoza and 199 hm³ or 24 percent in San Juan.[8] If all additional water requirements were met with ground water at a 70 percent average farm irrigation efficiency rate, the increased annual use of ground water as of 1985 would be 1,098 hm³ in Mendoza and 284 hm³ in San Juan.

With water use already in excess of the sum of likely average surface water supplies and recharge to the ground water stocks,[9] additional water requirements will be met largely with ground water stocks. If the additional annual ground water loss rose linearly from 1970 to 1985, the total water loss in any year from 1971 to 1985 would be defined by the equation:

[8] By allowing for differential growth rates among the various crop groups, the estimates take into account the water-saving effects of the change in the product mix. Alfalfa is treated as a separate crop group because of its importance for aggregate water use. The actual land planted to the crop groups as of 1969–70 in Mendoza and 1971–72 in San Juan were the bases from which the fifteen-year geometric rates were projected. Thus, the estimates referred to as 1985 actually correspond to the 1984–85 agricultural year in Mendoza and the 1986–87 agricultural year in San Juan. The use of 1985 is a notational simplification employed because the estimates are not projections of expected additions to water use but an idea of the impact of current growth forces on future water use.

[9] The quantitative justification for this statement, which does not allow for the possibility of an interbasin water transfer from the Grande River to the cultivated areas in southern Mendoza, is presented later in this section.

$$L_t = F + (A/15)t \qquad (4.1)$$

where $L_t =$ the total ground water loss (total outflow minus total inflow) in year t.

$t = 1$ in 1971; $t = 2$ in 1972; ...; $t = 15$ in 1985.

$F =$ the average annual ground water loss from the 1970 cropping pattern.

$A =$ annual water losses in 1985 resulting from changes in the cropping pattern between 1970 and 1985.

This equation says that depletion of ground water stocks in some future year will be the sum of net ground water use resulting from the cropping pattern in the initial period plus any changes in ground water use resulting from changes in the cropping pattern. The assumption that the values of A and F are independent is an oversimplification, but justifiable for the purpose of providing rough estimates of future ground water use under current incentives. The estimates of 1,098 hm³ in Mendoza and 284 hm³ in San Juan for parameter A (i.e., ground water use resulting from changes in the cropping pattern) were made without allowing for future river flows since water use in the initial period exceeds any likely surface water availability. However, parameter F, the net ground water use associated with the initial cropping pattern, is highly dependent on river flows. For example, higher river flows would both reduce pumping and increase the rate of recharge to an aquifer.

The interrelationship between river flows, total water use, and ground water stocks can be examined with some precision for several regions within Cuyo.[10] The following discussion focuses on the two most important regions, northern Mendoza and the region irrigated by the San Juan River. Ideally, the definition of a water region for the following

[10] The limiting factors for defining these areas are the availability of data on the size of the aquifers and the relation between surface water flows and ground water recharge. A program initiated in February 1965 between the United Nations and the government of Argentina developed detailed ground water data for five zones within Cuyo. The zones are: I. the Tulum and Ullum-Zonda valleys, which are the center of San Juan's agriculture and overlie ground water reserves of about 20,000 hm³; II. the Bermejo valley, which has very limited potential for the extraction of good quality ground water; III. Valle Fértil, which possesses several small but currently underutilized aquifers; IV. the lower basin of the Mendoza River, which possesses an aquifer with an estimated 20,000 hm³; and V. the Carrizal valley with an aquifer with an estimated 6,000 hm³. The first three zones are in the province of San Juan, and the last two are in the northern half of Mendoza province. The data and analysis of the ground water in these five zones up to the termination of the United Nations program in December 1970 are presented in Programa de las Naciones Unidas para el Desarrollo, *Investigación de las aguas subterráneas en el noroeste Argentina* (New York, 1972), Vols. 1–5. More recent unpublished data on the ground water in these zones are available from the offices of Investigación de las Aguas Subterráneas en el Noroeste Argentina located in Mendoza and San Juan.

discussion would be one in which every farmer using water from river R who could pump ground water fell within the limits of aquifer R' and vice versa. This, however, is not the situation for northern Mendoza, where there are at least three aquifers underlying the area irrigated by the Mendoza and Tunuyán rivers and the two which have been extensively studied are physically interconnected. The largest of these two aquifers receives its recharge from the other aquifer and infiltration from both the Mendoza and Tunuyán rivers.[11] Consequently, northern Mendoza minus an adjustment for a region around Valle de Uco, which falls within the area of a third aquifer of unspecified size, is treated as one water zone. In San Juan the definition of the water region was simpler. About 97 percent of the irrigated land in the province receives its water from the San Juan River or the aquifers in the Tulum and Ullum-Zonda valleys, which are recharged from the San Juan River or the lands irrigated by this river.

Estimates of the impact of current agricultural growth forces on the additional ground water extracted in 1985 from the two regions, parameter A in equation 4.1, are presented in the table immediately below, column 2. The derivation of these estimates starts with the estimates of additional ground water use for each province, assuming that the land planted to each crop group will grow at the 1947–48 to 1969–70 rates in Mendoza and 1960–61 to 1966–67 rates in San Juan. The provincial estimates are then reduced by a factor, estimating the percentage of the provincial totals that will fall within the two principal aquifers in northern Mendoza and the San Juan river basin. In Mendoza it is assumed that 70 percent of the increased provincial water requirements will fall within the relevant zone in northern Mendoza.[12]

[11] Another problem for separating the areas receiving water from the Mendoza and Tunuyán rivers is that some *departamentos*, which are the smallest units for which agricultural data are available, receive water from both the Mendoza and Tunuyán rivers. A *departamento* is roughly equivalent to a county in the United States.

[12] As of mid-1972 about 82 percent of the irrigation wells in Mendoza were in the departments of Capital, Godoy Cruz, Guaymallén, Las Heras, Luján, Maipú, Junín, Rivadavia, San Martín, Lavalle, Santa Rosa, La Paz, and Tupungato, the areas pumping from the two aquifers under consideration. According to data in Gobierno de Mendoza, Dirección de Estadísticas e Investigaciones Económicas, *Registro permanente de uso de la tierra, estadísticas agropecuarias*, (Estudio No. 77, 1971), p. 12, 58 percent of Mendoza's cultivated land was in these departments. The assumption that 70 percent of the provincial increase in water requirements will fall within this region is simply a guess based on these two percentages and knowledge that there is currently excess pumping capacity. A separate analysis of northern Mendoza requires departmental data which is available for 1960 and 1969 in the *Registro permanente de uso de la tierra*. If the 1960 to 1969 growth rates of the land planted to individual crop groups in northern Mendoza are projected to 1985, the implied increases in the area's plant water requirements are not significantly different from those presented in the table showing hypothetical water losses.

Thus, with a 70 percent farm irrigation efficiency the additional annual pumping from the two major aquifers in northern Mendoza would be 768 hm³ as of 1985. In San Juan it is assumed that all of the increased water requirements will fall within the San Juan river basin.[13] The estimated additional annual ground water pumping from the San Juan river basin is 284 hm³ in 1985 with a 70 percent farm irrigation efficiency.

	Additional annual loss in 1985	Average future annual loss from 1970 crop pattern	Total annual loss in 1985	Total loss from 1971 to 1985
Northern Mendoza	768	85	853	7,419
		300	1,068	10,644
San Juan	284	85	369	3,547
		200	484	5,272

Note: Figures are in millions of cubic meters.

Column 3 of the table above presents two alternative estimates for each region of the average annual ground water losses between 1971 and 1985 resulting from the 1970 cropping patterns, i.e., parameter F in equation 4.1. The actual net losses will be dependent on future flows of the Mendoza, Tunuyán, and San Juan rivers, which cannot be reliably forecast. The difference between optimistic and pessimistic river flow forecasts could conceivably imply values of F ranging from 0 to 350 hm³ for northern Mendoza and 0 to 250 hm³ for San Juan. The first estimate of the value of F used in the table is that the average annual ground water loss from the initial cropping pattern will be 85 hm³ in each region. These were the actual estimated annual losses during the years examined in the United Nations report, 1963–64 to 1969–70 in Mendoza and 1964–65 to 1968–69 in San Juan.[14] The average river flows during these survey years were considerably above the averages from 1967–68 to 1971–72 and were approximately the same as the averages since 1950.[15] The water requirements of the crops planted in 1970 were considerably higher in Mendoza and somewhat lower in San

[13] According to data from the 1968 grape-wine census only 0.6 percent of the vineyards, 3.0 percent of the surface water, and 0.6 percent of the ground water in the province of San Juan were in the departments of Iglesia, Jachal, and Valle Fértil, the only departments in the province not receiving water from the San Juan River or the aquifers recharged from this river. See Gobierno de San Juan, Secretaría Técnica de la Gobernación, Instituto de Investigaciones Económicas y Estadísticas, *Anuario estadístico 1971*, Cuardo 9, p. 65.

[14] Programa de las Naciones Unidas para el Desarrollo, *Investigación de las aguas subterráneas.* The average annual water deficits in Mendoza were 50 hm³ in zone IV and 35 hm³ in zone V.

[15] If we set the average annual river flows during the survey periods equal to 100, the respective flows from 1949–50 to 1971–72 and 1967–68 to 1971–72 averaged 103.9 and 83.7 for the Mendoza River, 96.5 and 84.6 for the Upper Tunuyán, and 101.7 and 51.9 for the San Juan.

Juan than the average requirements during the survey periods. On balance the estimates of 85 hm³ for the average annual future water losses resulting from a continuation of the 1970 cropping patterns assumes that average future surface water flows will be comparable to those since 1950. In view of the very low surface water flows in the most recent period and the 30 to 40 year declining trend in surface water flows, these assumptions are optimistic. For comparative purposes and to indicate the impact of particularly low river water flows, it is also assumed that the average annual ground water losses from the 1970 cropping pattern were 300 hm³ for northern Mendoza and 200 hm³ for the San Juan basin. These figures compare with the United Nations estimated losses from 1967–68 to 1968–69 of 338 hm³ for northern Mendoza and 225 hm³ for San Juan. The water flows during these two years as a percentage of the average during the entire survey periods were 75.4 for the Mendoza River, 70.0 for the Upper Tunuyán, and 54.5 for the San Juan River.

The total use of the ground water stocks from 1971 to 1985 under the assumptions above is defined by the equation

$$\sum_{1}^{15} L_t = 15F + 8A \tag{4.2}$$

The total estimated net water losses from 1971 to 1985, listed in column 5 of the preceding table, range from 7,419 to 10,644 hm³ in Mendoza and 3,547 to 5,272 hm³ in San Juan depending on the assumed river flows.

Since ground water losses mean little until they are related to ground water stocks or pumping depths, the following table relates the hypothetical net ground water losses presented in the preceding table to the stock of ground water in the aquifers.

	River flow assumption	Percent of depletion as of 1985	Year in which aquifers would be depleted by 75%	Year in which aquifers would be depleted by 100%
Northern Mendoza	optimistic	28.5	1999	2007
	pessimistic	40.9	1993	1999
San Juan	optimistic	17.7	2016	2030
	pessimistic	26.4	2005	2015

Note: The optimistic assumptions correspond to the case in the table on p. 64, in which the average future annual ground water losses from the 1970 crop pattern are 85 hm³ in both northern Mendoza and San Juan; and the pessimistic assumption assumes the average losses are 300 and 200 hm³ respectively.

It is assumed that the two aquifers in northern Mendoza start with a total of 26,000 hm³ and that the San Juan aquifer starts with 20,000 hm³ in 1970.[16] Column 3 indicates the percentage of the initial ground water stocks that would be used by 1985 under optimistic and pessimistic assumptions regarding surface water flows. This column indicates that from 28.5 to 40.9 percent of northern Mendoza's and 17.7 to 26.4 percent of San Juan's ground water would be used by 1985. Columns 4 and 5 of the table indicate the years in which the aquifers would be 75 and 100 percent depleted if the hypothetical annual loss rates did not change after 1985. The 100 percent depletion figures are purely illustrative since higher pumping costs, lower water quality, and inoperative pumps would alter the rate of ground water use long before the aquifers were pumped dry. The 75 percent depletion level is probably a conservative estimate of the point at which these factors would substantially alter ground water use even without a major change in government policies. Under the assumed growth rates the ground water would be 75 percent depleted within twenty-three to twenty-nine years in Mendoza and thirty-five to forty-six years in San Juan.

The lower hypothetical ground water losses summarized in the two tables above are relatively conservative estimates of the implications of current incentives for increases in agricultural water use. They are even more conservative as estimates of changes in total water use under current incentives, since they make no allowance for increases in other water uses. As of 1970 domestic, urban, and industrial water use in Cuyo amounted to only about 100 hm³, well below 5 percent of total water use in the region. One recent study, however, estimates that nonagricultural water use in the region will rise at 10 percent per annum.[17] With all additional water use requiring a comparable rise in ground water use, this growth in nonagricultural water demand would have a substantial impact on ground water stocks by 1985. For example, a 10 percent per annum growth in nonagricultural water use would add about 318 hm³ to the annual water demand in 1985 and 1,995 hm³ to total water use in Cuyo from 1971 to 1985. If the local

[16] These are the water volumes estimated by Programa de las Naciones Unidas, *Investigación de las aguas subterráneas.*

[17] Michel Jean Paul Ramlot, *Hacia un porvenir de la región cuyana* (Mendoza: n.p., 1972), p. 40. The petroleum industry alone may cause rapid increases in nonagricultural water use. One of the fastest growing industries within the region, petroleum is already a major consumer of ground water. Moreover, government arrangements with foreign companies virtually insure large increases in ground water use. For example, as an incentive for exploratory drilling, the government has granted foreign oil companies the right to exploit successful wells for a specified number of years. Since the wells become government property at the end of this period, generally fifteen years, the foreign companies attempt to maximize production prior to losing control. This results in the use of large quantities of ground water to maintain the pressure within the petroleum deposits. There are no restrictions on the use of ground water.

impact of this additional water demand were in proportion to the 1970 population distribution within Cuyo, 55 percent would be in northern Mendoza and 26 percent in the San Juan river basin. If one adds the nonagricultural to the agricultural water use estimates and assumes no increase in the annual water consumption after 1985, ground water stocks would be 75 percent depleted within twenty-one to twenty-six years in northern Mendoza and thirty-one to thirty-nine years in San Juan, depending on the surface water flows.

While such growth assumptions imply a rapid ground water use, the implied growth in the value of agricultural production is quite modest. For instance, with no allowance for technological change, the implied annual geometric growth rates of the value of agricultural production (to 1985) would be 2.3 percent in Mendoza and 2.1 percent in San Juan. If yields of the individual crop groups were to grow at historical rates, the growth of agricultural production would be 2.7 percent in Mendoza and 2.4 percent in San Juan. While the growth projections assume that cultivated land of individual crop groups grows at historical rates, the crop groups with the highest growth rates have greater weight in the future projections. Therefore, the implied growth of total cultivated land from 1970 to 1985 is 1.9 percent per annum in both provinces, substantially above recent historical rates. The implied annual growth of total agricultural water use is 1.6 percent in Mendoza and 1.5 percent in San Juan. Assuming no change in either land planted or water requirements after 1985, the implied annual growth rates from 1970 to 2000 for Mendoza and San Juan respectively are 1.2 and 1.0 percent for the value of agricultural production, 0.9 and 1.0 percent for land cultivated, and 0.8 and 0.7 percent for agricultural water use.

If the estimates were altered such that total cultivated land grew at only 1 percent per annum for the first fifteen years, ground water problems would be postponed, but not totally eliminated; e.g., in northern Mendoza with no allowance for nonagricultural water use, it would take an additional seven to seventeen years before the aquifers would be 75 percent depleted. If domestic and industrial water demand grew at 10 percent per annum for fifteen years, it would take only an additional six to ten years to reach this level of depletion. With total land growing at 1 percent per annum for fifteen years, the implied growth in the value of agricultural production in Mendoza would be only 1.6 percent with no allowance for technological change and 1.9 percent if yields of individual crop groups grew at recent historical rates.[18]

While the recent shortages of irrigation water have been more serious

---

[18] These calculations assume that the land planted to each crop group would be reduced by the same percentage.

in San Juan, the hypothetical losses suggested above indicate a more rapid future ground water depletion in Mendoza. The higher estimates for ground water losses in Mendoza are the result of the slightly higher growth rate of overall water use and the considerably larger initial overall water use to which these growth rates are applied. Since the estimates apply the growth rates to total water use and assume that all increases come from ground water, the projected rate of growth of ground water use is considerably higher in Mendoza.

The estimates in this section illustrate the future relationships among agricultural growth, total water use, and ground water stocks under current growth incentives. A number of important conclusions can be drawn from the preceding numerical exercises. First, even the modest agricultural growth rates of recent decades cannot be maintained for many more decades through a water-intensive growth pattern. Under the growth alternatives examined above, the region's ground water stocks would be fully depleted within thirty to sixty years. Second, before this stage were reached higher pumping costs, increased ground water salinity, and dry wells would be reflected in lower agricultural yields, higher costs, and crop losses. The quality of the ground water has already declined and adversely affected yields in some areas. Third, the investment losses from a development sequence similar to that just depicted could be enormous. By 1985 the region's agriculture would be overwhelmingly based on permanent crops and highly dependent on ground water even during years of above-average surface water flows. Permanent crops would account for nearly 85 percent of the cultivated land and over 90 percent of the value of agricultural production. In addition, the current $200 million investment in more than 20,000 irrigation wells would be considerably higher by 1985. Much of this investment in permanent crops and irrigation wells would never be recovered if the availability of good quality ground water declined rapidly. Fourth, the only likely means of avoiding the development outlook and investment losses described above is to have a major change in the programs which now subsidize agricultural development and discourage the adoption of water-saving technology in the region. Suggested policy revisions are developed in the following chapter.

NONWATER CONSTRAINTS TO AGRICULTURAL GROWTH

The discussion above makes an implicit assumption that water is the only relevant constraint to future agricultural growth. This assumption was made because of the prima facie evidence of the overriding importance of water to continued agricultural growth in the region and because the primary objective of this study is to examine the use of water and the interrelations between water use and agricultural growth. Nevertheless, before examining the efficiency of water use, one should at least note the major nonwater constraints to agricultural development in the region.

On the supply side there appears to be no productive factor, other than water, to impede the agricultural growth rates discussed above. Land is abundant. In recent years the private sector has invested large amounts in irrigation wells. Since the region now has the capacity to meet its short-run needs, the capital requirements associated with these agricultural growth rates should be less than the investment rates during recent dry years. Obtaining sufficient labor during the grape harvest is always a problem, but with a high enough wage, labor should continue to be available.

The major nonwater constraints to the growth patterns above are on the demand side. In particular there is considerable concern over the ability of the region to market the grapes at profitable price levels from the vines which have already been planted. Cuyo faces an inelastic domestic demand for grapes and wine, and exports have never exceeded 1 percent of Argentina's grape or wine production. A major frost, which has reduced the expected 1973 grape harvest in Mendoza by 20 percent, has temporarily abated fears of low prices and production gluts. But even without new vineyards, favorable growing conditions could bring much lower prices in the near future. Moreover, the agricultural growth assumptions in the previous section imply an annual increase of grape lands in Cuyo of 2.9 percent up to 1985. Even with no changes in grape yields and no net increase in grape plantings outside of the Cuyo region,[19] the annual rise in grape production during this period would be about 2.4 percent. The prospects for a comparable increase in domestic consumption at current prices are not good. With annual domestic wine consumption of about 93 liters per capita,[20] future increases in demand will probably depend primarily on population growth, which was only 1.56 percent per annum during the 1960s.

The growers, wineries, and government agencies concerned with the grape-wine market have recognized that a major export push is necessary if demand is not to become a major constraint on the region's growth. While Argentina produces both fine and common wines at

[19] From 1960 to 1971 vineyards in other areas of Argentina increased 17 percent.

[20] In 1970 Argentina had the third highest per capita wine consumption in the world after Italy with 115 liters and France with 107 liters. In the United States wine consumption was only 4.4 liters per capita in 1970. *Los Andes* (Mendoza, Argentina), December 8, 1972, p. 6.

highly competitive prices, the absence of established marketing channels and international consumer recognition inhibit export expansion. Some of the leading wineries have formed an export cooperative to promote and facilitate wine exports. In October 1971 a national decree-law (Ley 18,905) set up special lines of credit and tax incentives to encourage wine exports, nonwine uses of grapes, vertical integration in the grape-wine industry, and formation of stocks to reduce price fluctuations. The export results of these incentives have not been encouraging. Exports of grape products during the first nine months of 1972 were only about 2 percent above the levels of the comparable period in 1971, and total exports remain under 1 percent of production. While strength and rapid growth of the international wine market indicate the potential for a major export expansion of Cuyo's grape products, such an expansion probably will not materialize before domestic surpluses and depressed domestic grape prices stimulate greater concern and efforts for developing foreign markets.

The only other crop group projected to grow according to the above estimates of plantings is "other fruits." The projected increase over fifteen years is 30.7 percent. These fruits, especially peaches, apples, and plums, are the raw material for a substantial preservative and processing industry. Unlike the grape-wine industry, Cuyo's fruit preservative and processing industry is not in a monopolistic position within Argentina and has well established export markets for its products. Moreover, these export markets are apparently capable of absorbing greater production at current prices.[21] In general the market does not appear to be a serious constraint to the rates of expansion estimated above for "other fruits."

Perhaps the least likely aspect of the estimates in the previous section are that total land planted to vegetables in the region will continue to decline. Recent yield increases have increased the relative profitability of growing many vegetables, especially tomatoes and potatoes. Even with very conservative market projections there should be room for an expansion of lands planted to vegetables in Cuyo without a serious drop in prices.[22]

Overall the market does not appear to place a serious constraint on the fairly modest rates of agricultural expansion described in the previous section. If the expansion of vineyards slows due to low product

[21] In December 1971 the director of the Cámara de la Fruta Industrializada de Mendoza implied that the export possibilities for these products are enormous. See *Los Andes*, December 11, 1971, p. 8.

[22] For example, during 1972 Argentina spent millions of dollars importing potatoes. Currently potatoes account for about 16 percent of the land planted to vegetables in Cuyo, and the land could easily be expanded with the proper price incentives.

prices,[23] the slack in the overall expansion of agriculture is likely to be made up by other crops as long as the government maintains its subsidies for water use and the clearing and planting of new lands. The implicit assumption in the preceding section that water is the major constraint on overall agricultural growth in Cuyo appears justified.

SUMMARY

The combination of government investment incentives, relatively high grape prices, and the available supply of water provide favorable conditions for a renewed agricultural expansion in Cuyo. However, the potential for and implications of a continuation of the agricultural growth patterns of the past several decades are not good.

The most important source of agricultural growth in Cuyo over the last two decades has been the change in the relative product mix, primarily a shift from cereal and forages to grapes. Potentially, a continued shift to grapes could increase the value of agricultural production by an additional 30 percent. Complete crop specialization, however, is neither likely nor desirable. While some shift from cereals and forage to grapes and other crops with relatively high returns to water and land is likely to continue, changes in the relative product mix will undoubtedly have a much smaller impact on future agricultural growth in Cuyo. Since this is the only source of growth which clearly reduces average water requirements, comparable increases in the value of agricultural production are likely to require more water in the future than was true during the last several decades.

Although the short-term conditions are favorable for and indicate the likelihood of a substantial growth of cultivated land, the longer-run implications of such a water-intensive growth are ominous. The long-run problem stems from the combination of several factors. First, water use in Cuyo's principal irrigated areas already exceeds levels that can be maintained in the long run. Second, a continued water-intensive agricultural growth would greatly accelerate the use of ground water stocks. Third, long-term investments in land preparation, permanent crops, irrigation wells, and complementary urban areas have been and continue to be made with the expectation that an increasing quantity of water will be available for the foreseeable future. Much of this investment would be lost, and the entire region would suffer serious economic and social disruption, if a sharp reduction in water availability occurred. The poten-

[23] The historic rates of growth for vineyards in Mendoza which were used in the growth estimates of the previous section already reflect one period of surplus production and low product prices.

tial seriousness of the problem is demonstrated by calculations indicating that even the relatively modest agricultural growth rates of recent decades cannot be maintained for many more decades through a water-intensive growth pattern. By 1985 ground water use could reach levels that would deplete the usable ground water stocks within an additional ten to twenty years in at least two of Cuyo's three principal irrigated zones.

Water is clearly the major constraint on the region's continued agricultural development, and there is a great need for policies that would encourage water-saving investments rather than the current policies subsidizing a water-intensive growth.

water use 5
efficiency

EFFICIENCY CRITERIA

The development and use of water resources affect a number of societal concerns including income distribution, regional development, and the level of total national product. Since policy changes designed to alter water use are likely to have varying qualitative effects on some of these matters, and since they are seldom, if ever, defined such that quantitative comparisons can be made among them, abstraction is essential for examining the efficiency of water use. The most common abstraction adopted by economists is to evaluate efficiency in terms of maximizing the present discounted value of net national income at market prices over some time period. This section examines some of the advantages and limitations of this definition of efficiency and presents the conditions which must be satisfied to achieve such an efficient water use. Then, the second section evaluates current water use, government policies, and regulating institutions by the extent to which they impede or promote such an efficient water use. And the third section evaluates alternative means of improving water use efficiency in Cuyo. This third section reintroduces other societal concerns, in particular, income distribution and risk avoidance objectives in evaluating policy alternatives.[1]

Maximizing Net National Income over Time

One of several weaknesses of defining efficiency in terms of net national output is that the marginal utility of income is assumed to be constant and equal for all people, i.e., the distribution of income is not important.[2] If we avoid any assumption regarding the relative marginal utilities of income, we cannot proceed very far in evaluating water use. This can be demonstrated by considering the limitations of defining efficiency as any situation which satisfies the conditions of Pareto optimality. A Pareto optimum is a situation in which no one person can be made better off without making at least one person worse off. Suppose, quite realistically, that a redistribution of ground and surface water among existing farmers could be made such that there were no change in the quantity of water received by any farmer, but that the total cost to society of providing the water were less. If just one farmer experienced an increase in costs from this change, we could not describe it as an improvement or more efficient water use from the conditions of Pareto optimality alone. The system would be able to compensate the losers for their higher costs and still be able to improve the position of someone else. But it is not enough just to know that the system could compensate any losers. If we are to avoid distributional value judgments, actual compensation would have to be made before the new situation could unambiguously be called an "improvement." Since almost any redistribution of water either among farms or over time would, in the absence of compensating payments, make at least one person worse off, either now or in the future, and since adequate compensation frequently is not made, the Pareto optimal criterion does not take us very far in evaluating Cuyo's water use. To proceed further, an assumption regarding the relative marginal utilities of income is necessary. The most common and useful assumption, since it enables efficiency to be examined independently of distribution, is that

---

[1] The impact of government policies and agricultural trends on farm size are examined in Chapter 6.

[2] There are a number of other implicit assumptions in our definition of efficiency such as the independence of consumers' welfare, an underlying belief that the economy should serve the needs of its members, that the individual should determine what these needs are, and that market prices reflect the consumers' evaluation of the marginal benefits of goods. Other authors have discussed the assumptions underlying our definition of efficiency. A particularly good discussion within the context of water use is John Krutilla and Otto Eckstein, *Multiple Purpose River Development* (Baltimore: The Johns Hopkins Press, 1958), especially Chapter II.

the marginal utility of income is equal for everyone. This implies that we can define efficiency in terms of maximizing net national income.

The major advantage of this course is that we can readily derive specific criteria for evaluating any given water use. While other objectives of society are not directly included in the efficiency conditions, the use of this definition does not commit us to ignore them in the evaluation of water use. In fact, it could provide a more objective means of evaluating policy alternatives; the cost in terms of foregone national income of a policy designed to satisfy some other objective can be valuable information for policy formulation. The compatability between a water use strategy designed to maximize national income and other likely objectives of the region are examined later in this chapter.

Because agriculture accounts for over 95 percent of the water used in Cuyo, this sector is central to an efficient water use in the region. Nevertheless, it should be borne in mind that an efficient water use also requires that water be optimally distributed among the various sectors. While water constraints have probably not yet limited the growth of industry in Cuyo, increasing agricultural water requirements and laws giving agriculture priority over industrial water use indicate that readily available, good quality water may soon become a major problem for industrialization. We return to this point in Chapter 7.

The efficiency conditions are formulated in terms of social costs and benefits, which may differ substantially from private costs and benefits. For example, the social cost of using a unit of water at a given place and time includes both the cost of delivering the water to that location and the opportunity cost of not being able to use the water at some other location and time. The private cost of the water use includes the cost the farmer pays for receiving the water at his farm and the alternatives he must forego in using the water now at a given location. For several reasons private water use costs may not reflect social costs. First, the farmer may or may not be paying the full social cost of delivering the water to his farm. Second, and more important, the alternative uses of the water considered by a farmer generally do not take into account the full range of options available to the society. In the static framework the farmer's opportunity costs include only the option of allocating the water within his farm; they exclude the option of using it on some other farm where it may be more productive.[3] In the dynamic framework, a farmer includes the opportunity cost of not being able to use the water at some future time only if he has future property rights on the water.

---

[3] If water were bought and sold within a competitive framework and private and social benefits of water use were equal, the market mechanism would capture the static interfarm water use alternatives. However, in Cuyo, as well as in most other places in the world, water is not a competitively sold good.

Ground water in Cuyo is a common property resource, and a farmer's rights to this water extend only to what he pumps now. As a result private costs of current water use completely ignore the possible future value of water stored in an aquifer. The possible future value of water stored in an aquifer or behind a dam is central to efficient water use over time.

The common property aspect of ground water creates several important problems for achieving water use efficiency. In addition to a farmer's failure to allow for the future value of water in storage, a farmer does not consider that his pumping may increase the ground water costs of others interested in using the same aquifer. The problem is most serious when natural replenishment to the aquifer is insufficient to maintain water levels, which is now the case in Cuyo. Subsequent sections examine the inefficiencies resulting from the common property aspects of ground water and attempt to quantify the resulting differences between private and social ground water use costs within Cuyo.

While economic activity involves the use of resources through time, a useful abstraction for evaluating the efficiency of water use is to consider first the allocation of a given total flow per unit of time (i.e., within a static framework) and then the allocation over time (i.e., within a dynamic framework). An efficient water use would, of course, require efficiency in both the static and dynamic frameworks simultaneously. The following subsections present the static and dynamic conditions for an efficient water use.

Static Efficiency

The time period considered for the examination of water use within a static framework is the agricultural year. It is assumed that no net investment in irrigation infrastructure such as new wells and dams alters the availability or costs of water and that the total amount of water is fixed within the agricultural year.[4] It is also assumed that the timing of the water within the agricultural year is optimal or unimportant. To the extent that farmers are aware of the optimal irrigation requirements, this assumption is reasonable when ground water is used. However, only part of the annual river flows is available at the time that it can be utilized most efficiently by the plants. This part and, therefore, the overall efficiency of surface water use can be increased through the construction of dams to regulate the flows of river water. The resulting increase in the value of agricultural production is a major justification for the

---

[4] The optimal quantities of surface and ground water used in any given period would be derived from the dynamic efficiency criteria discussed later.

construction of such dams within the Cuyo area. A later chapter examines the possibilities for improving intra- and interannual surface water flows through dams. For the purpose of the current discussion of water use efficiency it is assumed that the intra-annual timing of the water distribution is optimal at the farm level within the capability of the system to control these flows.

The criteria for static efficiency must define a situation in which, for a given total annual water use, no change in either the source of or total quantity of water received by any farmer could increase the expected total net present discounted value of agricultural production.[5] If the cost and revenue curves are continuous at all points, such a situation would exist when, and only when, the ratio of the marginal revenue product (MRP) and marginal cost (MC) of water is equal in every use and when the ratio would be less than this level if water is not used. The ratio $MRP:MC$ of water is the value of the additional output that would be gained (lost) by spending one more (less) dollar on water. If this ratio were higher on farm A than farm B, water distribution would be inefficient in terms of our definition, since total output would be increased by spending one more dollar for water on farm A and one less dollar for water on farm B. The ratios of the marginal revenue products and marginal costs of ground and surface water must also be equal in every use for efficiency. If the ratio were higher for surface water, total output would be increased by spending one more dollar on surface water and one less dollar on ground water.

However, in the absence of a dam for storing surface water, the supply of surface water usable for agriculture is virtually fixed in the short run. In this case the short-run marginal costs of surface water, up to the quantity of water available, are just the delivery costs;[6] the marginal costs of additional surface water are infinite. Thus, the short-run cost curve for surface water is discontinuous, and the efficiency conditions above must be modified. Since the short-run costs of delivering surface water to lands served by the existing canal system are well below the pumping and user costs associated with ground water use, all surface water should be used before ground water is pumped. Consequently, in this case the assumption of a fixed total water supply implies a given breakdown between ground and surface water. With the supplies of

[5] When permanent crops are involved, it is clearly not sufficient to look at the returns in one year. Thus, even in the static sense the optimal water allocation must take into account the expected impact on future returns from permanent crops. Otherwise there would never be any water allocated to new crops with gestation periods in excess of one year.

[6] The social opportunity cost of delivering the water to one farm instead of another would be accounted for in the efficiency condition that the ratios of the $MRP:MC$ must be equal on all farms.

ground and surface water fixed in the short run, the ratios *MRP:MC* may differ for ground and surface water in the short-run, efficient water allocation. State efficiency then requires that: first, the ratio *MRP:MC* is equal for every use of surface water and equal for every use of ground water but not necessarily equal between the two sources; and, second, the ratio would be less than these respective levels for all possible alternative uses of ground and surface water.

Efficient water use is likely to imply that some farmers should not be receiving any water at all. Politically, however, such a change would be very difficult, if not impossible. Politically, change may be more feasible if every farmer had the expectation of receiving at least as much water as he would receive under the old system. Consequently, it is useful to focus on the criteria for minimizing the social costs of a given water distribution among farms through changes in the allocation of surface and ground water subject to the constraint that no farmer receive less water as a result of the reallocation. The least-cost criteria must define a situation in which, for a given distribution of water among the farms, it is impossible to reduce total costs by changing the source of ground and surface water among the farms. The conditions for optimal conjunctive water use are that the ratio of the marginal costs of ground and surface water be equal for all farmers using water from both sources, less than this level for all farmers using only ground water, and greater than this level for all farmers using only surface water.[7] If these conditions did not hold, a redistribution of the ground and surface water could decrease total costs with no reduction in the quantity of water received by any farmer.

Dynamic Efficiency

When water consumed in one period affects the costs or availability of water in another period, water use efficiency becomes intertemporal in nature. To the extent that water flows and use can be regulated over time, such as with water stored in an aquifer or behind a dam, both the total quantity of water used in any period and the mix of ground and surface water become potential variables central to the efficiency of water use. In addition, potential investments such as new irrigation wells, dams, lined canals, and new irrigation methods become relevant to the

---

[7] Cost minimization is, of course, also implied in the static efficiency criteria defined earlier which allow for altering the quantity as well as the source of water received by a farmer. It can easily be demonstrated mathematically that when the ratios *MRP:MC* of surface (ground) water are equal in every use, then, for any two farmers using both surface and ground water, the ratios of the marginal cost of ground and surface water must be equal for both farms.

intertemporal optimization process. Efficiency now requires not only satisfying the static criteria discussed above for allocating ground and surface water among farmers, but also determining the annual water releases and investment pattern that would maximize the present discounted value of water over time. This occurs only if the ratio of the present values of the marginal revenue product and the long-run marginal cost of water are equal in all periods and for both ground and surface water. If the ratio were higher for one period or source of water, the present value of production could be increased by spending relatively more money for water in this period or from this source.

The factors relevant for the maximization of the present discounted value of water in a region such as Cuyo are numerous and their interrelationship very complex. The discount rate is, of course, central to any evaluation of water use over time. A higher discount rate encourages current water use by attaching a relatively lower value to water stored either behind a dam or in an aquifer and by diminishing the importance of any increase in future costs resulting from current use. In addition, the profitability of investments in facilities to regulate water flows such as dams or to decrease water losses such as lined canals would decline as the interest rate rose. Since the interest rate is so important to water investment and use over time, it would be desirable to have some confidence in the rate of discount used. Unfortunately, the choice of the proper discount rate is a highly complicated issue. This issue has been discussed extensively in the economic literature, and there is nothing to be gained by repeating the arguments here.[8] In the absence of a well-established social rate of discount, it is useful to examine the sensitivity of the results to changes in the rate of interest.

Despite the oversimplifications adopted here which enable us to focus on the efficiency objectives without regard to income distribution or other objectives, the estimation of the benefits and costs of any given intertemporal water use and investment pattern is filled with difficult measurement problems. On the benefit side, it is helpful to divide the marginal revenue product of water (MRP_w) applied to a crop into its equivalent, the marginal physical product of the water (MPP_w) times the marginal revenue derived from the final unit of product (MR_q). Thus, the MRP_w is dependent on the shape within the relevant area of both the production and demand functions for a region's output. As was noted in the preceding chapters, the region's agriculture and particularly its agricultural growth is dominated by grapes. Since the demand

[8] An excellent summary of the principal issues and viewpoints involved in determining which rate of discount should be used appears in Orris C. Herfindahl and Allen V. Kneese, *Economic Theory of Natural Resources* (Columbus: Charles E. Merrill Publishing Co., 1974), pp. 204–221.

for Cuyo's grapes is not perfectly elastic and short-run grape production is positively related to water inputs, the marginal revenue of grapes at some period t would tend to decline as the amount of irrigation water applied to grapes in that period rose. The degree of the decline would depend on the short-run production and demand functions. In addition, since grapes are a permanent crop, to the extent that new plantings are related to total water availability, the total output of grapes and, therefore, the marginal revenue of grapes in period t would also be related to water releases in earlier periods. The optimum sequence of irrigation water use must take into account its impact on expected product prices over time. This is particularly important and difficult for a region such as Cuyo, where agricultural growth has been dominated by a permanent crop with an inelastic demand for the region's production.

The long-run marginal costs of both ground and surface water are also dependent on the sequence of water use and water-related investment. In the absence of a dam for storing and regulating river flows, surface water must be used as it becomes available, or it is lost to the region.[9] In figuring the long-run marginal cost of surface water, one must consider the possibility of constructing a dam for regulating the intra- and interannual flows. Even with the existence of surface storage, the rate of evaporation, which may run as high as 15 percent per year in an arid climate, provides a strong incentive for a rapid use of surface water. The future value of water stored behind a dam should be discounted by both the annual rate of evaporation and the social rate of discount. The total discount rate in this case is likely to be 20 to 25 percent per year, a strong deterrent to the interannual storage for irrigation purposes.[10] To the extent to which ground and surface water stocks are substitutable, such as with providing a source of water for future agricultural production and reducing the risk of low future water receipts, ground water stocks are generally preferable because of their low loss rates. Surface water stocks, however, may also have value for recreation, flood control, and power generation. In the case of a multipurpose dam the water should be managed to maximize total net benefits, not just the net benefits from irrigation. Evaluation of irrigation projects should include both the benefits of complementary water uses and the opportunity costs of not being able to use the water for other

[9] With the exception of the Grande River, the water is also lost to the nation since the other rivers generally run dry within the region.

[10] Cummings used an optimization model to determine the optimum use of a reservoir stock in northern Mexico. The criterion of "maximize the expected present value of income" called for exhausting the stock after at most three years. See Ronald Cummings, "Economic Aspects of Water Resource Management in Arid Environs," presented at the First World Symposium on Arid Zones, November 9–12, 1970, Mexico, D.F., pp. 8–9.

purposes. In this case, cost estimation also involves the problems of measuring benefits for which there are either no market prices or for which market prices provide no reliable guide as to social value. The optimal conjunctive management of ground and surface water stocks must take into account all these interrelationships and valuation problems.

The foregoing is meant to be merely a sampling of some of the difficulties likely to be encountered in an intertemporal evaluation of water use efficiency. Rather than amplifying on these problems in a general sense, which has been done by other authors,[11] it is more appropriate here to focus on the efficiency of water use in Cuyo.

WATER USE EFFICIENCY IN CUYO

Static Efficiency

1. Surface Water Water was not a limiting production factor in Cuyo during hundreds of years of agricultural development. Even in the mid-1930s, fifty years after the region's provincial governments first centralized and tightened controls on surface water use in the region, there was no real scarcity in the sense that water used by a farmer significantly affected the future or current supply of water. In the context of surplus river water, efficient water use entailed minimizing distribution costs, which comprised only the construction, maintenance, and administration costs of the irrigation canal system. There are obvious economies of scale in water distribution, and the provincial irrigation authorities probably did a good job in capturing these economies and passing the benefits on to the farmer.

The pricing policies of the provincial irrigation agencies were well suited to the situation in which water was not scarce. They charged farmers for the amortization, maintenance, and administration costs of the canal system in proportion to the number of hectares with water rights and the length of the canals required to deliver the water to the land. These charges were probably a close approximation of the social costs of the water delivered to the farms.[12] The annual charge per hectare was not a function of the amount of water received. As long as farmers received enough water for their land and new farmers were

---

[11] See, for example, Otto Eckstein, *Water Resource Development: The Economics of Project Evaluation* (Cambridge: Harvard University Press, 1958) and Krutilla and Eckstein, *Multiple Purpose River Development.*

[12] This assumes that labor, capital, and other inputs were priced at their social costs.

not prevented from using surface water under the same terms, both the private and social marginal costs of water were zero. Farmers probably applied water roughly up to the point where the marginal revenue product of water was zero, which, with surplus water, represented an efficient allocation from both the social and private points of view.

As was demonstrated in Chapter 2, for at least the past twenty-five years, the supply of surface water generally has not been sufficient to satisfy fully all users with water rights. Yet, surface water continues to be priced in the same manner. The annual charge for a hectare possessing water rights is still set to cover only the costs of amortizing, maintaining, and administering the canals. Since these charges are independent of water receipts, the explicit marginal cost of the water to a farmer, up to the amount he is alloted by the authorities, is zero, and there is no price at which he can legally obtain more surface water directly from the authorities.[13] The pricing system in effect assigns a zero value to a unit of water at some point on the river just above the irrigated areas. This price, however, is clearly not the social value of the water under conditions of water scarcity. Scarcity implies that water has a positive marginal revenue product in some actual or potential use. And when water is scarce, the social costs of distributing water to a farm include distribution losses due to evaporation and infiltration as well as the costs of amortizing, maintaining, and administering the canal system.

The emergence of increasing water scarcity and the maintenance of the water pricing and distribution system that emerged under conditions of nonscarcity have resulted in a gap between the private and social cost of water. This gap is maintained by the system of rationing. Surface water is distributed in proportion to the value of the water rights possessed by a farm.[14] These water rights were granted before water became a scarce factor of production in the region and when the provincial governments were interested in encouraging water use. Land use was supposedly the primary basis for granting water rights. This, however,

[13] A positive marginal revenue product for water opens the possibility that a farmer might attempt to bribe the irrigation authorities to leave the canal gates leading to his farm open longer. Bribes, however, are difficult since the water distribution off the local canals is controlled by the farmers with water rights. Changes in the scheduled water receipts are extremely difficult to arrange and require the approval of the other farmers served by the canal. However, tampering with the water flows is common, and violence stemming from water deliveries has occurred. Moreover, employing his survey data, Bertranou concludes that the difference of power of some groups over others was an important factor in the quantity of water received. Examining some of his other conclusions, one may presume that this power is positively related to farm size. See Armando Bertranou, "The Allocation of Irrigation Water in Mendoza, Argentina," a draft of April 1973 of a Ph.D. dissertation being prepared for the University of California, Davis, p. 14.

[14] Water rights are discussed in some detail in Chapter 3.

was obviously never strictly adhered to since the amount of land with water rights far exceeds the quantity of land cultivated and the amount of surface water that is ever likely to be available. Some farms possessed land with water rights well in excess of the land cultivated while others possessed no such cushion. Thus, as water grew scarce, many individual farmers continued to feel no water scarcity and undoubtedly continued to apply water up to the point where the marginal revenue product of water reached zero. At the same time water applied to other lands had a positive marginal revenue product, and other potentially profitable uses of water were frustrated by the lack of surface water.

Gradually, the increase in plantings on farms with water rights and the decline in the total surface water flows in the region affected more and more farmers. Although the explicit marginal cost of water may have been zero for the quantity received, farms with insufficient water to plant all the land desired had implicit, or opportunity, costs for using the water. It is reasonable to assume that individual farmers allocated the water on their farms in order to maximize net returns which would entail equating the ratio of the marginal revenue product and marginal cost of water in every use. Intrafarm efficiency, however, does not imply interfarm efficiency. Social opportunity costs of a given water use allow for alternative water uses throughout the region and not just the intrafarm alternatives.

Land with water rights is supposedly allocated a certain portion of the available surface water measured at the start of the irrigation system. Since the canal system is long and distribution losses great, the water actually received for land with comparable water rights will be greater in the upper part of the canal system than it is in the lower regions. For example, in a recent year a hectare with permanent water rights from the Mendoza River received about 10,000 m^3 in the upper reaches of the canal system and about 4 to 5,000 m^3 towards the end of the system.[15] While the current system of water distribution results in much lower water distribution losses than would result from attempting to deliver the same quantity of water to each hectare possessing comparable water rights, which is what the law actually calls for, the current system does not produce an efficient allocation of surface water. Large quantities of water are transported great distances with correspondingly large distribution losses. Moreover, because of the rationing system, there is no necessary relation between the social costs of delivering water to a farm and its productivity on that farm. If a farm in the lower reaches of the irrigation system possessed water rights well in excess of

[15] These data were provided by Armando Bertranou and are based on farm surveys. Water from the Mendoza River travels about 80 additional km to reach the lower irrigated areas, which accounts for large water losses.

the land cultivated, it might use water virtually to the point where its marginal revenue product approached zero despite the high social costs of delivering water to the farm. On the other hand, a farm where the social costs of delivering water are much lower may have a relatively high *MRP* of water. The coexistence of such farms is a clear violation of the static efficiency criteria which state that the ratio of the marginal revenue product and marginal cost of surface water must be equal in every use.

The coexistence of farms with very different ratios of the marginal revenue product and marginal cost of water should produce some incentive to transfer water or water rights privately. For example, both farmers might benefit if a farmer with poor land on the lower part of the canal system could sell his water rights to a farmer with good land in the upper part of the canal system. Any such transfer, however, is prohibited by law. The water rights belong to the land and cannot be transferred. If a farmer is to benefit from the water right, he must receive it at his farm. Once the water is delivered to a farm, there is no economical means of selling and delivering the water to another farm.

2. Ground Water In contrast to the controls on surface water, there are virtually no government restrictions on ground water use. A farmer's ground water use is limited only by the availability of a well, motor, and pump and his willingness to pay the costs of operating the pump.

The static efficiency criteria for using ground water require that the ratio of the marginal revenue product and marginal cost of ground water be equal in every use. An individual farmer attempting to maximize profits will tend to satisfy these criteria from the perspective of private benefits and costs. That is, a farmer would maximize net profits by pumping up to the point where his marginal cost of pumping a unit of water equaled his marginal revenue product of water and by distributing the water among his crops such that the ratio of his marginal revenue product to his marginal cost of ground water was equal in every use.

The social inefficiency in the pumping and use of ground water within an agricultural year results from the divergence between private and social costs.[16] The private marginal cost of ground water is essentially just the cost of the power to run the pump. Although it is beyond the scope of this study to derive the social cost of power in Cuyo, it is relevant to note that: the power company is planning additional capacity; the company is not noted for making large returns on its investment; and electric power rates for irrigation pumping are set well below rates

[16] It is assumed in this discussion that market prices reflect both the social and private benefits of production.

charged other users in the region. Consequently, we might expect that at least for peak-time consumption, the social costs of power are closer to the rates charged nonfarm users. The divergence between farm and nonfarm power rates is substantial. The marginal cost per kilowatt is 29 to 434 percent higher for residential use, 75 to 610 percent higher for commercial use, and 21 to 391 percent higher for industrial use.[17]

The divergence between marginal social and private ground water costs is increased further since one farmer's pumping imposes external diseconomies on others because of the common pool problem. Quantitatively, the most important divergence between private and social ground water costs stems from the individual farmer's failure to attach any value to water stored in an aquifer. This problem is intertemporal in nature and is examined below under dynamic efficiency. However, even when the water table is not falling from one year to another, one farmer's pumping may produce external diseconomies. Except in the case where the water in an aquifer flows through the region much like a river, one farmer's pumping will lower the water table at least temporarily and, thereby, increase the pumping costs of other farms. The aquifer underlying the area irrigated by the Mendoza River demonstrates the importance of the characteristics of the aquifer on the external diseconomies of pumping. In the upper, unconfined region of the aquifer, water flows fairly rapidly, and pumping does not significantly affect the pumping depths in that region. However, in the lower, confined region the water moves very slowly, and pumping depths are more sensitive to the rate of use of the water. The external diseconomies of pumping in both regions are felt primarily by pumpers in the lower parts of the aquifer. The effect on neighboring pumps is very pronounced during the actual period of pumping, since the pumping causes a conical depression in the water table, centered around an operating pump.

Dr. Zapata has estimated the externality resulting from the intra-annual decline in the water table for two regions overlying the confined aquifer in northern Mendoza. He concluded "that the discrepancy between private and social costs of additional withdrawals in Mendoza is of the order of magnitude of 30 percent of private costs."[18] Dr. Zapata's estimates are intended to be a conservative indication of externalities when current pumping has only a transitory effect on the level of the water table. Moreover, his estimates implicitly assume that private and

---

[17] These calculations are based on rates in Mendoza that went into effect in January 1972. Marginal power costs vary with consumption, and the range of comparative costs compares the high agricultural rate with the low rate of other users and vice versa.

[18] Juan Antonio Zapata, "The Economics of Pump Irrigation: The Case of Mendoza, Argentina" (Ph.D. dissertation, University of Chicago, 1969), p. 3.

social power costs are equal. If private power costs are less than social costs, which previous discussion indicates is probably the case, the discrepancy between private and social pumping costs would be greater. If we assume that the discrepancy between private and social costs is 30 percent when private power costs are equated to social costs and that average residential power rates reflect the marginal social costs of power, then electric power costs on the 20-hectare farm should be increased by 95 percent to close the gap between private and social costs of ground water pumping.[19] This is a very crude estimate of the increase in private pumping costs necessary to equate private and social pumping costs when there is no interannual decline in the water tables.

3. Conjunctive Use Determination of an efficient conjunctive use of ground and surface water within the static framework is a problem in cost minimization. Because of political and institutional constraints or societal goals other than the maximization of the present discounted value of net national income, it may be impossible or undesirable to effect a change which would reduce the amount of water previously available to any farm. Nevertheless, within these constraints, it may be possible to reduce the total social costs of delivering water by altering the locations using ground and surface water.[20]

With surface water distributed according to a system of water rights

---

[19] The power costs for pumping 10,330 m³ of water a height of 30 meters would average $49.5 if the residential power rates were paid on the 20-hectare farm. If this rate represents the social cost of power during the hours of peak use, an additional 30 percent for the discrepancy between private and social costs of ground water use resulting from the externalities would raise the annual cost of the water (exclusive of the capital costs of the well, pump, and motor) to $64.4 per hectare. This cost compares to the current power costs of $14.8 with off-peak agricultural rates and $33.0 with regular agricultural power rates. Since average power rates currently vary according to farm size and pumping depth, the increases in water costs resulting from the imposition of residential power rates and a user tax on ground water use would also vary. Chapter 6 examines the impact of social water costs on farms of different size and with different pumping depths.

[20] The quantity of surface water in the region refers to the flow at some point on the rivers above the irrigation area, i.e., the first diverting canal. While this flow is assumed to be fixed in the short run, the total quantity of water received by farmers would be increased by reducing delivery losses due to evaporation and infiltration. These delivery losses are one of the major components of the marginal social costs of surface water use. The social cost of losing a unit of water in the delivery to a farm is the marginal revenue product of water. However, if infiltration increases usable ground water storage, which it does in the area of the unconfined aquifer, the water is not lost to the system. While a farmer views such infiltration as a complete loss since he has no property rights on its future use, the social cost of water infiltration which recharges the aquifer is the social cost of pumping the water back to the surface. In the intertemporal context when ground water tables are declining, the optimal conjunctive use of ground and surface water must take into account whether or not water infiltration ends up as recharge to the aquifers.

granted under conditions of water surpluses and with no regulation on the drilling and pumping of irrigation wells, it is hardly surprising that something approaching a least-cost distribution of ground and surface water has not emerged. The type of change that would reduce the overall cost of the intra-annual water distribution can be readily identified for northern Mendoza. In comparison to the costs of delivering water to a farm in the lower regions of the irrigated area, surface water costs are lower and ground water costs higher in the upper regions. Drilling and pumping depths in the upper portions of this irrigated area are generally three to five times the depths in the lower irrigated areas. Based on the estimates and assumptions of Table 2.9, the annual cost of irrigating 20 hectares with a pumping depth of 30 meters, which is common in some of the lower irrigated areas, is about 56 percent of the cost at 90 meters; the estimated energy costs at 30 meters are only 32 percent of the cost at 90 meters.[21] Moreover, surface water distribution losses increase with the distance the water travels to reach the farm. Delivery losses to areas in the lower irrigated regions are usually large. For instance, just the infiltration losses of sending water from the Dique Cipolletti, the main diversion dam on the Mendoza River, to the Nuevo California canal, a distance of about 80 km, are estimated at 41.4 percent. Infiltration losses along a 50-km stretch of the Tunuyán River irrigation system are estimated at 28.7 percent.[22] Of the infiltration referred to above, only part of the water from the Mendoza River recharges the usable aquifers; none of the water lost from the Tunuyán recharges the usable aquifers. Clearly, the least-cost conditions for an efficient conjunctive use of ground and surface water are being violated when substantial quantities of ground water are pumped in the upper irrigated regions and substantial quantities of surface water are delivered to the lower regions. Total water costs could be reduced and the amount of water received at the farm increased by delivering more river water to the upper regions and pumping relatively more water in the lower regions.

[21] These data refer to private ground water costs. For reasons indicated earlier, social costs would be considerably higher. Although the use of social costs might not significantly alter the percentage cost differences among pumping depths, the absolute differences among social pumping costs would probably increase. The differences in the total annualized water costs presented in Table 2.9 are almost certainly underestimated since the drilling depth for all wells is assumed to be 220 meters. Dynamic pumping depths for northern Mendoza vary from about 30 to 190 meters.

[22] The loss estimates for the Tunuyán River are from Ing. David Pedro Dimov, "Pérdidas en ríos y cauces de riego en la Provincia de Mendoza. Hídrometria. Distintos casos comprobados. Beneficios del revestimiento de canales," (a folder in the files of Sección Hidrología del Departamento General de Irrigación de la Provincia de Mendoza, Mendoza, November 30, 1966). The estimates for the Mendoza River are from a map prepared by Ing. Lotera, Departamento General de Irrigación de la Provincia de Mendoza, November 1970.

Bertranou has estimated that an improved conjunctive use of ground and surface water could increase the usable quantity of water received by farmers in northern Mendoza by approximately 5 percent with no change in total costs, or alternatively water delivery costs could be reduced by about 5 percent with no change in the quantity of water received by any farmer.[23]

Dynamic Efficiency

The preceding discussion on static water use efficiency assumed that the total quantity of water used and the infrastructures were fixed. In the dynamic context, however, the determination of the quantities of ground and surface water used in any year and the rate of investment in agriculture and water infrastructure are key variables for achieving efficiency. For long-run water use efficiency these variables should be adjusted such that the ratio of the present values of the marginal revenue product to the long-run marginal cost of water are equal in every use.

Dams currently permit the regulation of intra- and interannual surface water flows from the Atuel and Lower Tunuyán rivers. There are two dams on the Atuel River: the Nihuil with a capacity of 260 hm³ and the Valle Grande with a capacity of 180 hm³. The Nihuil is operated solely for the purpose of generating power, while the Valle Grande, farther downstream, is operated solely for irrigation. The capacity of the Valle Grande is considered by the irrigation authorities to be sufficient only for intra-annual control of river flows. The recently completed dam, El Carrizal on the Tunuyán River, is large enough, with storage capacity of about 390 hm³, to permit significant control of interannual river flows. Although the generators are not yet operative, El Carrizal is projected to have a hydroelectric potential of 17 MW and an average annual energy production of 50 GWh. The reservoir, about an hour's drive from the city of Mendoza, is also expected to become a major recreation center.

The first priority for the operation of El Carrizal dam is irrigation. With estimates of the monthly water requirements of the crops in the area and projections of the monthly river flows for the agricultural year, the provincial authorities hope to make the irrigation flows coincide with requirements. The objective is to regulate the intra-annual water flows from the point of view of optimizing the current year's agricultural production. Although years of unusually high river flows such as 1972–

[23] This estimate was obtained in a conversation with Armando Bertranou in Mendoza in June 1973. Bertranou's estimates are based on analysis being undertaken for his Ph.D. dissertation entitled "The Allocation of Irrigation Water in Mendoza, Argentina."

73 will bring an increase in interannual storage, there is no objective to even out interannual flows or leave a margin of protection against very low future flows.[24] In the years for which there is an excess of water available, the total quantity of water released for agriculture will be guided by estimates of crop requirements and, more important, the requests of the farmers. That is, as long as there is water available, the total quantity of water released would tend to rise up to the point where there were virtually no further complaints of inadequate water. Legally, power and recreation uses of the water will be purely residual and will not affect the amount of water released. In practice, however, it is likely that power requirements will play some role in water releases.[25]

There are several reasons for expecting that the methods of dam operation discussed above may be suboptimal. If farmers fail to consider that current water use has an opportunity cost because of the uncertainties of future water availability, they are likely to request water releases that would maximize only their net agricultural returns during the current agricultural year. If their requests were granted and there were sufficient water available, water would be released until its marginal revenue product approached zero. In comparison, during years of low water availability the marginal returns to water might be fairly high. In addition, zero is clearly not the real value of power and water recreation facilities in Mendoza, and by attaching an effective zero value to these uses in regulating a dam, water use is likely to be suboptimal.

On the other hand, in view of the overwhelming importance of agriculture within the region, the high rate that should be used to discount any future values attached to water stored behind a dam, the availability of the aquifers and large investments in irrigation wells to compensate for the risk of low river flows, and the difficulties of evaluating the effects of alternative rates of water use on other potential benefits such as recreation and power, the operation of the dams in order to roughly maximize intra-annual agricultural returns may be a reasonable first approximation to an overall efficient use.

The advisability of undertaking additional investments that would affect water availability and use, such as new dams and the lining of irrigation canals, depends on the results of a benefit-cost analysis of the individual projects. If the discounted benefits exceeded the costs, the project would improve the overall efficiency of water use. The diffi-

---

[24] Significant interannual control of the Lower Tunuyán River is now becoming a possibility since it was only in the current agricultural year, 1972–73, that the water level behind the dam surpassed its dead storage level.

[25] The information on the operation of the dams was obtained during a discussion with officials of the Departamento General de Irrigación, Mendoza.

culties, however, lie in insuring that, first, the benefits and costs are properly defined and evaluated, and, second, all the viable alternatives, such as the use of ground instead of surface water storage, are considered.[26] The major water infrastructure projects under construction in and proposed for the region are examined in Chapter 7. The analysis in Chapter 7 demonstrates that the conception and design of the projects do not consider the full range of costs, benefits, and alternatives that could be taken readily into account. Consequently, these investments are likely to result in an inefficient use of the region's resources.

Government policies provide substantial subsidies for agricultural expansion and water use in Cuyo. Private ground water costs for many potential investors are effectively reduced by about 35 to 55 percent through the credit, tax, and power pricing policies.[27] New investments in permanent crops, which now almost certainly require ground water, are also being subsidized through the provision of agricultural credit at negative real rates of interest and the right to deduct investment costs twice from taxable income.[28] Even if farmers expect government subsidies to continue indefinitely at current levels, the present value of the increased profit potential from these subsidies is greater in earlier than in later years because of the operation of the rate of discount. Thus, farmers maximizing the net present discounted returns of agricultural investments over time would shift agricultural investment toward the present, shortening the life of the aquifers.

The inefficiencies in ground water use are compounded by the external diseconomies and user costs associated with pumping. A rough estimate of the externalities resulting from intra-annual declines in ground water levels was provided above. However, with interannual declines in the water tables, two factors increase further the gap between social and private ground water costs. First, additional withdrawals will impose costs on other users in future years as well as during the year of pumping. Second, since a farmer has no property rights on water left in the aquifer, private costs ignore the potential future value of this water. An important element in the value of this water is its potential use as a hedge against the risk of low future surface water recipts. Moreover, the tendency for the quality of the water pumped at any time to be positively related to the quantity of the water in the aquifer increases the magnitude of the social cost of current water use.

---

[26] The reader is again referred to two excellent books on the evaluation of water projects: Eckstein, *Water Resource Development*, and Krutilla and Eckstein, *Multiple Purpose River Development*.

[27] See Table 3.4, p. 51.

[28] The profitability of growing grapes with and without the subsidies is examined in Chapter 6.

Unfortunately, there are no estimates of the magnitude of the gap between social and private costs of ground water use in Cuyo within a dynamic framework. However, quantitative studies of other regions indicate that just the future scarcity value of water stored in the aquifer is probably substantial. For example, a model of the use of the ground water in Hermosillo, Mexico,[29] indicated that with optimal use the future scarcity value of the water stored in the aquifer rose from $0.08 to $4.00 per 100 m³ over a thirty-five-year period. Over the thirty-five years the model calls for depletion of about 88 percent of the water initially stored in the aquifer. The scarcity value of the water in storage at the start of the second year is $0.35 per 100 m³, roughly 4.4 times private pumping costs. The scarcity value of the water stored in Cuyo's aquifers is currently probably not as high as the second year value for Hermosillo since the rate of mining in Cuyo recently was only about 0.5 percent compared to the initial 3.4 percent annual rate in Hermosillo. Yet, under the growth assumptions used to estimate future ground water use in Chapter 4, northern Mendoza will have reached Hermosillo's initial rate of ground water mining within eight to eleven years depending on whether the pessimistic or optimistic assumptions regarding future surface water flows are used. And with these growth rates 90 percent of the water in the aquifers in northern Mendoza will have been mined within twenty-seven to thirty-four years. Moreover, the fact that the crops are annual in Hermosillo and predominantly permanent in Cuyo would tend to inflate the relative scarcity value in Cuyo for comparable levels of water storage and annual mining rates.

The prospect of even more rapid declines in water tables in the near future indicates that the gap between private and social ground water costs will become increasingly important. The current growth forces and government policies examined in earlier chapters are leading to a situation in which the external diseconomies may be reflected in more than just marginal increases in pumping costs to all farmers. Reductions in water quality and dry wells could bring widespread investment losses in permanent crops, wells, and other long-term fixed agricultural investments. And since the prosperity of the urban sector is closely tied to rural welfare, additional losses in long-term fixed capital could also occur in the urban sector.

The conclusion that the aquifers are currently being overpumped from an economic point of view does not imply that pumping should now be reduced to the level of natural recharge. The mining of ground water

[29] Ronald Cummings and others, "Administración y desarrollo de los recursos hidráulicos en el noroeste de México: Un análisis de alternativas," in mimeograph. Column 4 of Table 8.8 indicates the scarcity value of water under the optimal exploitation of the aquifer in Hermosillo.

is no different in principle than the mining of a mineral. Both resources have a value in use, and this value tends to be greater in the near future than in later years because of the operation of the interest rate. The major problem with the mining of ground water is that users tend to ignore many important costs of current use because of the commonality problem. Even if all these costs were internalized to the users, one would expect some ground water mining. The rate of mining, however, would be considerably less than under current conditions. Eventually an economic and hydrologic equilibrium would be reached when higher water costs resulting from increased pumping costs and declining water quality eliminated marginal producers, encouraged remaining users to seek less water-intensive uses, and discouraged new investors from the area.

The gap between private and social water costs also discourages on-farm investments which would improve water use efficiency. Low private marginal water costs provide virtually no incentive to invest in such irrigation systems as sprinkler or controlled-drip which offer substantial potential for increasing output per unit of water. The subsidization of irrigation wells, land clearing, and planting of permanent crops encourages the irrigation of more land and the use of more water per unit of land than is optimal. Without such subsidies, relatively more farm expenditures would probably be directed into areas such as hail protection, fertilizer, and pesticides that could increase agricultural output per unit of water. The profitability and its sensitivity to water costs of some on-farm investments that would increase output per unit of water are examined in Chapter 7.

The ground water investment pattern in Cuyo has also been socially inefficient in its failure to incorporate the large economies of scale in ground water extraction. For example, with a small pump the estimated per hectare annual ground water costs for irrigating just 5 hectares are 300 to 378 percent higher than the cost on 20 hectares and 474 to 597 percent higher than the cost on 36 hectares.[30] Larger pumps probably provide even lower annual water costs on larger farms. Yet, many small motors and pumps have been installed which operate well below capacity even during dry years. The basic reason, discussed in detail in Chapter 2, is that during recent dry years many farm operators had to choose between losing permanent crops or drilling a well. Under these conditions it became profitable to drill a well for irrigating as little as 5 hectares. However, without the rescue component of water demand, ground water costs are prohibitively high for 5 hectares.[31] Given the

[30] Based on the cost estimates in Table 2.10, p. 29.
[31] See the discussion on farm profitability in Chapter 6, pp. 115–116.

magnitude of economies of scale, it would have been cheaper from the social point of view if fewer wells had been drilled and the same quantity of ground water had been pumped from fewer wells operating closer to capacity. Theoretically, this might have been achieved if either fewer farms had been completely dependent on ground water or the government had drilled the wells and distributed the water through the irrigation canals. The provincial governments, especially the San Juan government, have installed batteries of large irrigation wells to supplement surface water flows. Yet the expenditure of tens of millions of dollars on such wells and government pumping has only marginally reduced the farmer's risk of inadequate surface water receipts, and it has not prevented the drilling of large numbers of small wells. From the efficiency point of view, water distribution losses limit the net economies of scale of using government wells.

IMPROVING WATER USE EFFICIENCY IN CUYO

Efficiency and Other Social Objectives

The prior discussion argued that water use in Cuyo is inefficient in terms of the objective of maximizing the present discounted value of national income. The combination of natural market failures and government policies which limit the operation of the market system and further distort the relation between private and social costs results in numerous and sizable deviations between actual and efficient (defined in terms of the efficiency conditions developed above) water use. However, maximizing the value of output at market prices is generally not the only objective of a society. It may not even be one of the most important objectives. Consequently, while an alternative water use might generate substantial increases in national income, it may or may not represent an improved social use of the water.

While government policies such as lower power prices for agricultural users, subsidized credit, and tax subsidies for drilling irrigation wells increase the gap between the private and social costs of ground water and contribute to a higher-than-efficient water use, the motives for these policies are undoubtedly complex; e.g., often, special subsidies to the agricultural sector are viewed as necessary incentives to a sector where market and weather uncertainties result in unusually high individual risk. There may be a desire to subsidize rural life and small farmers for noneconomic reasons. For example, a major objective of the tax subsidy is to encourage investment in nontraditional areas. Furthermore, the surface water rationing system in Cuyo undoubtedly protects small farmers who could not survive if they were charged the full scarcity value of the water.

The following examines the impact of major policies affecting water use in Cuyo on four alternative social objectives: development of arid lands, rural development, rural income stability, and aid to small farmers. These objectives were selected because of prima facie evidence that they are or have been objectives in Argentina. There is no attempt to determine the relative importance policy makers attach to these objectives. Three questions are asked: What are the impacts of policies affecting water use on these alternative objectives? Are there more "efficient" ways to achieve these objectives? And in the absence of more "efficient" alternatives, what is the cost in terms of foregone national income of these other social benefits?

The national government's interest in promoting the development of arid lands was manifested in a 1966 law granting tax credits for investment in such areas. However, if we take anything but a very short-run perspective, there are certainly more efficient ways to achieve this end. Moreover, current policies may actually be counterproductive to the region's long-run development. An earlier argument offered that water is the major constraint to continued agricultural development in Cuyo and that current policies encourage high water use rates for a given level of production. Consequently, current policies are actually hampering the long-run growth potential of the region by encouraging a prodigious use of its most limiting resource. Continued development of the region's agriculture requires a more economical water use; policies encouraging such a growth would promote both a more efficient water use and a more viable development of the region's agriculture.[32]

Subsidized agricultural credit and subsidies for rural electrification and power use are evidence of interest in stimulating rural development. Again, if we take anything but a very short-run perspective, there is no inconsistency between rural development in Cuyo and efficient water use. For the same reasons given above for arid lands, long-run rural development in Cuyo will not be fostered by squandering the region's scarcest resource.

Some of the policies which have increased water use have probably stabilized farm incomes. For instance, subsidies for irrigation wells and continuation of the historical pricing system for surface water have cushioned farm incomes from changes in water costs. Moreover, ground water subsidies and government irrigation wells to reinforce canal flows undoubtedly reduced crop losses during the recent unusually dry period, thereby tending to stabilize farm incomes. It is not clear, however, that

[32] Chapter 7 considers some of the possible investments which would increase yields per unit of water.

these policies will contribute to long-run income stability in the region. Current agricultural investment and water use incentives are leading to a situation in which the region's agriculture is becoming increasingly concentrated in permanent crops and increasingly dependent on a declining supply of ground water. It is possible that, within several decades, an increase in ground water could not offset a sharp decline in surface water, regardless of any government action. The result could be large losses in permanent crops and other urban and rural capital. This prospect indicates that a cost of achieving short-run income stability through water cost subsidies may be greater long-run instability.

The greatest sources of farm income instability stem from product price fluctuations and changes in yields resulting from weather factors, not from changes in factor prices. For example, from 1960 to 1969 the average percentage deviation from the mean was 22.4 percent for grape prices (in constant 1969 U.S. dollars) and 9.9 percent for grape yields. Moreover, these fluctuations did not tend to offset each other, since the average percentage deviation from the mean of gross revenue per hectare was 28.0 percent. A 15 percent change in either grape prices or yields would be equivalent to a change of $125 per hectare in water costs,[33] about twelve times the current cost of surface water and roughly equivalent to the estimated annualized per hectare cost of ground water on a 20-hectare farm.

Policy makers have recognized that grape and wine price stability is central to income stability within Cuyo. Vertical integration, encouraged by economic incentives, has been one approach to grape price stability. The operations of two provincial wineries, Giol in Mendoza and C.A.V.I.C. in San Juan, are of even greater potential importance for the stability of grape and wine prices. These wineries currently have sufficient market leverage to set and maintain minimum grape prices, and the additions being made to wine storage capacity will provide the capability for effecting greater interannual stability in wine prices. These are clearly much more promising means of achieving income stability within Cuyo than the reduction of water cost increases, and they have the advantage of not generating further inefficiencies in water use. The problems are to determine the long-run equilibrium price and to avoid political pressures to attempt to support prices at higher levels. Efforts to support prices above the long-run equilibrium level are likely to increase long-run price instability and create additional inefficiencies.[34]

---

[33] This assumes a grape price of $49/MT, the average from 1960 to 1969, and a yield of 17 MT/ha, a good but reasonable average annual yield with the overhead-trellis system of growing grapes.

[34] See the discussion in Chapter 3, p. 53.

Hail and frost losses are major sources of yield instability. Reduction in these losses would both stabilize incomes and increase production per unit of water. Hail damage to grapes can be substantially reduced through the installation of protective screening. This involves a substantial investment, which could be subsidized by the government as a means of stabilizing incomes. Higher water costs would also encourage such investments since reducing hail losses is one means of increasing production per unit of water.

Greater stability in water receipts would also contribute to stability in yields and income. Government wells to reinforce canal flows in dry years and dams to regulate interannual stream flows are important means of stabilizing water receipts. These investments can be consistent with achieving an efficient water use.

Official policy regarding farm size and income distribution is not at all clear. A progressive income tax, generally only paid by larger farmers, is the only policy clearly favoring the smaller farmer. On the other hand, vertical integration in the grape-wine industry is encouraged by credit and tax incentives. These policies alone do not necessarily distort relative factor use; the policies with a more direct effect on water use have a mixed impact on income distribution and farm size. While none of these policies benefit just small farmers, the maintenance of low surface water costs in spite of the increasing social value of water probably has meant the difference between financial survival and collapse for many small farmers. The real beneficiaries, however, are the owners of the land with water rights—farmers of all sizes as well as many urban, absentee land owners. On the other hand, the credit and tax investment policies which subsidize ground water use are overwhelmingly biased in favor of the large farmer. Access to credit depends on a farmer's collateral, and the tax investment incentive tends to offset the equalizing impact of the progressive income tax while reducing the relative cost of ground water. Whatever the society's objectives may be regarding income distribution and farm size, they could certainly be achieved equally well, and perhaps better, by policies which encourage a more efficient water use in the region. For example, the credit and tax investment incentives could be made available exclusively for water-saving investments, and more credit could be directed to small farmers.

In summary, there are no obvious nonefficiency objectives justifying the current policies encouraging water use inefficiency. Moreover, current policies appear to be inconsistent with long-run income stability, as well as with regional and rural development. Alternative income distributions do not require water use inefficiency.

In addition to the varied social objectives complicating the evaluation of alternative water uses, there are political and institutional constraints limiting the feasible range of alternatives. Policies condemned as stimuli for inefficiency in water use are certainly not viewed as failures by farmers. These subsidies tend to reduce production costs and increase the profits of farmers; any attempt to eliminate them without offsetting subsidies would produce loud protests. Farmers tend to feel that the government should act to offset the cost increase and uncertainties of adequate water receipts that emerged for reasons beyond their control. From the farmers' point of view the most logical way to offset these rising costs and uncertainties is to attack them directly. Thus, subsidies for irrigation wells, lower agricultural power rates, and government wells to reinforce canal flows are viewed as logical government responses to the emergence of water scarcity.

An improved water use within Cuyo can be approached through direct and indirect government controls. The advantages and disadvantages of these two approaches, taking into account effects on efficiency and nonefficiency objectives as well as political and institutional constraints, are examined below.

The Market Mechanism and Indirect Controls

Agricultural studies have generally found that farmers with the technical sophistication and capital required for irrigated farming act as profit maximizers. Two recent studies indicate this sensitivity in Cuyo: Llop has found that the quantity of land planted to grapes is significantly related to grape prices; Bertranou has discovered that the quantity of water applied to crops is sensitive to the marginal cost of water.[35] Thus, we can expect that on-farm water use and agricultural investment in Cuyo are sensitive to change in farmers' prices, costs, and overall profit expectations.

Economists have proved that under the highly abstract conditions of perfect competition, the price system produces an efficient allocation of resources. With perfect competition, prices reflect social as well as private values and costs, and individual farmers seeking to maximize their own profits allocate resources in a manner that also maximizes the social discounted value of production.[36] Unfortunately, however, as indicated in the previous discussion of water use in Cuyo, there are numerous important divergences between private and social costs in

[35] Armando Llop, "The Grape Wine Economy in Argentina: An Econometric Approach," and Armando Bertranou, "The Allocation of Irrigation Water in Mendoza, Argentina." Both studies are Ph.D. dissertations being prepared for the University of California, Davis.

[36] A particularly useful discussion of the price system under conditions relevant to water resource management is found in John Krutilla and Otto Eckstein, *Multiple Purpose River Development,* chapters II and III.

areas central to water use. These divergences are due both to government policies which distort the investment signals transmitted by the price system and to natural failures in the market system, such as the existence of external diseconomies, economies of scale, and the user cost associated with private use of a common property resource.

The most important of the natural market failures results from the private use of an aquifer in which the water level is falling interannually. Private costs in this case do not reflect either the additional costs one farmer's pumping imposes on other users or the potential future value of water in storage. Single ownership and exploitation of the aquifer would internalize these costs and tend to result in an efficient use of the water for the resulting production level. However, if the single owner possessed monopoly powers, other forms of inefficiency would result. Moreover, this solution is clearly not a practicable alternative for Cuyo, where the major water basins include thousands of farmers. Alternatively, a tax on pumping could close the gap between private and social ground water costs. But how high should the tax be? If the tax were set too high, it would discourage ground water use to less than efficient levels; if set too low, ground water use would continue to exceed efficient levels. Moreover, the social costs and, therefore, the ideal tax would change each year as the water table levels and other pertinent variables changed. The ideal tax would also probably vary from farm to farm. In practice, however, it would undoubtedly be necessary to set a single tax rate or schedule.

Earlier discussion held that in the absence of interannual declines of the water tables private pumping costs on the 20-hectare farm would have to be increased to about $65 per hectare for pumping 10,330 m³ a height of 30 meters.[37] About $15 of this would represent the externalities of the water use and the rest the social power and pump costs. Moreover, it was argued that the external diseconomies and user costs associated with ground water pumping from an aquifer which is declining interannually are even greater than the intra-annual distortions. Just the scarcity value of the water in storage could soon amount to $35 for 10,330 m³.[38] Consequently the user tax required to equate private and social costs of ground water use would approach $50 per 10,330 m³. The combination of residential power rates and a $50 user tax would raise the annual costs of ground water use excluding the cost of the well, pump, and motor to about $100 per hectare on the 20-hectare farm. This cost compares to the current costs of about $33 with regular agricultural rates and $15 with off-peak pumping rates.

Administratively, the water use tax would require water meters. If

[37] See p. 86, note 19.
[38] See p. 91.

widespread tampering with the meters were avoidable, the improvements in water use efficiency resulting from the tax would far exceed the costs of the meters and administration. Politically, however, any government-imposed cost increase is going to be unpopular. A $67 increase in per hectare production costs from the higher power rates and the tax on ground water use would be equivalent to about 8 percent of the average gross revenue from a vineyard averaging 17 MT per hectare per year and nearly 16 percent of the gross revenue for a vineyard yielding 8.8 MT per year, the average yield for Mendoza. Such an increase would probably eliminate some marginal farmers; it would force others to seek methods of reducing relative water costs. Both results would be desirable for improving water use efficiency. However, both results, especially the elimination of some farmers, might be inconsistent with the society's objectives regarding the distribution and stability of farm incomes. If this were the case, the impact of the cost increases could be eliminated or reduced through direct payments to farmers. However, if these payments are not to eliminate the incentive to reduce ground water use per unit of output, the tax must be dependent on, and the offsetting payment completely independent of, ground water use.

Government credit and tax subsidies also lead to overinvestment in irrigation wells, pumps, and motors. This source of inefficiency could be corrected simply by eliminating the subsidies for this form of investment. If such a change were presented as a measure to protect investments already sunk in irrigation wells, it should encounter little political resistence. The beneficiaries would include most farmers with irrigation wells. These farmers are probably far more numerous than the potential investors who would face increased costs by the elimination of the subsidy. Furthermore, since the subsidies are biased in favor of large farmers and corporations, their elimination might be consistent with social income distribution objectives.

Perfect competition also breaks down in the use of surface water because of the large economies of scale in its distribution. To capture these economies of scale, the government assumed control of surface water distribution and the construction of the major canals. The canals were built and the water distributed on the basis of water rights granted before water became a scarce resource in the region. No allowance is made for differences in water productivity and distribution losses among the different lands, and there is no mechanism for transferring a water right to more productive land.

Private investment alone and a reliance on the free-market system would not have resulted in an efficient development of a surface water distribution system. Nevertheless, the introduction of some form of competitive surface water pricing could substantially improve the efficiency of the future distribution of surface water. For example, the right to sell surface water rights, subject to approval of the regulating agency that the transfer could be accommodated by the existing distribution network and would not result in significant losses to third parties, could produce a more efficient conjunctive use of ground and surface water. It would become more profitable for farmers to transfer water rights from land with relatively low productive potential or high water distribution losses to land with a higher productivity and lower distribution losses. Water rights would tend to become concentrated on good lands in the upper portion of the distribution system, while ground water use would tend to concentrate in the areas with lower pumping depths. In the absence of effects on third parties, no farmer would be directly hurt and many would benefit by the creation of a market in surface water rights.

When the transfer of water rights generates significant effects on third parties (i.e., externalities), trading in water rights does not necessarily lead to an improved social water use. In this case it is important to distinguish between technological and pecuniary external effects. For example, if a transfer of water rights from a downstream to an upstream user reduced the quality of water to other users this would be a technological loss or a real loss to society. In this case the transfer results in a more efficient water use only if the benefits of transfer more than compensate for the losses. The market mechanism, however, would not take the external effects into account since by definition they are external to the trading parties. If the neighbors of the farmer selling water rights must pay more for canal maintenance because these costs are then divided among fewer users, this would be a pecuniary external effect and not a real productive loss to society. The pecuniary externality creates a distribution, but not an efficiency, problem. If deemed desirable, the change in income could be offset with payments to third parties.

There is no reason to expect significant technological externalities from trading in water rights in Cuyo. However, if farmers continued to pay the costs of maintaining the principal irrigation canals according to the length of the canals leading to their land and the percentage of land using the canals, there would be both pecuniary external economies and diseconomies. These externalities could be readily avoided by changing the basis of charging surface water users. However, if downstream users were forced to pay higher canal maintenance costs, this would increase the incentive for additional sales of water rights. Consequently, the move toward an efficient allocation of surface water might be more rapid.

The combination of a user tax on ground water pumping and trading in surface water rights would lead toward an optimal conjunctive use of ground and surface water. Considerably higher pumping costs in the upper reaches of the irrigated region would give these farmers greater incentive to substitute ground with surface water. The incentive would be even greater if interannual surface water receipts were regulated through dams or government irrigation wells. The price they would be willing to pay for these rights would easily enable the downstream farmers to switch entirely to ground water despite the increase in their pumping costs. Moreover, the combination of these two measures would tend to equate private with social water costs on every farm. Even if a farmer were given rights to more water than he could possibly use, the opportunity to sell this water would tend to internalize the social value of this water to the farmer. He would benefit by selling any of the water which could make a higher net return in an alternative use. The internalization of these social costs is essential for encouraging on-farm water use efficiency and investments required for a less water-intensive growth in the region.

Another theoretically possible method for improving the efficiency of surface water use and the conjunctive use of surface and ground water would be to auction the water rights at some regular interval such as monthly or annually. For instance, if the rights to certain quantities of river water, measured at some point on the river above the irrigated lands, were auctioned annually, the farmers with the most productive uses after allowance for differences in distribution losses would presumably make the highest bids and receive the water. Thus, the water would be directed to its most productive uses and farmers' water costs would reflect the full social costs of delivering water to farms.

It is unlikely, however, that any system of water auctioning would be practical—politically or administratively. Farmers could be expected to object vigorously to any such scheme since it would mean large increases in their water costs as the scarcity value of the water was transferred to the government. Although farmers as a group could be reimbursed for this loss in a manner that would not distort water use, an auctioning system would produce uncertainties in water costs and receipts. Any system increasing the risks of farming would be strongly resisted. The administrative obstacles to water auctioning would be even greater. It would be virtually impossible to insure that the many thousands of small farmers all had the opportunity to participate in the auctioning process on a comparable basis. It would also greatly complicate the regulating agency's task of delivering the water to the proper lands.

In summary, three generalizations regarding the operation of the market mechanism in water use in Cuyo are clear: the assumptions of the perfectly competitive model are not sufficiently satisfied for the market system alone to bring about an efficient water use; the market system could play a much more effective role in encouraging water use efficiency; even a well-patched market system is certain to fall short of achieving an optimum efficient water use. Considerable improvements in efficiency could be gained by eliminating the indirect policy measures which distort the efficient allocation of water through the market mechanism, imposing a tax to narrow the gap between the private and social costs of water use caused by natural market failures, and providing some means of selling surface water rights. The major obstacles in using the market mechanism to effect increases in water use efficiency lie in quantifying the social costs and benefits, implementing and collecting a tax on ground water use, and changing the laws which make surface water rights inseparable from the land.

Direct Controls

While indirect controls work through the market system and, if successful, improve it, direct controls attempt to eliminate the role of the market. Government fiats allocate resources, and, in fully centralized economies, determine what goods are to be produced and how.

Currently, the provincial governments directly control the allocation of surface water within Cuyo and exert some slight influence over ground water use through government-owned irrigation wells that reinforce surface water flows in some areas. Water use efficiency has never been a factor in the design of these controls. Historical claims are the only criteria for allocating surface water. The major justification for the government drilling of irrigation wells has been to reinforce water supplies to land where recent low surface water receipts jeopardized the historical claims to surface water.

Government also directly influences water use through investments in major water-related infrastructure such as dams and large canals. To the extent that the projects are undertaken on the basis of benefit-cost analyses, there is an attempt to allocate government investment funds efficiently. However, the justification for some of the projects undertaken or contemplated, such as the El Carrizal and Potrerillos dams and the lining of the major irrigation canals, would hardly qualify as benefit-cost analysis. In general, water use efficiency has played little role in the design and operation of water infrastructure.[39]

Although efficiency considerations have never entered prominently, if at all, into the development of direct controls of water use in Cuyo, the mounting costs of inefficiency are calling this neglect into question. Change may become more acceptable.

[39] The support for this statement is provided in the first section of Chapter 7.

Ideally, with complete information on the benefits from and costs of delivering water to every unit of land at all points of time, the government could devise an optimal program for water-related investments and distribution of the water both spatially and temporally. This ideal is, of course, impossible for many reasons. First, the enormous amount of data required for determining an efficient allocation of the water within one agricultural year could not be fully attained even at great cost and time. The optimal use over time would also depend on unknowns such as future water receipts, demands, and changes in technologies which can be estimated only with considerable imprecision. And even if all the information were available, it would be a herculean, if not impossible, task to develop a model and derive an optimal solution. Finally, even if the model were constructed and the water distributed efficiently over time and space, this alone would not insure an efficient use of the water. Unless the costs of the water to each farmer reflected social costs, on-farm investment decisions would tend to result in an inefficient use of the water.

While the judicious use of direct controls to distribute water are bound to leave us some distance from an optimum, they may well lead us in that direction. Much progress has been made in developing models to aid in the administration of a multipurpose dam and in the determination of the optimal conjunctive use of ground and surface water and the optimal intertemporal use of water stored in the ground or in a reservoir. Indeed, a group of economists from the National University of Cuyo in Mendoza are developing a model to determine the optimal conjunctive use of ground and surface water for the irrigated zone in the north of Mendoza province. All such models are necessarily highly abstract. Yet, by focusing on the most important factors for efficient water use, the models can be reduced to a manageable scale and still provide specific guidelines for improving water use efficiency.

The model being developed for northern Mendoza should indicate how changes in the conjunctive use of ground and surface water could yield large savings in terms of lower water distribution losses and pumping costs. Its recommendations undoubtedly will call for the increased use of surface water in the upper reaches of the irrigation system and relatively greater pumping in the lower reaches.

Politically, however, it would be very difficult to effect such a change without making concessions to farmers that might offset any improvements in the overall efficiency of water use. For example, there would be a huge uproar if the government simply attempted to transfer the water rights from the lower to upper irrigated areas, leaving it up to the farmers in the lower region to come up with ground water. Even in the lower parts of the irrigation system the private costs of surface water are currently well below the private costs of ground water. Secondly, because of economies of scale in ground water drilling, it would be inefficient and unreasonable to expect small farmers to drill their own wells. Consequently, the government would almost certainly have to undertake the ground water pumping required to compensate farmers for the loss of surface water rights. Any attempt by the government to recover the full costs of providing this ground water would be strongly resisted since this would mean much higher water costs to farmers in the lower areas. A third potential problem would be to avoid large increases in the number of operational irrigation wells. If a large increase is to be avoided, there must be some provision for transferring the pumps and motors currently used to pump ground water in the upper areas to the lower areas. Yet such a move would likely be resisted since additional rights to surface water and the availability of a pump for ground water may not be perfectly substitutable in the minds of farmers. The pump adds a degree of insurance that many farmers find valuable in view of the erratic nature of surface water receipts. In summary, all farmers would expect to benefit from, or at least not be made any worse off by, a change in the conjunctive use of ground and surface water. Satisfying these expectations would almost certainly mean decreases in private water costs and increases in the rate of ground water use. Any increase in the gap between private and social water costs would further discourage efficient on-farm water use. Unless these problems are adequately solved, it is not clear that a government-imposed improvement in the conjunctive use of ground and surface water actually would improve the overall efficiency of water use.

Direct controls over ground water use within Cuyo have been rumored and, if imposed, are, at first, likely to take the form of limitations or outright prohibitions on new wells. Prohibitions or strict limitations on new wells would be relatively easy to enforce and would offer substantial political advantages. Drilling prohibitions would tend to protect prior investment in wells; as the number of well owners rises and the threat of higher pumping costs and dry wells increases, these farmers are likely to demand limitations on new drilling. The farmers benefiting from a prohibition are likely to be more numerous and politically influential than the potential investors hurt by such a limitation.

However, the prohibition of new wells may or may not be economically advisable from a social perspective. It would certainly eliminate or reduce the current overinvestment in ground water equipment. But it is not clear that zero would be the optimal rate of ground water investment. In addition, a drilling prohibition suffers from the same efficiency disadvantage as the current system of surface water rationing: it provides no means for transferring ground water to more productive uses, and it does not close the gap between private and social water costs which discourages farmers from undertaking on-farm, water-saving investments. A more flexible system of control over new wells would be more efficient only if efficiency criteria were the basis for permitting new drilling. But in this case, the easiest and surest way to introduce efficiency criteria would be to use indirect controls to narrow the gap between social and private drilling and pumping costs.

With about 20,000 irrigation wells in the region, the pumping capacity already exists for rapid drawdowns of many water tables. This capacity raises the possibility of using some form of quota system to regulate pumping. Pumping quotas would not be easy to enforce. Meters, which would involve the same costs and control problems mentioned in connection with the imposition of a user tax, would be required. But the most difficult problems for achieving greater efficiency through quotas are determining "to whom" and "how many" quotas. From an efficiency point of view, the "to whom" problem is unimportant if owners are allowed to sell their quotas. Regardless of the initial distribution, the quotas would tend to end up in the hands of the farmers who could make the most money from the water since they would be able to pay the highest price. With a market for water quotas, a farmer's opportunity costs tend to reflect the social costs of the water use, encouraging more on-farm water-saving investment. In the absence of a market for ground water rights, however, an inefficient allocation of the water is virtually certain. Even if the government desired to make the most efficient allocation of the quotas, it does not have nor could it reasonably expect to obtain the detailed information on entrepreneurial and farming abilities and soil qualities, which are necessary to make the efficient distribution directly. Moreover, changes in technology and all the other factors pertinent to an efficient distribution would alter the efficient distribution of the quotas over time. For example, as the ground water tables fell, pumping depths and water quality would be affected differently in different regions. The changes would be very difficult to predict with any precision and difficult to keep abreast of as they happened. Unless there were a market in ground water quotas, there would be no reasonable means of adjusting to such changes. The question of "how many" quotas to issue is essential to an efficient intertemporal use of the ground water. If the quotas were set equal to the safe-yield of the aquifer, this would preserve the long-run water level and the future value of the quotas. But this does not make any more economic sense than would preventing the mining of a mineral. Ideally, ground water use would initially rise as the agricultural economy grew, reach a peak after a substantial portion of the water was extracted, and taper off until use was equivalent to the long-run safe-yield of the aquifer. Determination of the optimum rate of mining and, therefore, the optimum number of quotas at any given time, is comparable in difficulty to determining the optimum user tax.

It was argued above that when direct controls such as quotas are used to distribute ground and surface water, a market in these quotas would tend to internalize the social cost of the water to the user and thereby encourage more efficient on-farm water use. In the absence of such a market, a farmer's alternative uses of the water are limited to his farm; for some farmers the net marginal value of water may be very low. In such cases farmers have little incentive to use the water efficiently or to make water-saving investments. For example, field water efficiency rates may remain very low for lack of land leveling, and large quantities of water may be used on such crops as alfalfa which generally provide a low return to water. Yet, regardless of the magnitude of these inefficiencies, it is very unlikely that the Argentine government would attempt to impose extensive direct controls over the on-farm decisions of what and how to produce. On several occasions in the past the provincial governments have imposed limitations on the quantities and varieties of grapes that could be planted. However, with the possible exception of controls on the drilling of irrigation wells and ground water pumping, it is unlikely that either national or provincial government would attempt to make further inroads through direct controls into on-farm investment decisions. Indeed, both the experience of countries attempting to impose direct control over the agricultural sector and the historical performance of government-run enterprise in Argentina indicate that extensive government control of farming would be disastrous for agricultural efficiency in Cuyo. The most promising methods of encouraging on-farm water use efficiency are to internalize the full social cost of water use through either a user tax or a market in ground and surface water rights.

SOME CONCLUSIONS

The inefficiencies of water use and agricultural development within Cuyo are not the result of backward farmers adopting inefficient or outdated techniques. To the contrary, the farmers generally are efficient in terms of their objective of maximizing individual profits. The inefficiencies stem from the failure of the prices directing on-farm investment and production to reflect social values and from the direct government controls on water use. Moreover, current policies are not justified as means for fulfilling nonefficiency objectives of the society.

In some situations direct government controls are necessary, e.g., intertemporal releases of reservoir water almost certainly must be determined by some central authority. It would be administratively impractical to enable individual farmers to purchase additional water for some period such as a month or year. In such cases the development of mathematical models can be very useful for insuring that releases are set in accordance with some predetermined set of criteria and not, as currently seems to be the case, left up to the whim of an administrator or the pleas of conflicting interest groups.

The case for using indirect or direct controls to improve the optimal conjunctive use of ground and surface water is complicated. Because of the economies of scale in water distribution and the nature of the existing canal system, the government must operate the diversion canals. And because of natural market failures, there is a strong case for some form of government control over ground water use. The important issue is whether the government should be the sole or primary determiner of where ground and surface water is to be used. If the government assumed this role, the determination of an efficient allocation of the ground and surface water within a static framework would be extremely complicated for a region such as northern Mendoza; the problems increase severalfold for an intertemporal analysis. To account adequately for the major relevant factors requires the use of a sophisticated model. The disadvantages of modeling in this instance are not so much in the abstractions necessary as in the scarce resources demanded, highly trained personnel and computer time, and in the long period required for collecting data and developing and solving the model. More important objections to relying on direct government controls to allocate the water are these: in an effort to gain political acceptance of a major readjustment, administrators will likely grant some farmers concessions, which could actually decrease the on-farm and interannual efficiency of water use; and the use of direct controls over one aspect of water use presents the possibility of distorting some other aspect of water use. For example, the current system of regulating surface water distorts on-farm investment incentives, and, very likely, direct controls to limit drilling investment and ground water pumping would worsen the timing of pumping and the locating of wells.

If there were no suitable alternatives, the comments above would merely indicate some of the costs and possible pitfalls of using direct controls for improving the conjunctive use of ground and surface water. But there are alternatives. For surface water a preferable alternative is creation of a market in water rights and elimination of the laws attaching the water rights to the land. Although the changes in water use resulting from creation of such a market in surface water rights might not be as dramatic and complete as with a government decreed change, the advantages include elimination of the great time and costs required to estimate optimal surface water distribution, easier political accept-ance without the attachment of self-defeating concessions to particular interest groups, an automatic means of adjusting to future changes in the conditions affecting the optimal conjunctive use, internalization of the social cost of the water use,[40] and release of highly trained personnel to work on other tasks required for achieving water use, such as studies of the policy changes required to close the gap between private and social ground water costs and the estimation of the optimal rate of ground water mining.

For ground water there are two clearly preferable alternatives to government decrees controlling pumping and drilling—permitting the sale of the drilling and pumping quotas independent of the land or taxing drilling and pumping in order to equate the private and social costs. Features common to both approaches are reliance on market forces as opposed to government decrees to achieve efficiency, internalization of the social costs of drilling and pumping, dependence on water meters for control, and annual adjustment of the ideal tax and quantity of quotas, as changes in water stocks, product prices, interest rates, and so on alter the optimal rate of mining of the aquifers. If the government desired or felt compelled to prevent any significant redistribution of income, the granting of pumping quotas on the basis of historical use would be preferable. However, if the government were unconcerned with or wanted to alter income distribution, auctioning of the pumping quotas or a user tax would transfer the scarcity value of the water to the government. These funds could then be used to alter the income distribution in the desired manner.[41] Politically, the auctioning of the pumping quotas and user tax approaches would encounter resistance from current well owners. Quotas for drilling new wells, however, could

---

[40] When the water is not completely consumed in an economic sense, as is the case with drainage water, which becomes available to other farmers or infiltration to the aquifer, achieving water use efficiency is greatly complicated. Theoretically, the use of direct controls for improving water use efficiency could take into account the nonconsumptive component, including changes in water quality, of any water use. In practice, however, crude approximations of the impact of these factors on efficiency are the best that can be expected. When the nonconsumptive effects vary among farmers, it would be very difficult to take them into account when market forces allocate the water. In these cases private costs will not accurately reflect social costs and an optimum water use will not be achieved. However, unless these factors are very important, the market alternatives under consideration should result in substantial improvements in water use efficiency.

[41] Economies of scale in ground water extraction present the possibility of a conflict between efficiency and income distribution objectives when market forces are used to control ground water use. This conflict, however, could be resolved by permitting farmers to buy ground water rights from the government for delivery through existing canals and the formation of pumping cooperatives among farmers on adjoining lands.

probably be auctioned without arousing the opposition of any sizable group.

Indirect controls over factor and product prices and credit terms are definitely preferable to direct controls over farmers' planting decisions for achieving efficiency in on-farm investment and production. Efforts to impose extensive direct controls over on-farm decisions are likely to lead to greater inefficiency.

The greatest obstacle to achieving a more efficient water use and agricultural development within Cuyo is the political environment within which important economic decisions are made. Economic policies are largely a reaction to the lobbying, pleas, and even rioting of special interest groups. The importance of these forces was evident in the setting of electric rates for Mendoza in 1972 and grape prices in 1972 and 1973. Objective economic analysis of alternative policies either is not made or carries little weight in the decisions. Within such a decision-making environment, there is little hope for improving water use efficiency through either direct or indirect controls.

farm level
implications
of rising water costs
and alternative
government policies

The overall impact of government policies and changes in underlying factor conditions on the region's development depends on the decisions of thousands of farmers responding to their individual investment opportunities. Expected farmers' profits provide the incentive to adopt a particular technology or alter the rate and direction of investment. Consequently, to understand better the implications of current trends and investment incentives and evaluate policy alternatives, it is essential to examine the impact of policies and factor prices on the profitability of various farming alternatives. Such an examination requires a microeconomic look at farm profits under alternative conditions. This chapter attempts to quantify the impact of different water costs and government policies on (1) the profits of a representative 10-hectare vineyard, (2) the optimal farm size, and (3) the relative profitability of permanent and annual crops. This analysis supports some of the prior conclusions such as how the higher water costs associated with ground water use have altered the rate and direction of agricultural investment and how subsidies and natural market failures associated with ground water use have altered water use patterns. Moreover, the data and conclusions of this chapter are used in the following chapter to examine the profitability and, therefore, the likelihood of acceptance of alternative irrigation technologies under current and social water costs.

RETURNS FROM GRAPE GROWING

This section examines the impact of alternative water costs and government policies on the profitability of grapes. While costs and revenues obviously vary substantially among farms and even from year to year on the same farm, these complications are initially ignored. Using cost and revenue estimates for a hypothetical, representative 10-hectare farm, the sensitivity of profits to changes in yields, prices, water costs, and the ability of a farmer to benefit from government investment incentives are examined.

There is no attempt to examine whether grapes are the best agricultural investment in the region; nor is there any attempt to determine the optimal cropping pattern. On-farm income studies have almost invariably demonstrated that farmers' cropping patterns and factor utilization are well adapted to the conditions and technology within which they must operate. There is no reason to expect that Cuyo is an exception to this. Indeed, the available data indicate that grapes are a very attractive investment in Cuyo. Moreover, the well-established marketing system for grapes is undoubtedly an important attraction for farmers who might otherwise have difficulty in marketing their production at profitable prices.

Costs, Revenues, and Profits for a Hypothetical Vineyard

Table 6.1 presents the estimated costs per hectare of planting and cultivating 10 hectares of grapes using the overhead-trellis planting system.[1] These estimates include all costs except the cost of the land.

---

[1] A 10-hectare farm is used initially because it is representative of a large number of vineyards in the region and cost data were available for this size vineyard. The impact of economies of scale, especially those deriving from ground water use, are examined later in this chapter.

The local name for the overhead-trellis system of grape growing is *parral*. It involves the construction of an overhead trellis to support the vines. The most common alternative system in the region is *contraespaldera* which involves the construction of a wire fence to support the vines. As the height of the fence increases, the expected grape yields, as well as the initial construction and material costs, rise. The *parral* system involves the highest initial costs and offers the highest expected yields of any system used in the region. The relative profitability of the alternative growing systems depends primarily on the yield difference,

Table 6.1 Production Costs for a Hypothetical Vineyard[a]

(in 1969 dollars per hectare)

	Year 1	Year 2	Year 3	Years 4 to 30
Land preparation, planting and cultivation[b]	193.3	153.2	145.0	169.1
Construction of overhead trellis[c]	171.2	26.1	—	—
Materials[d]	731.7	280.0	158.8	90.1
Annual cost of buildings, equipment and work animals[e]	47.3	47.3	47.3	47.3
Water[f]	10.0	10.0	10.0	10.0
Total Costs	1,153.5	516.6	361.1	316.5

[a] The costs are based on the overhead-trellis (*parral*) planting system and a farm with 10 hectares of grapes. The costs of the land and harvest are excluded. Harvest costs are excluded since the examination of profitability uses prices of grapes on the vine. The treatment of land costs is discussed in the text. The primary source of the estimates is José P. Morelli, "Inversión privada en viticultura," *Revista de investigaciones agropecuarias* (Buenos Aires: INTA, 1970), Serie 6, Economía y Administración Rural, Vol. 4, No. 2, tables 10, 11, and 12. The 1968 peso costs were converted to 1969 dollars at 343 pesos to one dollar.

[b] With the exception of $29 in the first year for tractor rental to prepare the land, these costs are for labor. The land preparation costs do not allow for land leveling or clearing of heavy brush. Labor is priced at $3.7 per eight-hour day regardless of whether the work is done by the owner or hired help. The number of hours required and tractor costs are based on data in ibid., Table 12 and p. 84.

[c] These costs are based on data in ibid., pp. 93–94.

[d] The materials include seed, fertilizer, insecticides, herbicides, and the wood and wire for constructing the trellis. The wood and wire are the most important cost items during the first two years. The data also include an allowance for the wood and labor required to maintain the trellis after the third year. The data are from ibid., pp. 90, 92, 94, and 95.

[e] These costs include the estimated interest, amortization, and maintenance costs of a perimeter fence, shed, tools, work animals, corral, and harness. There are economies of scale for some of these items; the calculations are based on a farm with 10 cultivated hectares. The annual costs were calculated from data for the initial purchase or construction costs and life expectancy of individual items using a 10 percent discount rate. The major source of the basic data is ibid., tables 10, 11, and 12. Alternative cost estimates were obtained from nonpublished sources. In some cases averages were used for initial costs.

[f] In 1970 water rights in Mendoza cost from $3.4 to $25.9 per hectare.

Land with water rights in Mendoza costs approximately $1,000 per hectare. For an individual farmer the opportunity cost of this money or the rent paid on the land is a cost of production. For the whole society, however, the value of the land for nonagricultural purposes is very low

---

discount rate, time horizon, and price of grapes. If the yields of the *contraespaldera* system are 80 percent of the *parral* yields, then *parral* would be more profitable than *contraespaldera* at a 10 percent discount rate and time horizon of eight years or longer. If the difference in the revenue from the two systems dropped in half, *parral* would be more profitable at a 10 percent discount rate only if the time horizon were extended to fourteen years or longer.

if not zero; the price of or rent for the land is really a return to farming.[2] Indeed, in the Cuyo area agricultural land values are largely determined by the profitability of growing grapes. Consequently, if the cost of the land is included in production costs, then any decrease in other costs or increase in grape prices and average yields would be reflected in an increase in the value of the land with water, and there would be no corresponding increase in the profits from grapes. Grape profits would simply reflect a normal return to the owners' labor and management. Although this may be relevant for individual farmers, it does not reflect the social returns to grapes or agriculture in general. Thus, in order to examine the returns to agriculture under alternative water costs and government policies, the following discussion focuses on the return to land planted to grapes.

Table 6.2 indicates the gross and net returns per hectare to grape growing over a thirty-year period on a hypothetical farm. The major assumptions are that production costs are similar to those in Table 6.1, growers receive $49 per metric ton of grapes on the vine (the average growers' price from 1960 to 1969), and the yields are those presented in column 2 of Table 6.2.[3] The final column of Table 6.2, the cumulative sum of the present value of the profits, indicates that the internal rate of return is slightly over 10 percent for a time horizon of nine years. The

[2] Agricultural land with surface water rights is perfectly inelastic in supply within Cuyo while land with ground water potential is still plentiful. Competition should establish relative land prices such that an investor is indifferent between buying land with water rights or other land and drilling a well. If the overall profitability of farming rises due to improved technology or higher prices, the value of land with water rights or an operational irrigation well would temporarily rise. Gradually as new wells were drilled and new lands brought under cultivation, agricultural returns and, therefore, land prices would fall. In Cuyo, however, the longer run means a sharp reduction in the availability of ground water; increased water scarcity might force a decline in the total cultivated area. In this case higher agricultural returns in the region would increase the value of land with water and encourage new plantings in other regions.

[3] The implied average annual production over the thirty years is 17.90 MT per hectare. This yield compares with the actual average (including all systems of grape growing) of 8.79 MT per hectare in Mendoza and 13.97 MT per hectare in San Juan from 1960 to 1972. There is no way to determine the actual average yields from the land using the overhead-trellis system. However, in Mendoza the average yield for grapes grown with the overhead-trellis system should be substantially above the overall average for the province since more than three-fourths of the vineyards are planted with systems with considerably lower average yields. San Juan's average yield for trellis-grown grapes should be much closer to the overall average, because nearly 88 percent of their land under grapes uses this system. While the yields implied in Table 6.2 are undoubtedly above the average, they are not exceptionally high; some vineyards yield 30 MT or more per hectare during the vine's most productive period. The 17.9 MT yields are more relevant than the provincial averages for evaluating new investments which is the basis of the subsequent analysis.

Table 6.2 Profits for a Hypothetical Vineyard[a]

Year	Yield[b] (tons/ha)	Revenue[c] ($/ha)	Profit[d] ($/ha)	Present value of profits as of year 1 (10% discount rate) ($/ha)	Cumulative sum of present value of profits ($/ha)
1	—	—	−1,154	−1,154	−1,154
2	—	—	−517	−470	−1,623
3	2.13	104	−257	−221	−1,844
4	10.63	521	204	153	−1,691
5	17.01	833	517	353	−1,338
6	21.26	1,042	725	450	−888
7	21.26	1,042	725	409	−478
8	21.26	1,042	725	372	−106
9	21.26	1,042	725	338	232
10	21.26	1,042	725	308	540
11	21.26	1,042	725	280	819
12	21.18	1,038	721	253	1,072
13	21.09	1,033	717	228	1,301
14	21.01	1,029	713	207	1,507
15	20.92	1,025	709	187	1,694
16	20.84	1,021	705	169	1,862
17	20.71	1,015	698	152	2,014
18	20.58	1,008	692	137	2,151
19	20.45	1,002	685	123	2,274
20	20.33	996	680	111	2,385
21	20.20	990	673	100	2,486
22	20.00	980	663	90	2,575
23	19.81	971	654	80	2,655
24	19.61	961	644	72	2,727
25	19.41	951	635	64	2,792
26	19.21	941	625	58	2,849
27	18.95	929	612	51	2,901
28	18.69	916	599	46	2,947
29	18.43	903	586	41	2,987
30	18.17	890	574	36	3,023

[a] The data are based on the overhead-trellis planting system and a farm with 10 hectares of grapes. Minor differences in the data exist because of rounding. The dollars are deflated to 1969.

[b] The yields are from Morelli, "Inversión privada en viticultura," p. 69. These yield estimates allow for an average loss of 18.8 percent due to frost and hail.

[c] This assumes a price of $49 per metric ton, the average growers' price for grapes on the vine from 1960 to 1969.

[d] This column subtracts the cost estimates of Table 6.1 from the revenue estimates in this table.

internal rate of return would be 15 percent for a time horizon of ten years and 22 percent for twenty years.

Profitability is, of course, extremely sensitive to the price and yield. The internal rate of return over twenty years with good grape yields would drop to 18 percent with a 15 percent fall and increase to 25 percent with a 15 percent rise in growers' prices. If average grape yields are reduced by half, returns fall sharply. Even with allowance for lower production costs on a farm with half the yields,[4] the internal rate of return would reach 10 percent only with a twenty-eight-year time horizon. These yields of half the levels assumed in Table 6.2 are approximately equivalent to the average for all vineyards in Mendoza; they are probably well below the yields of vineyards planted with the overhead-trellis system. Consequently, farmers with average or below average yields can expect a reasonable return on their investment only if no allowance is made for the cost of the land.

Effects of Ground Water Costs on Profits on a 10-Hectare Farm

The use of ground water substantially increases the production costs of the 10-hectare farm depicted in tables 6.1 and 6.2. In the absence of credit and tax subsidies, annual water costs on a 10-hectare farm pumping water a height of 30 meters range from $1,970 to $2,470.[5] This compares to a cost of about $100 on a farm receiving surface water. The internal rate of return with a twenty-year time horizon (using all assumptions for the farm depicted in tables 6.1 and 6.2 except water cost) is 11 percent with water costs of $247 per hectare and 13 percent with water costs of $197 per hectare.

The per hectare costs of irrigating just 5 hectares with ground water would be nearly double the water cost for 10 hectares.[6] The higher water costs are prohibitively expensive for planting grapes; even with a thirty-year time horizon, the internal rate of return would be well under 10 percent. Yet, if a farm with 10 hectares of grapes were suddenly confronted with surface water receipts sufficient for only 5 hectares, investment in ground water would be profitable if the alternative meant the loss of 5 hectares of good-yielding grapes. For example, if we assumed that the farm described in Table 6.2 were faced with the alternative of abandoning 5 hectares of grapes after the tenth year or drilling a well to supplement the surface water, the well clearly would be more profitable. At a 10 percent discount rate the net present value of the

[4] These calculations assume that the lower yields would be accompanied by a 50 percent reduction in the cost of fertilizer, pesticides, and herbicides, an annual saving of three labor days per hectare, because of the reduced use of these inputs, and a 30 percent reduction in the annualized cost of the buildings, equipment, and work animals.

[5] The ground water costs are based on estimates from tables 2.8 and 2.10. The higher figure includes $501 for the annual cost of a storage pool. Both figures assume that pumping is done during the hours of low energy rates. The assumption of off-peak pumping without a storage pool is more realistic for a farm of 10 hectares or less than for the 20-hectare farm considered in Table 2.8.

[6] Based on data in Table 2.10.

Table 6.3 Estimated Ground Water Costs on a 10-Hectare Farm with
Varying Subsidies

(in 1969 dollars per hectare)

	Without storage pool	With storage pool
No subsidy[a]	197	247
Credit subsidy[b]	154	192
Tax subsidy[c]	156	194
Credit and tax subsidies[d]	112	138

   [a] From Table 2.10.
   [b] Calculated from data in tables 2.10 and 3.1 assuming a bank lending rate of 15 percent and a nominal discount rate of 40 percent.
   [c] Calculated from data in tables 2.10 and 3.2 assuming a marginal tax rate of 33 percent and a nominal discount rate of 40 percent.
   [d] The cost reductions from the credit and tax subsidies are additive.

return over the following twenty years would be nearly $15,000 greater from drilling the well than the alternative of abandoning 5 hectares.

On a relatively inefficient vineyard (a farm with the overhead-trellis planting system and yields averaging 8.84 metric tons per hectare) ground water costs are prohibitive for a 10-hectare farm. With a thirty-year time horizon, the present discounted value of the investment would be minus nearly $2,000 per hectare at a 10 percent discount rate. Moreover, such a farm would limit its losses by abandoning 5 hectares of grapes rather than drilling a well to save the low producing vines.

For farms that have an operational irrigation well with excess pumping capacity, marginal water costs are very low. The marginal water cost with a pumping height of 30 meters would be just under $10 per hectare with off-peak energy rates and range from $10 to $29 per hectare with daytime pumping. The internal rates of return to a good vineyard with these water costs would range from 21 to 22 percent.

Government Policies and Farm Profits

One of the most important factors in a farmer's production costs in Cuyo is his ability to take advantage of agricultural credit subsidies and tax investment incentives. Chapter 3 examined the importance of credit and tax policies for a farmer's ground water costs. Table 6.3 presents estimated ground water costs on a 10-hectare farm with and without the subsidies. Annual ground water costs with no storage pool would be reduced about $430 by the credit subsidy and $410 by the tax subsidy. A farmer able to take advantage of both subsidies would reduce annual production costs by $840, about 10 percent of the average annual revenue of a good vineyard. This saving would increase the expected pretax internal rate of return on the 10-hectare farm over a twenty-year time horizon from about 13 to 17 percent, a substantial additional incentive for investment in grapes and ground water. The subsidies would also substantially reduce the cost of a storage pool. For the case of the 10-hectare farm with the pool, the credit and tax subsidies combined reduce production costs about $1,090 and increase the pretax internal rate of return from 11 to nearly 16 percent.

The credit and tax investment incentives are not limited to subsidizing ground water costs. Many investors are able to obtain credit for other agricultural costs. If a farmer obtained 70 percent financing of the costs of the irrigation well and other production costs incurred during the first two years, this credit subsidy alone would raise the internal rate of return to a 10-hectare vineyard using ground water with no storage pool from 13 to over 17 percent.[7] The tax investment incentive, which permits investors to deduct certain costs twice from taxable income, also applies to the costs of land clearing and leveling, installing irrigation canals, electrification, and planting and cultivating permanent crops until productive. For an investor with a 33 percent marginal tax rate, the tax incentive alone raises the pretax internal rate of return to grapes on the 10-hectare farm using ground water from 13 to more than 18 percent. The combined impact of the tax and credit incentives raises the pretax internal rate of return to 25 percent, a return nearly 4 percent higher than the estimated return when farmers pay the nominal surface water charges but receive no tax and credit subsidies. Even with the additional cost of the storage pool, under the preceding assumptions the credit and tax subsidies increase the internal rate of return to 24 percent.

These profit estimates for a farm using ground water already allow for the low electric power rates charged agricultural users. Annual costs would rise if farmers paid the rates charged any other power users. For example, Table 6.4 indicates the average power cost of pumping 10,330 m^3 of water a height of 30 meters would be $49.5 per hectare with residential power rates. This power cost would raise costs by $29 per hectare on the 10-hectare farm. An increase in annual water costs from $197 to $226 per hectare would decrease the internal rate of return on the 10-hectare vineyard with good grape yields from about 13 to 12 percent. This cost increase, equivalent to about 3.4 percent of the average annual revenue from a good vineyard, might mean the difference between drilling and not drilling an irrigation well for some marginal investors.

If this were the extent of the rise in production costs, the impact of

---

[7] All the estimates in this paragraph assume a 15 percent lending rate and a 40 percent nominal discount rate.

Table 6.4 Estimated Annual Power Costs as a Function of Pumping Depth with Residential Power Rates[a]

(in 1969 dollars per hectare)

Pumping depth (meters)	25 hp Motor		60 hp Motor	
	Pumping cost[b]	Cost increase[c]	Pumping cost[b]	Cost increase[c]
30	49.5	29.0	43.1	10.5
50	81.2	54.7	77.7	37.9
70	129.7	94.0	130.7	79.5
90			174.7	114.2
110			211.9	143.6

[a] This table is based on a cost of $34.85 per 1000 kW. This cost is the average power cost on the 20 hectare farm described in Table 2.8 if residential power rates are charged. The residential rate structure has a fixed bimonthly charge and increasing marginal rates after 100, 120, and 150 kWh consumed bimonthly. The calculations in this table, however, assume the average power cost is constant regardless of the amount of power consumed.

[b] The data underlying the derivation of the power requirements are presented in the notes to tables 2.8 and 2.9. It is assumed that 10,330 m³ of water are pumped per hectare.

[c] The cost increase is the difference between the power costs with the assumed residential rates and agricultural rates for a 10-hectare farm. With agricultural power rates, the fixed component of the power cost on the 10-hectare farm is $11.1 with the 25-hp motor and $23.5 with the 60-hp motor. The changes in the variable power costs with pumping depths are proportional to the increased power requirements. The assumptions regarding hourly water flows and the power requirements for the various pumping depths are presented in the notes to tables 2.8 and 2.9.

the higher power rates on the total number of wells drilled would probably not be great. However, since power consumption per unit of water rises with the pumping depth, the size of the cost increase would rise with the pumping distance. Table 6.4 presents estimates of the pumping costs per hectare for various pumping depths when farmers are charged residential power rates. The higher power rates would increase the incentive to locate relatively more of the new wells in areas with shallower pumping depths. Indeed, the magnitude of the power costs would be a substantial deterrent to drilling new wells with pumping depths of 90 meters or more. Power costs of $175 per hectare would increase the annualized cost of water on the 10-hectare farm with a 60-hp motor to about $380 per hectare. These costs would reduce the internal rate of return to a good vineyard to about 5 percent.

The preceding estimates of water costs assume annual pumping of 10,330 m³ per hectare, the estimated requirement for irrigating grapes in Mendoza with a 70 percent farm efficiency rate. The actual amount of water pumped per hectare, however, depends on various factors including the marginal cost of pumping and the water requirements of the crop under cultivation. Under the current rate structure more than half the annual power costs on the hypothetical 10-hectare farm are independent of the quantity of water pumped. Thus, marginal power costs are currently very low. If the annual cost of pumping 10,330 m³ of water a height of 30 meters were raised to $49.5, and if the rates were set such that the marginal and average power costs were equal, the higher rates would increase marginal water costs more than 400 percent. Such an increase in marginal water costs would affect the optimal cropping pattern and the optimal amount of water pumped for a given crop. Consequently, higher pumping rates should decrease the average quantity of water pumped from a well and, therefore, the total quantity of water pumped in the region.

Normal responses to a sharp change in a factor price are to plant relatively more crops with a higher return to the more expensive factor and to substitute relatively cheap for expensive inputs. The higher water costs discussed here are not likely to result in immediate abandonment or eradication of crops already under cultivation since, with the exception of alfalfa, the higher water costs are not apt to be a high percentage of either the expected revenue from crops already under cultivation or the irrecoverable costs associated with their planting and cultivation. However, as the time horizon increases and more costs become variable, the higher water costs become more pertinent for determining the total quantity of land to be planted and the crop composition. Substantial changes in the plantings of annual crops might come within a year. In particular, much of the alfalfa would be an obvious target for replacement. With a 70 percent irrigation efficiency and 30-meter pumping depth, the annual pumping costs for irrigating a hectare of alfalfa would be about $74, about 45 percent of the average annual revenue from a hectare of alfalfa in Mendoza. However, even with the current low agricultural power rates, ground water costs are probably too high for use on alfalfa with the possible exception of the alfalfa used by the dairy industry. The region's permanent crops, on the other hand, offer relatively high returns to water and have high fixed costs representing long-term investments. Higher pumping costs would encourage farmers to remove or abandon old and relatively unproductive trees and vines somewhat sooner, but the effect in any one year would be minor.

Water, of course, cannot be eliminated from the productive process through factor substitution. However, the farm efficiency of water can be increased through investments such as canal lining, new irrigation methods, and land leveling. Higher water prices would increase the profitability of these water-saving investments. Furthermore, the quantity of water delivered to the plants can and should be reduced until the marginal revenue product of the water is equal to the higher marginal cost of the water.

FARM LEVEL IMPLICATIONS 119

Bertranou has used observations of pumping costs and water applications per hectare to estimate demand curves for irrigation water in several areas of northern Mendoza.[8] His estimates of the price elasticities of demand for irrigation water, evaluated at the mean of the sample values, range from -0.26 to -1.33, with most between -0.5 and -0.7. However, to determine the impact of a substantial price increase on the quantity of water applied per hectare on a given crop, one would need to know the arc elasticity of demand between the two price levels.[9] The absolute value of the relevant arc elasticity would undoubtedly rise as the time horizon increased. For example, a farmer's immediate response to the price rise is likely to be a reduction in the quantity of water pumped and delivered to the plants already under cultivation. Investments to increase farm water use efficiency involve a time lag. And for the region, the labor and capital required for these investments are apt to be inelastic in supply in the short run and elastic in the long run. Moreover, the higher water costs should encourage the search for new technology to reduce water use or increase output per unit of water. For all these reasons the relevant arc elasticity of demand for water per hectare would be substantially greater in the long run than the elasticity relevant for measuring the response in the first month or year. Yet, even in the long run, the relevant arc elasticity of demand for water applied to a hectare of grapes for a 400 percent price increase is not likely to be as high as -0.5. A 400 percent price rise with an arc elasticity of -0.5 would reduce pumping by half. If a farm had been pumping 10,330 m^3 of water per hectare of grapes annually, even with 100 percent water use efficiency, a 50 percent decline in pumping would leave the vines 30 percent below the estimated ideal water requirements of grapes in Mendoza. Such a drastic decrease in water available to the vines, particularly if maintained for several years, would probably result in significant reductions in production. Since the cost of not reducing pumping in the face of the higher water price would be equivalent to only 3.4 percent of the average annual production of a good vine, this should be the maximum short-run decline in production resulting from such a rise in water costs.

[8] Armando Bertranou, "The Allocation of Irrigation Water in Mendoza, Argentina," a draft as of April 1973 of a Ph.D. dissertation being prepared for the University of California, Davis, Table 5.2.

[9] Arc elasticity of demand is defined as

$$\left(\frac{q_2 - q_1}{q_2 + q_1} \right) \div \left(\frac{p_2 - p_1}{p_2 + p_1} \right)$$

where q is the quantity demanded, p is the price, and the subscripts 1 and 2 refer to the initial and final levels of the variables. The point of elasticity is the value of this expression as Δp approaches zero where $\Delta p = p_2 - p_1$.

Table 6.5 Estimated Social Costs of Ground Water Use for a 10-Hectare
Farm for Varying Pumping Depths

(in 1969 dollars per hectare)

| Pumping depth (meters) | Annualized capital cost[a] | Variable costs | | | Total annual cost |
		Energy cost[b]	User tax[c]	Total variable cost	
Small motor (25 hp)					
30	177	50	50	100	277
50	177	81	50	131	308
70	177	130	50	180	357
Large motor (60 hp)					
30	205	43	50	93	298
50	205	78	50	128	333
70	205	131	50	181	386
90	205	175	50	225	430
110	205	212	50	262	467

[a] These estimates are based on data in tables 2.8, 2.9, and 2.10 and assume no storage pool.

[b] From Table 6.4.

[c] The basis for the assumption of the $50 per 10,330 m³ of water use is presented in Chapter 5, p. 98.

Social Water Costs and Farm Profits

Chapter 5 demonstrated that social water costs are currently higher than private water costs in Cuyo. To increase private ground water costs to the level of social costs, the government could eliminate investment subsidies for irrigation wells, equate private power costs to the social cost of power, and impose a tax on pumping equivalent to the external diseconomies and the user cost of private ground water use. The capital costs presented in Table 2.10 estimate the nonsubsidized costs of a well, motor, and pump. The estimates in Table 6.4 represent the social power costs of pumping 10,330 m³ of water various heights given that residential power rates are a reasonable proxy for the social costs of power. And $50 per 10,330 m³ of water is probably a reasonable first approximation of the magnitude of the external diseconomies and user cost associated with ground water pumping from Cuyo's major aquifers.[10] Under these assumptions, Table 6.5 summarizes the total and variable social costs of ground water use on a 10-hectare farm pumping 10,330 m³ of water various heights.

Internalizing the social cost of ground water to the farmer would have a substantial impact on potential investors. A ground water cost of $277 per hectare would reduce the internal rate of return on the

[10] See Chapter 5, p. 98.

10-hectare farm with good grape yields to just under 10 percent. Since this return makes no allowance for the cost of the land, it is hardly an attractive investment incentive. However, if the credit and tax subsidies were available for nonwater costs, the internal rate of return would be about 15 percent.[11] With a pumping depth of 90 meters the annual water cost would be $430 per hectare. The internal rate of return on the 10-hectare farm with water costs of $430 per hectare would be about 2 percent with no subsidies for nonwater costs and about 6.5 percent with the credit and tax subsidies for nonwater costs.

The impact of social water costs on a farm with an operational irrigation well would also be substantial. Under the above assumptions for social costs, the annual cost of pumping 10,330 m^3 of water a height of 30 meters would be about $100. This cost compares to the current estimated cost of about $20.5 on the 10-hectare farm pumping during the hours of low power rates and the cost of $49.5 with residential power rates but no water use tax. Moreover, if the water use tax were constant per unit of water pumped and the new power rate structure equated the marginal and average power costs for all users,[12] the social rate structure would represent more than an eightfold increase in marginal ground water costs on the farm above. As Table 6.5 indicates, the variable social costs of ground water rise rapidly as the pumping depth rises. As a percentage of the average gross revenue to a vineyard averaging 17.9 MT per hectare, the variable water costs would be about 11 percent at 30 meters and 26 percent at 90 meters. Nevertheless, the incentive to expand cultivation and water use would be substantial even with social water costs if a farmer had a well with excess pumping capacity. With marginal water costs of $100 per hectare, the internal rate of return to a good vineyard would be over 17 percent.

The internalization of social water costs to farmers would also bring sharp increases in the private costs of surface water. Equating private and social surface water costs would entail charging farmers more for distribution as well as internalizing the full social scarcity value of the

---

[11] The returns with the credit and tax subsidies assume a 33 percent marginal tax rate, 15 percent bank lending rate, 40 percent nominal discount rate, five-year financing of 70 percent of nonwater production costs incurred during the first two years, and a deduction from taxable income with a one-year lag of the nonwater production costs incurred during the first three years.

[12] For equating social and private costs there should be no discounts to large pumpers and water users either through the user tax or power rates. Within the relevant range for any one pumper, the user cost and externality which the tax is designed to price would be virtually constant for each unit withdrawn. Once the power lines are in place there is no economic reason for differential power rates dependent on the quantity consumed. There are, however, economic reasons for charging different power rates depending on the hour of use since the social cost of power consumption is lower during the hours of low overall consumption.

water. Distribution charges would have to be increased to allow for water losses as well as the cost of administration, amortization, and maintenance of the canals. The scarcity value of water could be internalized either through a user tax or permission to sell water rights independent of the land.

The much higher marginal water costs that would result from internalizing social costs to the farmers would provide strong incentives for increasing the returns to water and reducing the on-farm water losses. The qualitative responses of farmers would be similar to those described earlier regarding the impact of residential power rates. The incentives for change, however, would be greater with social costs since marginal ground water costs would be even higher and surface water costs would rise as well. The sharp rise in marginal water costs would encourage the drilling of any new wells primarily in areas with relatively short pumping distances, investments to increase farm water use efficiency, reductions in the quantity of water applied to the plant, and, if permitted legally, the sale of surface water rights from areas at the end to areas at the beginning of the irrigation system. Within the first year the major effect on the quantity of water consumed probably would result from the reduction in plantings of crops such as alfalfa requiring large quantities of water. In the longer run the impact on the profitability of adopting water-saving techniques would be crucial to the rate of water use. The profitability of water-saving techniques and the impact of different water costs on this profitability are examined in the following chapter.

PROFITABILITY AND FARM SIZE

Farm Size in Cuyo

The tremendous inequality in rural land holdings within the Cuyo region is indicated in Table 6.6. As of 1960 44 percent of all farms were 5 hectares or less and accounted for only 0.4 percent of the land. In contrast, 2.9 percent of the farms accounted for 91.7 percent of the land. These data, however, are not a good indication of the degree of economic concentration in agriculture. Without water, agricultural land in the region has little value, provides virtually no productive employment, and produces very little output. Consequently, the value of production from extensive livestock grazing over 1,000 hectares without irrigation water might be less than the value from a small vineyard.

The data most relevant to economic concentration, economic viability of farms, and the incorporation of economies of scale would be farm

Table 6.6 Farm Size in Cuyo as of 1960

Farm size in hectares	Farms	Hectares	Percentages of	
			Farms	Hectares
Mendoza				
0 to 5	9,989	26,584	39.2	0.3
5 to 25	10,681	132,456	41.9	1.5
25 to 100	2,734	132,592	10.7	1.5
100 to 1,000	1,112	418,099	4.4	4.8
over 1,000	977	8,061,780	3.8	91.9
Mendoza totals	25,493	8,771,511	100.0	100.0
San Juan				
0 to 5	5,859	12,984	55.7	0.6
5 to 25	3,220	35,458	30.6	1.7
25 to 100	1,015	49,207	9.7	2.3
100 to 1,000	364	90,298	3.5	4.3
over 1,000	53	1,917,599	0.5	91.1
San Juan totals	10,511	2,105,546	100.0	100.0
Cuyo				
0 to 5	15,848	39,568	44.0	0.4
5 to 25	13,901	167,914	38.6	1.5
25 to 100	3,749	181,799	10.4	1.7
100 to 1,000	1,476	508,397	4.1	4.7
over 1,000	1,030	9,979,379	2.9	91.7
Regional totals	36,004	10,877,057	100.0	100.0

Source: Dirección Nacional de Estadística y Censos, *Censo nacional agropecuario 1960* (Buenos Aires, 1964), Vol. 1, pp. 4–5.

size measured according to the quantity of land under cultivation. Unfortunately, such data are not available. However, with the data on farm size in Table 6.6 and the data indicating farm size according to the number of hectares planted to grapes in Table 6.7, one can get some idea of the economic concentration within agriculture. Table 6.7 indicates that in 1968 65 percent of the farms growing grapes in Cuyo had 5 hectares or less planted to grapes and 84 percent had 10 hectares or less; 22 percent of the land planted to grapes was on farms with 5 hectares of grapes or less and 41 percent on farms with 10 hectares or less. Many of these farms, however, had land planted to other crops; a farm with 5 hectares or less of grapes could range from a small farm insufficient to support adequately one family to a sizeable, diversified farm with grapes covering only a small part of the total cultivated area. Nevertheless, since grapes accounted for about 58 percent of total cultivated area in the region in 1968, it is likely that farms of 10 hectares or less accounted for about 75 percent of the farms and 25 percent of the cultivated land. Moreover, the combination of data on farm sizes according to the number of vineyards and total area (cultivated and uncultivated) indicates that in 1960 at least 37 percent of all

Table 6.7 Farm Sizes According to Land Planted to Grapes in 1968

Land planted to grapes (in hectares)	Farms	Hectares planted to grapes	Percentages of Farms	Percentages of Land planted
Mendoza				
0 to 5	16,369	42,455	62.1	20.3
5 to 10	5,504	40,088	20.9	19.1
10 to 15	1,821	22,447	6.9	10.7
15 to 25	1,386	26,948	5.3	12.9
25 to 50	782	27,171	3.0	13.0
50 to 100	338	23,065	1.3	11.0
over 100	147	27,341	0.6	13.0
Totals	26,347	209,515	100.0	100.0
San Juan				
0 to 5	6,922	15,278	72.8	27.8
5 to 10	1,387	10,040	14.6	18.3
10 to 15	470	5,801	4.9	10.6
15 to 25	376	7,193	4.0	13.1
25 to 50	245	8,525	2.6	15.5
50 to 100	86	5,685	0.9	10.4
over 100	17	2,370	0.2	4.3
Totals	9,503	54,892	100.0	100.0
Cuyo				
0 to 5	23,291	57,733	65.0	21.8
5 to 10	6,891	50,128	19.2	19.0
10 to 15	2,291	28,248	6.4	10.7
15 to 25	1,762	34,141	4.9	12.9
25 to 50	1,027	35,696	2.9	13.5
50 to 100	424	28,750	1.2	10.9
over 100	164	29,711	0.5	11.2
Totals	35,850	264,407	100.0	100.0

Source: Instituto Nacional Vitivinicultura, *Censo vitícola nacional III: 1968*, Mendoza.

farms growing grapes had 5 hectares or less of cultivated land. The percentage might have been as high as 49 percent.[13]

Economies of Scale with Surface Water

Optimal farm size and economic viability are relative terms. Farms of 100 hectares may be inefficiently small and nonviable for producing grains under conditions of relatively expensive labor and inexpensive capital. Efficient production, however, is reached on much smaller

[13] The 1960 census data indicate that 15,848 farms, 44 percent of all farms within Cuyo, had 5 hectares or less. Data from the Instituto Nacional Vitivinicultura (internal document "Formulario 195," p. 26) indicates that as of December 31, 1960, there were 32,198 farms growing grapes in the region, 90 percent of the total number of farms listed in the 1960 agricultural census. Consequently, at least 37 percent of all farms growing grapes had no more than 5 hectares of land, both cultivated and uncultivated. The percentage would be higher if there were farms with fewer than 5 hectares that did not grow grapes.

farms with crops such as grapes, the production of which cannot be so readily and completely mechanized, and where labor and animal power are economically attractive alternatives to tractors. The economic viability of a small farm depends on assumptions regarding the minimum rate of return to investment, income levels, average family size, and labor occupation rates. In addition, the most efficient farm size and the minimum economically profitable farm size for growing a given crop vary with other factors such as farm management, natural soil productivity, and water supply.

There are no significant on-farm economies or diseconomies of scale stemming from the use of surface water in Cuyo. The substantial economies of scale associated with the distribution of surface water to farms are captured by government investments. The per unit water charge to farmers is independent of farm size and the number of hectares with water rights. There are, however, other sources of economies of scale. For example, the length of a perimeter fence around a square plot is 400 meters for 1 hectare and 800 meters for 4 hectares, one animal with implements could work about 7 hectares and a tractor considerably more. Diseconomies of scale, due primarily to administrative limitations and worker incentives on large farms, set in at some point, eventually offsetting additional economies to larger farms.

Economies and diseconomies of scale vary among farms and cannot be quantified with any precision. Nevertheless, the following generalizations, based on a recent study of profitability and farm size for vineyards[14] and other information regarding efficiency rates of specific major productive factors such as labor, animals, and tractors, appear warranted for vineyards using surface water and with no allowance for the impact of government credit and tax policies on profits. First, farms of 5 hectares and less are insufficient to provide productive employment to a family. Excluding the harvest 5 hectares of grapes require about 225

[14] Adolfo M. de Torrontegui and Teodoro A. Tonina used farm surveys to examine the relation between profits and vineyard size in Mendoza. Their conclusions are summarized in Instituto Nacional de Tecnología Agropecuaria (INTA), *Programa "Vid"*, March 1972, pp. 48–49. Major conclusions of this study are the following: a farm with less than 5 hectares worked directly by the owner and family is not a viable economic unit since the family must augment its income with other activities; a farm from 5 to 10 hectares, which is generally worked by contract using animal power, does not constitute a viable economic unit when yields are less than 10 tons per hectare; a 9.5-hectare farm is the minimum economically profitable unit; a 23-hectare farm maximizes the rate of profit; and 90 hectares is the maximum size for which profits are greater than zero. Another publication by the same authors which is relevant to the issues of economies of scale is "Análisis económico de fincas vitifrutícolas en tres departamentos de la provincia de Mendoza," *Revista de investigaciones agropecuarias* (Buenos Aires: INTA, 1969), Serie 6, Economía y Administración Rural, Vol. 3, No. 3.

labor days once the vines have entered the productive stage. This would not even fully employ one worker. Second, a 10-hectare farm with good yields is sufficient to provide employment and a good living for a small family. Economies of scale for larger farms using animal power are probably not great and might be offset by the added problems associated with hiring outside labor. Third, economies of scale using tractor power can be achieved on about 30 hectares. However, in the absence of credit and tax subsidies which can substantially reduce the farmer's cost of a tractor, tractors offer little advantage over animal power for performing most farm tasks. Tractors have a comparative advantage in performing heavy tasks such as earth moving and land leveling. Farmers, however, can generally rent tractors for such tasks or contract a company to perform the work. In summary, economies of scale in the absence of ground water costs and government policies are not great. However, at least 37 percent and probably as many as 50 percent of all farms in the region are not of sufficient size to fully employ a small family.

Impact of Ground Water on Optimum Farm Size

Important economies of scale due largely to the indivisibility of an economically efficient well emerge with ground water pumping. Sometimes these scale economies have been captured by government wells or consortiums of ground water users, and the benefits have been passed on to small farmers. Many farmers, however, must drill their own wells to insure an adequate water supply. The unit cost of the water to such farmers depends strongly on the quantity of water pumped. With the assumption that 10,330 m^3 of water are pumped for each hectare, Table 6.8 indicates the estimated annualized ground water costs for various farm sizes in the absence of tax and credit subsidies and the impact of these costs on the profitability of grape growing when ground water costs are the only source of cost differences among the farms. The annual per hectare ground water costs range from $386 for 5 hectares to $81 for 36 hectares under the most conservative estimate of economies of scale and a pumping height of 30 meters. As a percentage of the average annual gross revenue from a good vineyard these annual ground water costs range from 44.0 percent for 5 hectares to 9.3 percent for 36 hectares. Farms of 10 hectares and less which are dependent on ground water clearly face a substantial competitive disadvantage. When the ground water costs are the only source of cost differences among farms, the internal rates of return to a good vineyard are less than 5 percent for the 5-hectare farm, 13 percent for 10 hectares, 16 percent for 20 hectares, and 18 percent for 36 hectares.

Table 6.8 Ground Water Costs and Returns to
Grape Production for Various Farm Sizes

Farm size (hectares)	Annual ground water costs[a] ($/ha)	Internal rate of return to grape production[b] (percent)
5	386	5
	486	0
10	197	13
	248	11
15	135	16
	168	14
20	128	16
30	92	18
36	81	18

[a] These are the estimated annualized costs of pumping 10,330 m³ of water a height of 30 meters. The cost data are from Table 2.10 with minor differences due to rounding. Off-peak pumping rates are assumed when possible. The low cost estimates for the farms of 5, 10, and 15 hectares assume no storage pool; all other estimates assume a storage pool.

[b] With the exception of the water costs, all revenues and costs are assumed to be the same as the data for the 10-hectare farm in tables 6.1 and 6.2.

Impact of Government Policies on Optimum Farm Size

The electricity rate schedule also contributes to economies of scale for irrigating up to 20 hectares. For example, the approximate annual energy costs per hectare (for pumping 10,330 m³ per hectare a height of 30 meters) are $31.4 for 5 hectares, $20.5 for 10 hectares, $16.7 for 15 hectares, and $14.9 for 20 hectares. These estimates assume pumping only during the hours of off-peak power rates and assume a 25-hp motor for all farm sizes. The economy of scale is due to a fixed component in agricultural power charges dependent on the capacity of the motor. This average fixed power cost amounts to $22.1 for 5 hectares, $11.1 for 10 hectares, and $5.6 for 20 hectares. Average energy costs rise for farms larger than 20 hectares since the progressively higher water requirements necessitate pumping during the hours of higher power rates. The higher variable charges more than offset the lower average fixed charge, and the average annual energy costs per hectare are $16.7 for 30 hectares and $18.3 for 36 hectares.[15] The electricity rate schedule,

[15] These figures are based on the energy cost data in Table 2.10, which assumes pumping is done during the hours of low power rates if possible. If we assume all farmers pump during the hours of peak energy rates, the economies of scale resulting from the rate structure would be greater than indicated in the text since the marginal power rate for daytime use declines for agricultural users as consumption rises. Consequently, both the average fixed and marginal power costs would be lower on the larger farms.

Table 6.9 Internal Rates of Return to Various Size Vineyards with the Credit Subsidy

Farm size[a] (hectares)	Rates of Return[b]	
	Credit subsidy on water costs only[c]	Credit subsidy on water costs and other costs incurred during the first two years of planting[d]
10	$\begin{cases} 15 \\ 13 \end{cases}$	$\begin{cases} 18 \\ 16 \end{cases}$
15	$\begin{cases} 17 \\ 16 \end{cases}$	$\begin{cases} 20 \\ 19 \end{cases}$
20	17	21
30	19	22
36	19	23

[a] The estimates for the 5-hectare farm are omitted since it is unlikely that subsidized credit would be granted for such a small farm.

[b] With the exception of water costs, the basic, nonsubsidized costs and returns are identical to those in tables 6.1 and 6.2. The high estimated returns for the 10 and 15 hectare farms assume no storage pool; all other estimates assume a storage pool. It is assumed that pumping occurs during the hours of off-peak power rates to the extent possible.

[c] The underlying assumptions regarding the credit subsidy are based on the assumptions in Table 3.1 assuming a bank lending rate of 15 percent and nominal discount rate of 40 percent.

[d] This assumes that the subsidized credit is also available for the costs incurred during the first two years of planting a new vineyard. Consequently, the costs of years 1 and 2 presented in Table 6.1 are reduced by 24.5 percent by the availability of credit.

however, is clearly not the major source of economies of scale resulting from ground water use. If the average power cost were reduced to the cost on the 20-hectare farm, the annual per hectare ground water costs on the 5-hectare farm would still be 2.9 times those on the 20-hectare farm and 4.6 times those on the 36-hectare farm. The internal rate of return to the 5-hectare vineyard with good yields and ground water would still only be 5 percent with the lower power costs.

Availability of subsidized agricultural credit is a major source of cost and profit differences among farms. Ability to repay is the primary basis for providing credit. Consequently, the small farmer with little collateral and high average ground water costs is seldom granted the highly subsidized credit channeled through the banking institutions. Thus, access to credit tends to magnify the profit differentials among different size farms using ground water. Table 6.9 indicates the impact of the credit subsidy on the rate of return to various size vineyards. Subsidized credit for the well, motor, and pump increases the internal rate of return 1 to 2 percent. If credit is also available for the production costs during the first two years of planting, the return increases 4 to 5 percent. The internal rates of return with subsidized credit for the water and initial planting costs range from 21 to 23 percent on the 20- and

36-hectare vineyards. These are strong investment incentives, especially in comparison to the returns without the credit subsidy of less than 5 percent on the 5-hectare vineyard and from 11 to 13 percent on the 10-hectare vineyard.

The previous profit calculations have been based on pretax earnings while farmers presumably are interested in maximizing posttax income. As long as the tax is levied on gross profits and is equally enforced, the imposition of a progressive income or profit tax alters only the absolute and relative profitability, not the ranking, of various investments and farm sizes. Income tax collections, however, tend to be less than perfect in rural areas. Administratively, it is difficult to quantify rural earnings and to identify delinquent taxpayers. Small farmers find it particularly easy to avoid payment since it is generally too difficult and not worth the expense to determine their liability and make them pay. Consequently, the income tax tends to diminish the posttax profitability differences among farms of various size and in some cases may actually make the smaller, less conspicuous farm a more attractive investment.

The investment tax credit mitigates the impact of the income tax. Moreover, if the tax credit discriminates among eligible investments, the credit may affect the ranking as well as the relative and absolute profitability of alternative investments. For example, the tax credit in Cuyo increases the relative profitability of permanent compared to annual crops and the use of tractors compared to labor. To the extent that a larger farm is likely to have a higher percentage of costs eligible for the tax credit, such as with the purchase of a tractor, the credit increases the relative profitability of the larger farm.

The combination of being able to deduct rural investments from nonrural income and the lax enforcement of the rural income tax is a substantial incentive for agricultural investment. Table 6.10 indicates the pretax internal rates of return to various size vineyards using ground water for a hypothetical investor benefiting from the tax credit. The returns for the investor with a 33 percent marginal tax rate range from 17 to 24 percent, returns 5 to 6 percent higher than the comparable returns without either the tax or credit subsidies.

The investor able to benefit from the tax credit is also very likely to have excellent access to subsidized credit. The impact of the combination of the two subsidies on an investment in various size vineyards is indicated in Table 6.11. For the investor able to benefit from both subsidies, the investment in a vineyard of 10 hectares or more can be very profitable. For the hypothetical investor considered in Table 6.11, the pretax returns to the land and entrepreneurial inputs are 24 to 25 percent on a 10-hectare farm and 30 percent on farms of 30 hectares or more. These returns are 12 to 13 percent above the returns with no

Table 6.10 Internal Rates of Return to Various Size Vineyards with the Tax Credit Subsidy

Farm size[a] (hectares)	Rate of return[b]
10[b]	19 17
15[b]	21 20
20	22
30	23
36	24

Note: It is assumed that the tax credit reduces eligible costs by 23.6 percent. This assumes a 33 percent marginal tax rate, 40 percent nominal discount rate, and that the taxes saved would otherwise have been paid one year after the eligible investment is made. The percentage savings for alternative assumptions are presented in Table 3.2. The eligible investments include the capital costs of the ground water presented in Table 2.10 and the nonwater costs incurred during the first three years presented in Table 6.1.

[a] The 5-hectare farm is excluded since the high ground water costs make it an unlikely investment.

[b] With the exception of water costs, the basic, nonsubsidized costs and revenues are identical to those in tables 6.1 and 6.2. The high estimated returns for the 10- and 15-hectare farms assume no storage pool; all other estimates assume a storage pool. It is assumed that pumping occurs during the hours of off-peak power rates to the extent possible.

subsidies presented in Table 6.8 and compare favorably with the return of 22 percent with no credit and tax subsidies but free water.

Impact of Social Water Costs on Various Size Vineyards

Earlier discussions suggested that for private water costs to reflect social costs there should be no tax or credit subsidies for irrigation wells, power costs should be approximately doubled, and a user tax of about $50 per 10,330 m³ of water pumped should be imposed.[16] Table 6.12 presents estimated social costs of pumping 10,330 m³ of water a height of 30 meters for various size farms and the impact of the respective annual water costs on the internal rate of return to a good vineyard. The social costs of the water range from $454 per hectare on the 5-hectare farm to $163 per hectare on the 36-hectare farm. The return with no allowance for land costs to the 5-hectare vineyard is only 1 percent. However, the comparable return rises to 10 percent for the

[16] See the discussion under the section entitled "Social Water Costs and Farm Profits" on pp. 121–123.

Table 6.11 Internal Rates of Return to Various Size Vineyards with the Credit and Tax Credit Subsidies[a]

| | Rates of return | |
Farm size (hectares)	Subsidies on water costs only	Subsidies on water costs and initial planting costs
10	$\begin{cases} 17 \\ 16 \end{cases}$	$\begin{cases} 25 \\ 24 \end{cases}$
15	$\begin{cases} 18 \\ 18 \end{cases}$	$\begin{cases} 28 \\ 27 \end{cases}$
20	19	29
30	20	30
36	20	30

[a] The assumptions regarding costs, revenues, and terms of the credit and tax subsidies are similar to those in tables 6.9 and 6.10.

Table 6.12 Internal Rates of Return to Various Size Vineyards Paying Social Ground Water Costs

| Farm size (hectares) | Annual social ground water costs (1969 dollars per hectare) | | | Internal rate of return[c] |
	Capital[a]	Variable[b]	Total	
5	354	100	454	1
10	177	100	277	10
15	118	100	218	12
20	114	100	214	12
30	76	100	176	14
36	63	100	163	14

[a] The estimates of capital costs are from Table 2.10. Since marginal power costs are assumed to be equal regardless of the timing or quantity of pumping, the storage pool is unnecessary for avoiding night irrigation on farms of 15 hectares or less. Consequently, the capital costs for the farms of 15 hectares or less do not include a storage pool. The costs on the larger farms include a storage pool since otherwise some night pumping and higher labor costs would be required to pump the necessary quantity of water with the assumed motor and pump size.

[b] Based on the assumptions of Table 6.5 the total variable cost of pumping 10,330 m³ of water a height of 30 meters is $100. Half this amount is the user tax and the other half the social cost of the power.

[c] Except for water costs, the revenues and costs are identical to those presented in tables 6.1 and 6.2.

10-hectare vineyard and 14 percent for the 30- and 36-hectare vineyards. Moreover, if the credit and tax subsidies are available to defray the initial land preparation and planting costs,[17] the returns with social water costs would range from 15 percent on the 10-hectare vineyard to 22 percent on the 36-hectare vineyard, substantial incentives for continued investment.

[17] The cost reductions resulting from the credit and tax subsidies are based on the assumptions used in tables 6.9 and 6.10.

As Table 6.5 indicates the social water costs rise rapidly with the pumping depth. Compared to the costs at 30 meters, annual water costs per hectare would be $80 higher at 70 meters and $162 higher at 110 meters regardless of the farm size. The returns to the 36-hectare vineyard paying social water costs and receiving no tax and credit subsidies would be 11 percent at 70 meters and 7 percent at 110 meters. Consequently, in the absence of additional subsidies we would expect few new irrigation wells to be drilled in areas with pumping depths of 70 meters or more if farmers paid the social costs of pumping and using water.

PERMANENT VERSUS ANNUAL CROPS

An earlier chapter (Chapter 2) revealed the dominance of permanent crops in Cuyo's agricultural production and recent agricultural growth. In Mendoza permanent crops accounted for about 76 percent of the cultivated land and 85 percent of the value of production in 1970, and permanent crops accounted for about 99 percent of the growth in the value of agricultural production since 1948. In San Juan, permanent crops assume an even greater relative importance, and they accounted for over 100 percent of the growth in the value of agricultural production since 1955.[18] This dominance of permanent crops is testimony to their profitability within the region, especially the profitability of grapes. This profitability, however, is not entirely the result of natural competitive advantages of permanent over annual crops in the region. Government tax and credit policies have enhanced the relative financial attractiveness of permanent crops, at least since 1966.

To demonstrate the impact of the credit and tax subsidies on the relative profitability of permanent and annual crops, it is helpful to compare the revenues and costs from the vineyard described in tables 6.1 and 6.2 to the revenues and costs of an annual crop. Table 6.13 presents estimated annual costs of producing tomatoes with average yields of 30 metric tons per hectare. These cost data are intended to approximate the costs of an annual crop under assumptions similar to those adopted in Table 6.1 for grapes. Consequently, there is no allowance for land costs, and the yields assume above average technology and applications of inputs such as fertilizer. The annual water requirements of the two crops are roughly the same making it reasonable to ignore differences in annual water costs. With an average price of $30 per metric ton, the average price received by tomato growers from 1961 to 1968, the annual profit to the land and entrepreneurial ability would be $333 per hectare.

[18] Tables 2.1 through 2.4 indicate the importance of the major crop groups.

Table 6.13 Production Costs for Tomatoes

(in dollars per hectare)

Labor costs[a]	395.9
excluding harvest	236.8
harvest	159.1
Materials	114.2
seed, manure and tractor rental for land preparation	42.8
fertilizer and pesticides	71.4
Annual cost of buildings, equipment and work animals[b]	47.3
Water cost	10.0
Total annual cost	567.4

[a] The physical labor requirements and the cost of the materials used are based on data in M. N. Firpo's "Listado de gastos de cultivos hortícolas," Instituto Nacional de Tecnología Agropecuaria, Cuyo, October 1970, in mimeograph. The data are applicable for tomato production with the techniques recommended by INTA; the expected yields are 30 MT per hectare which compares with the average yield during recent years of about 20 MT. The labor requirements are sixty-four days prior to harvest and forty-three days for the harvest. A wage rate of $3.7 per 8-hour day is assumed.

[b] Water costs and the annual cost of the buildings, equipment, and work animals are assumed to be identical to the comparable costs for grape production listed in Table 6.1.

Over a twenty-year time horizon, a discount rate of about 6.5 percent would equate the present discounted value of the grape returns indicated in Table 6.2 and a profit of $333 per year for twenty years from growing tomatoes. Consequently, if there were no difference in risk, tomato production would be preferable if the rate of interest were over 6.5 percent; grapes would be preferable if the interest rate were less. Since water requirements are approximately equal for the two crops, an increase in water costs due to higher charges for surface water or ground water use would not affect this result unless the annual water costs were high enough to eliminate the profits from tomatoes. Water costs above $343 per year per hectare would result in losses for tomatoes and reduce the internal rate of return to grapes below 6.5 percent. As a result, neither investment would be attractive.

The above profit estimates do not take into account the impact of credit and tax policies on the relative returns to annual and permanent crops. Subsidized credit and tax credit subsidies would increase the profitability of both crops. The impact on permanent crops, however, is likely to be greater since a higher portion of their costs are eligible for the subsidies, and the time stream of their costs and revenues make the returns to permanent crops very susceptible to the magnitude of the losses incurred in the initial years. Many of the expenses associated with planting on virgin land would be similar for both tomatoes and grapes. For example, the costs of land clearing and leveling, irrigation wells, and canal construction would be comparable, and the impact of credit and tax subsidies on these expenses would be similar. Moreover, short-term production credit and tax credits for fertilizer and pesticide costs would not significantly alter the relative attractiveness of the two alternative investments. The major alteration in relative profitability comes from providing subsidized credit for the costs of the trellis used to support the grapes and allowing tax deductions for all costs associated with the planting of a permanent crop until the time it enters into production. If the credit subsidy reduced the costs of the overhead trellis by 24.5 percent, this would reduce grape production costs by $188 in year 1 and $71 in year 2.[19] This cost reduction would increase to nearly 8 percent the maximum rate of interest for which grapes are more profitable than tomatoes. The availability of the tax credit for all grape production costs during the first three years and the fertilizer and pesticide costs of tomato production[20] increase the maximum rate of interest for which grapes are more profitable to just over 8 percent. The combination of the credit and tax subsidies increases this maximum interest rate to nearly 10 percent.

The data above refer to only one factor relevant for determining which crop a farmer should plant and are intended to be merely illustrative of the impact of the credit and tax subsidies on the relative profitability of permanent and annual crops. Maximization of the rate of return on investment is likely to be a more important criterion on a large farm or for an absentee landowner. A farmer with little land may be more interested in maximizing his total annual income from farming his land. Since the labor requirements are considerably higher for tomatoes than the annual requirements for a productive vineyard, this criterion alone greatly enhances the relative attractiveness of tomatoes on a small farm. However, for a farmer with more land who is interested in limiting his dependence on outside labor, the higher labor requirements of tomatoes would be a disadvantage. The well-established marketing system for grapes and greater stability of grape prices[21] are important factors contributing to the attractiveness of grapes. These advantages are in part the result of government policies. In Mendoza the provincial winery, Giol, sets minimum prices for grapes and hopes to stabilize grape and wine prices through construction of additional wine storage facilities and wine inventory adjustments. Overall, the combina-

---

[19] The assumptions regarding credit terms are similar to those in Table 3.1 with a bank lending rate of 15 percent and a nominal discount rate of 40 percent. The labor and materials for constructing the trellis amount to $767 in year 1 and $289 in year 2.

[20] Based on the assumptions in Table 3.2, a 33 percent marginal tax rate and a 40 percent nominal discount rate, the real cost to the farmer of items eligible for the tax credit is reduced by 23.6 percent. The cost items are presented in tables 6.1 and 6.13.

[21] The standard deviation of growers' prices from 1959 to 1968 was 42.5 percent of the average price for tomatoes and 27.7 percent for grapes.

tion of the paternal attitude of the local governments toward the grape and wine producers as well as the federal tax and credit subsidies favoring permanent crops have biased the region's agriculture toward permanent crops in general and grapes in particular.

SUMMARY AND CONCLUSIONS

There are few important economies of scale on a farm receiving surface water in Cuyo. Water costs are very low, and even an inefficient farmer can live reasonably well from 10 hectares. Moreover, limited urban employment opportunities keep on the land many farmers who are not doing well economically, and the inability to transfer water rights to different land often keeps these people working on poor land. There are no strong incentives for consolidation or elimination of inefficient producers receiving surface water. While high rates of inflation make land and permanent crops attractive investments, a low-yielding, 5-hectare vineyard which cannot readily be incorporated into a larger farm has limited investment appeal. In addition, the difficulty in finding alternative investments that would not result in the erosion of the real value of their capital might make small farmers reluctant to sell.

Economies of scale and production efficiency assume greater importance when ground water is used. It generally does not pay to drill a well for a small or inefficient farm. The exception to this is when ground water means the difference between saving and losing permanent crops. The well becomes profitable if it means the difference between saving 5 hectares of good yielding or 10 hectares of average yielding grapes. Since further increases in cultivated land within the region generally require ground water, new investment in such land should be located where marginal water costs are relatively low. These conditions exist primarily on farms with excess pumping capacity and on relatively large, efficient farms. Moreover, these conditions can often be created through government investment in wells or consortiums of water users.

The ability to take advantage of credit and tax subsidies is one of the most important factors in the expected profits of expanding agricultural production. These policies tend to favor the larger, more prosperous investors and encourage the planting of permanent as opposed to annual crops. The expected real return to grapes might reach 30 percent if an investor can take advantage of both the tax and credit subsidies.

Both the level and structure of electric power rates for agricultural users make marginal ground water costs on a farm with an operational irrigation well very low. These low marginal power costs encourage the installation of wells in areas with higher pumping distances, the cultivation of crops with higher water requirements per value of output, and the application of more water per crop than would result if farmers paid social energy costs. Moreover, these low marginal power costs discourage investments in alternative irrigation systems which would increase the efficiency of water use.

The imposition of social water costs would bring major changes in rural profits, investment incentives, and cropping patterns. Social water costs would increase marginal water costs substantially, as much as eightfold for ground water users. Such cost increases would probably eliminate many inefficient farmers. The prices for land with surface water rights would fall since current prices include the scarcity value of water. Social water costs would undoubtedly slow the overall expansion of cultivated land. The impact on the overall growth of agricultural production, however, would be tempered by the increased incentive to introduce new technology and switch to crops with higher returns per unit of land and water. If the cost changes were coupled with the right to transfer water rights independent of the land, considerable improvements in water use efficiency would result from transferring water to lands with lower distribution losses and higher productive potential. The impact on the overall growth in the value of agricultural production would be uncertain in the short term. However, these changes would clearly curb the expansion of overall water use and make possible greater long-term expansion of the region's agriculture. Of course, ultimately, the level of agricultural production would be constrained by annual water receipts to the region.

alternative growth 7 patterns within Cuyo

Some conclusions of the preceding analysis are that water is the major constraint on future agricultural expansion in Cuyo; current levels of water use cannot be maintained indefinitely with the existing infrastructure; current incentives encourage expansion of cultivation and provide little incentive for conserving water use; and continued water-intensive agricultural growth could reduce within several decades the supply of good quality ground water to levels that would not only terminate but might even force a major reversal of this growth pattern. This chapter examines alternative growth patterns for the region. The first section focuses on methods of increasing the quantity of water available to the farms; the second section examines the possibilities for increasing the value of production per unit of water through either on-farm changes or shifts to nonagricultural water uses.

INCREASING THE AVAILABILITY OF WATER

The effective quantity of water available to the region's farms can be increased through investments such as dams to control inter and intra-annual water flows, investments in canals to reduce water distribution losses, and an interbasin water transfer. As decreasing river flows curbed growth and threatened prior cropping patterns during the past decade, interest in such investments increased markedly.

Investment in Dams

Dams within Cuyo have been prompted by the need for power as well as irrigation. The hydroelectric potential of Cuyo's rivers is envisioned as a major source of power in an interconnected national power grid that will eventually link all Argentina's major power producing and consuming areas. However, the law grants potable and irrigation water uses priority over power generation in the use of the region's rivers. Since the combined demand for potable and irrigation water already exceeds the normal flows of the region's rivers, hydroelectric works legally may not be detrimental to the supply of these water demands. Consequently, dams which give priority in their operation to the supply of potable and irrigation water are practically legal prerequisites for harnessing the power potential of the region's rivers. With the combined needs for irrigation water and energy stimulating investments, dams are now either completed, in construction, or being studied for every major river within Cuyo.

Until 1972 there was only one completed dam within the region for regulating temporal river flows for agricultural purposes. This dam, Valle Grande on the Atuel River, was completed about 1965. Valle Grande dam has had little impact on agricultural water use. The flow of the Atuel River is controlled primarily by a dam farther upstream, El Nihuil, which is operated solely to produce hydroelectric power. However, since irrigation has priority over power generation in the use of water, Agua y Energía Eléctrica, the national power company, was required to construct Valle Grande to compensate for the effects of El Nihuil on irrigation water. Valle Grande's capacity of 188 hm³ is considered inadequate for controlling interannual water flows. Moreover, for more than half its working years, river flows have been so low in relation to the demand for irrigation water that Valle Grande dam has had little impact on intra-annual irrigation water flows. During years of relatively abundant river flows the dam is used to make irrigation water receipts coincide more closely with crop requirements; the dam has not significantly altered the quantity of land that can be safely irrigated with the water from the Atuel River.

El Carrizal, the first multipurpose dam in the region, was completed in 1972. El Carrizal cost about 70 million new pesos without the power installations,[1] has a storage capacity of 390 hm³, and is expected to increase the agricultural production potential of areas irrigated with the water of the Tunuyán River by 20 percent. The hydroelectric output from El Carrizal will be small with a capacity of only 17 MW (megawatts) and an expected average annual production of about 50 GWh (billion watt hours). However, the presence of El Carrizal for regulating agricultural water flows will permit the national power company to construct dams farther upstream which can be operated solely for producing power. Indeed, within two years the company expects to begin construction on Los Blancos dam on the Upper Tunuyán River. This project will cost an estimated $60 million and will generate an average of 680 GWh per year.

In 1972 construction was started on two other multipurpose dams within the region, Los Reyunos on the Diamante River and Ullum on the San Juan River. Los Reyunos, which is expected to cost about $25 million, will have a storage capacity of about 220 hm³ and will reportedly increase from 70,000 to 90,000 hectares the land that can be safely irrigated from the Diamante River. The hydroelectric capacity will be 216 MW and the expected average annual power production 302 GWh.[2] Ullum, which is expected to cost about $40 million, will have a storage capacity of 440 hm³ and will reportedly increase by 28,500 hectares the land that can safely be irrigated from the San Juan River. The hydroelectric capacity will be 47 MW and the expected average annual production 147 GWh.[3]

[1] The value of the peso varied from about 2.2 to 6.2 pesos per 1969 dollar during the period of construction. The cost in 1969 dollars was probably nearly $20 million. The data on the El Carrizal dam were provided by the office which is currently charged with overseeing the studies and construction on the Potrerillos dam for the province of Mendoza. This office performed the same function for El Carrizal dam during its construction.

[2] Construction on Agua del Toro dam, upstream on the Diamante River from the Los Reyunos site, was initiated and will be completed before Los Reyunos. Although Agua del Toro will eventually be used almost exclusively for producing power, its operation will legally have to give priority to potable and irrigation water supplies until Los Reyunos is operational. The Agua del Toro dam will have a storage capacity of 375 hm³ and will generate an average of 315 GWh per year when operated solely for power production. Agua y Energía Eléctrica has plans for constructing at least two other hydroelectric dams on the Diamante River over the next thirty years. The data on the Los Reyunos dam are from articles in *Los Andes* on July 30 and 31 and August 1, 1972. The data on the Los Blancos and Agua del Toro dams come from Agua y Energía Eléctrica, Estudios y Proyectos Zona Centro-Cuyo.

[3] The estimated impact of the Ullum dam on the region's agriculture is from *Projecto quebrada de Ullum,* Estudio de Factibilidad (San Juan: Gobierno de la Provincia de San Juan, 1969), a study prepared by Edison Harza. The cost estimate is from the Mendoza newspaper *Los Andes*, September 14, 1971, and the

Two other multipurpose dams are currently being proposed for the region and might well enter the construction stage within several years. These dams are Potrerillos on the Mendoza River and Cuesta del Viento on the Jachal River.[4] Although the dimensions of these dams are still provisional, the most recent plan for Potrerillos would cost an estimated 1.3 billion new pesos at 1973 prices, or well over $100 million, provide a storage capacity of 840 hm^3, have a peak power capacity of 134 MW, and produce an estimated 399 GWh per year. The dam would increase the reliability of water receipts to land with water rights for the Mendoza River and would reportedly increase the agricultural production potential of this river by about 15 percent. The dam being proposed for the Jachal River would cost an estimated $8 million excluding the hydroelectric installations, have a storage capacity of 215 hm^3, increase the area that can be cultivated from the river flow by about 2,700 hectares to a total of 10,300 hectares, and produce an estimated 25.9 GWh per year.

These agricultural benefits of the multipurpose dams are difficult to quantify with any precision and may well have been overestimated in the project proposals. Even without the dams, the water in the rivers for which multipurpose dams are proposed has been fully used during years of normal and subnormal river flows. Only during years with above average river flows such as 1972–73 does a substantial quantity of water flow out of the region. During years with large river flows, the dams would enable water otherwise lost to the region to be stored for future use within the region. On the other hand, evaporation losses from the water stored behind the dam will at least partly offset the advantages stemming from the interannual storage of water. Test tanks at the site of the El Carrizal dam lost an average of 2.4 meters per year from 1960 to 1968. Although the actual losses from the dam would be less, the evaporation loss rate could average as much as 10 to 15 percent of the average quantity of water stored. Moreover, the presence of additional dams for hydroelectric generation would increase evaporation losses in the region even more. The major agricultural benefits from the dams will be in the improved intra-annual timing of the irrigation water receipts and reduced risk of inadequate water receipts on land with surface water rights. On many of these farms, however, irrigation wells

---

power figures are from the Buenos Aires newspaper *La Nación*, December 13, 1972, Section 2.

[4] The data on the projected dam at Potrerillos were obtained in May 1973 from the office which is in charge of overseeing this project for the government of Mendoza. The data on the proposed dam at Cuesta del Viento are from Consejo Federal de Inversiones, *Estudio de prefactibilidad técnico—Económico de una presa de embalse sobre el río Jachal, provincia de San Juan,* Vols. 1–5, prepared by Harza de Argentina, S.A., Técnica Consultora, 1971.

have already reduced the risk of inadequate or poorly timed water receipts. The impact of the dams on recharge to the aquifers is unknown, and there has been no consideration of using artificial ground water recharge combined with pumping to achieve the substantial agricultural benefits which are claimed for these dams.

Lining of Canals

The construction and lining of irrigation canals are also means of improving the distribution and use of water. The first investments in the irrigation distribution system antedate the arrival of European settlers to the region. However, most of the current irrigation network has been built during the past century, and substantial net investments in the system continue to be made. Until the last two to three decades, investments in irrigation infrastructure were designed primarily to expand the areas to which river water could be delivered. In more recent years the investments have been designed more for reducing water losses and improving the regulatory capability within the areas already under irrigation.

In Mendoza, for example, major primary canals of about 33 km each are under construction along the left banks of the Tunuyán and Diamante rivers. These cement canals, which will replace sections of their respective river beds in the irrigation systems, are expected to cost about \$250,000 per km with an average capacity of about 50 m^3 of water per second. The canals are expected to reduce annual maintenance costs by as much as 70 percent and enable water deliveries to reflect much more closely the legal rights of farmers. The major justification of the projects, however, is the elimination of water infiltration losses, which currently amount to 25 to 30 percent of the water passing the length of the river beds to be bypassed by the canals. Indeed, an official report states that these water savings are sufficient to justify construction of the canals along the Tunuyán River in the absence of any other benefits.[5]

Reduced infiltration losses represent a net gain in usable water to the region and not just a net gain to farmers with surface water rights only if the infiltration does not recharge the region's usable aquifers. This consideration, however, which is extremely important for measuring the total net benefits from the canals, was not mentioned in the project proposals and was not a factor in the investment decision. In the case of the canal along the Tunuyán River it appears that most, if not all, of

[5] The following information on these canals was obtained in May 1973 from conversations with and reports provided by personnel of the Dirección de Hidráulica, Ministerio de Obras y Servicios Públicos, Gobierno de Mendoza.

the sections of the river being bypassed overlie the confined aquifer.[6] Thus, the reduced infiltration losses represent net water savings to the region. However, the aquifers in the southern parts of Mendoza are not well enough defined to know if the reduced infiltration represents a net saving of water available to the region.

The provincial governments have spent about $1.5 to $2 million per year on these two primary canals; in addition, they have lined many smaller canals to reduce infiltration losses. In 1972 the Mendoza government spent the equivalent of about $250,000 on other projects designed primarily to reduce water infiltration losses. From May 1971 to May 1973 the Departamento de Hidráulica in San Juan spent nearly 6 million pesos (roughly $1 million) for lining three canals. The criteria used in both provinces for selecting which canals to line take into account the impact on surface water only; the criteria ignore whether or not the water infiltration recharges the region's usable aquifers.

Interbasin Water Transfers

The most ambitious water projects under consideration involve interbasin water transfers from the Grande to the Atuel rivers. The Grande River has an average annual flow of about 120.6 m³/sec. measured at Bardas Blancas (see Figure 2), a flow more than twice that of any of the other rivers in the region.[7] Virtually none of the water of the Grande River is currently used within the province of Mendoza since the terrain and climate of its river basin discourage agriculture. This situation suggests the possible desirability of transferring some of the water from the Grande River into another river basin where suitable agricultural land is abundant, the climate is more favorable for agriculture, and water is valuable and a major limiting factor on the area's growth. The first study of the physical possibility of such a transfer dates from 1911. However, the interest of the Mendoza government in such a transfer increased notably over the past two decades and particularly during the last five years as water became more valuable within Mendoza and downstream use threatened to preempt Mendoza's rights to the water.[8] In 1969 Mendoza contracted a consulting firm, Harza

[6] Infiltration above a confined aquifer does not recharge the aquifer.

[7] The average annual flows in m³/sec. of the other major rivers in Cuyo are approximately 29 for the Atuel, 39 for the Diamante, 54 for the Mendoza, 32 for the Lower Tunuyán, and 47 for the San Juan.

[8] A listing of the various studies undertaken and commissions formed to study the feasibility of transferring water from the Grande River and its tributaries to other regions of Mendoza is presented in Joaquín M. R. López, "Trasvase de cuencas en Mendoza: Estudios, proyectos, perspectivas," a paper presented for the jornadas "El agua y el futuro regional," Mendoza, April 14, 1973, pp. 13–16.

Table 7.1 Alternative Projects for Transferring Water from the Grande to Atuel Rivers

| Alter-native | Major construction works | Water transfer (m³/sec.) | Additional land to be irrigated (1,000 ha)[a] | | | Additional power production (GWh/year) |
			With infra-structure[b]	New areas	Total	
I	Estrechura dam tunnel 18.5 km	24	44.2 (60.8)	— (5.0)	44.2 (65.8)	819
II	Estrechura and Valenzuela dams tunnels 27 km	40	60.8 (80.3)	6.7 (25.0)	67.5 (105.3)	1,272
III	Portezuelo and Bardas Blancas dams tunnel 30 km canals 40 km	105	80.3 (80.3)	49.6 (98.3)	129.9 (178.6)	3,282
IV	Estrechura, Portezuelo, and Bardas Blancas dams tunnels 48.5 km canals 40 km	105	80.3 (80.3)	49.6 (98.3)	129.9 (178.6)	3,139
V	Estrechura, Valenzuela, Portezuelo, and Bardas Blancas dams tunnels 57 km canals 40 km	105	80.3 (80.3)	49.6 (98.3)	129.9 (178.6)	3,033

Source: All the above data were obtained from the files of the Comité Ejecutivo Técnico de Aprovechamiento de los Ríos Colorado, Grande y Barrancas (C.E.T.A.R.C.) in Mendoza.

[a] The figures in parentheses indicate the additional land that could be irrigated with the various products if the canals in the irrigated areas were lined to prevent infiltration water losses.

[b] With infrastructure refers to areas which can be irrigated with the existing water distribution infrastructure.

de Argentina, S.A., to summarize the available data and alternatives for such a transfer. Harza submitted a preliminary report in June 1972 focusing on the four alternatives considered the most feasible and economical. These alternatives as well as a fifth alternative for which the Mendoza government requested more information are described briefly below, and some of their principal characteristics are summarized in tables 7.1 and 7.2. Figure 2 indicates the location of the various projects.

Alternative I calls for the construction of the Estrechura dam with a capacity of 760 hm³ to capture and control the flows of the Cobre, Tordillo, Santa Elena, and Las Cargas tributaries. With the construction of an 18.5-km tunnel through the mountains, an average of 24 m³ of

Table 7.2 Costs of Alternative Projects for Transferring Water from the Grande to Atuel Rivers

(in millions of 1969 dollars)[a]

Alternative	Costs of infrastructure for the water transfer and power production		Other costs[b]	Total costs[c]
I	a. Estrechura dam and tunnel to the Salado River	66.3	10.6	88.4
	b. Nihuil power station	11.5	(44.5)	(122.3)
	Subtotal	77.8		
II	a. Estrechura dam, tunnel to the Salado River, and Los Morros power station	76.0		
	b. Valenzuela dam, tunnel and aqueduct to Estrechura	15.7	14.4 (56.2)	135.9 (177.7)
	c. Nihuil IV power station	29.8		
	Subtotal	121.5		
III	a. Dam and power station at Portezuelo del Viento	107.8		
	b. Bardas Blancas dam, tunnels and canals to the Atuel River	226.8	30.5 (91.5)	522.5 (583.5)
	c. Construction at Nihuil and Valle Grande	157.4		
	Subtotal	492.0		
IV	a. Same as item I-a	66.3		
	b. Dam and power station at Portezuelo del Viento	56.4	30.5 (91.5)	509.5 (570.5)
	c. Bardas Blancas dam, tunnels and canals to the Atuel River	200.2		
	d. Construction at Nihuil and Valle Grande	156.1		
	Subtotal	479.0		
V	a. Same as II-a plus II-b	91.7		
	b. Dam and power station at Portezuelo del Viento	44.4	30.5 (91.5)	511.3 (572.3)
	c. Bardas Blancas dam, tunnels and canals to Atuel River	189.5		
	d. Construction at Nihuil and Valle Grande	155.2		
	Subtotal	480.8		

Sources: The data were obtained from the files of the Comité Ejecutivo Técnico de Aprovechamiento de los Ríos Colorado, Grande y Barrancas (C.E.T.A.R.C.) in Mendoza. The data for alternatives I to IV are from Capítulo 15 of the Harza study and the data for the last alternative are from a file labeled "Alternativa V."

[a] The original cost estimates are based on prices as of December 1971. These peso costs have been converted into 1969 dollars at the rate of 5 pesos to 1 dollar.

[b] Other costs include the costs of drainage and improvements in and expansion of the water distribution network. The figures in parentheses also include the costs for lining the canals in the water distribution network.

[c] The total cost figures in parentheses include the costs for lining canals in the irrigation system.

water per second could be transferred to the Salado River, a tributary of the Atuel. This project would cost an estimated $88.4 million and would permit cultivation of 44,200 additional hectares. The lining of irrigation canals in the cultivated areas would add an estimated $33.9 million to

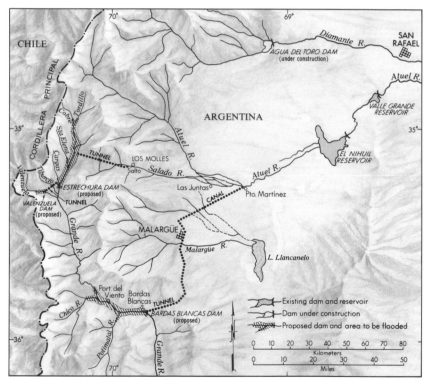

Figure 2 Proposed Interbasin Water Transfer Projects

the cost and 21,600 hectares to the land that could be irrigated from the surface water.

Alternative II also calls for construction of a dam at Estrechura and a tunnel of 18.5 km to carry water from behind the dam to the Salado River. However, the capacity of the dam would be enlarged to 960 hm³, and the tunnel would be enlarged to carry an average flow of 40 m³ per second. The additional water would come from the Valenzuela tributary and would require a dam on the Valenzuela River and about 9 additional km of tunnels and aqueducts to transfer this water to that stored behind the Estrechura dam. The second alternative would cost about $136 million and add about 67,500 hectares to the cultivable land. The lining of canals in the irrigated areas adds an estimated $41.8 million to the total cost of the project and 37,800 hectares to the land that can be cultivated.

Alternative III calls for the construction of dams along the Grande River at Portezuelo del Viento with a capacity of 2,699 hm³ and Bardas Blancas with a capacity of 305 hm³. With the construction of about 30 km of tunnel through the mountains and another 40 km of canals, an average of 105 m³ of water per second could be transferred from the Grande to the Atuel rivers. This project would cost an estimated $522.5 million and irrigate an additional 129,900 hectares. Canal lining would add an estimated $61 million to the cost and 48,700 hectares to the land that could be cultivated.

Alternative IV is a combination of alternatives I and III. The dam, tunnel, and water transfer from Estrechura would be identical to alternative I. Since an average of 24 m³ of water per second would be diverted at Estrechura, only about 80 m³ of water per second could be transferred from Bardas Blancas. While the dam at Bardas Blancas would have the same capacity as in alternative III, the capacity of the Portezuelo dam would be reduced to 1,100 hm³, and the capacity of the tunnel and canal to carry water from Bardas Blancas to the Atuel River would be smaller. This entire project would cost an estimated $509.5 million and irrigate an additional 129,900 hectares. This cost is $13 million less than the estimate for alternative III; the additional land that could be irrigated is approximately the same for both alternatives III and IV. The increases in the costs and cultivable land from lining the canals in the irrigated areas would be identical for alternatives III and IV.

Alternative V is a combination of alternatives II and III. The dams, tunnels, and water transfers from Valenzuela and Estrechura would be identical to alternative II. In addition to these transfers, 65 m³ of water per second would be diverted from Bardas Blancas to the Atuel River. The size and cost of the tunnels and canals and the latter dam would be smaller than those for either alternatives III or IV. Alternative V would cost an estimated $511.3 million, a figure between the estimates for alternatives III and IV. The impacts on irrigation with and without the lining of the canals in the irrigated areas would be comparable to the impacts under alternatives III and IV.

All the above alternatives would substantially increase the hydro-electric production of the area. In addition to enabling the water transfers, several of the construction projects, especially the dam at Portezuelo, would be equipped to generate power. Moreover, the water transfer would greatly enhance the hydroelectric potential of the Atuel River and the power plant already installed at El Nihuil. The estimated increase in the average annual energy production within the region ranges from 819 GWh with the first alternative to 3,282 GWh with the third alternative.

The second alternative, which would transfer about 40 m^3 of water per second, is currently considered the most profitable by the Mendoza authorities. Demand estimates indicate that the increased power and irrigation water provided by this transfer would be readily absorbed after the estimated seven-year construction period. The expected returns are higher and the estimated per hectare water costs considerably lower for the first two alternatives than for the last three. For example, the average total project costs per additional hectare that can be irrigated would be $2,000 for alternative I, $2,013 for alternative II, and approximately $4,000 for the other alternatives without the lining of the canals in the irrigated zones. The average costs per hectare are lower when canal lining is included; the estimated average costs are $1,688 for alternative II, and about $3,200 for the last three alternatives.[9]

The second alternative has the additional advantage for the province of Mendoza of maximizing the quantity of water transferred subject to their current rights on the water in the Grande River. Since the water being considered for transfer would otherwise flow into other provinces, the use of the water is subject to national law. Mendoza has already been granted rights to enough of the water to enable the province to undertake either of the first two interbasin transfers discussed above. However, the more ambitious projects calling for the transfer of 105 m^3 of water per second would require an agreement by the national government worked out with the other affected provinces.

The estimated marginal costs for transferring more than 40 m^3 of water per second from the Grande River are two to three times the average costs per hectare for alternatives I or II. For example, if Mendoza initially undertook the second alternative, the marginal cost

[9] These costs include the costs of the power installations.

per hectare of later transferring an additional 65 m³ of water from Bardas Blancas (i.e., the second stage of alternative V) would be about $6,013 without and $5,381 with canal lining. Even if half these costs could be written off as being attributable to additional power production,[10] the additional irrigation water is expensive. A 10 percent interest charge on half the initial construction costs would imply average annual water costs of about $270 to $300 per hectare. As was indicated in Chapter 6, these water cost levels would make it difficult for an efficient grape producer to earn as much as a 10 percent return to his land. Moreover, the social cost of the water would be much higher than these levels, which make no allowance for the cost of maintaining and amortizing the facilities, the opportunity cost of the water, or the time lag between the investment expenses and the availability of the water. While Mendoza now favors alternative II, the province does not intend to limit its claim on the water of the Grande River to just 40 m³ per second. Indeed, changes in technology and factor and product prices may later make the additional transfer of 65 m³ per second from Bardas Blancas an attractive investment for the province.

Mendoza's economic evaluations of the use of the Grande River assume that the opportunity cost of the water transferred to the Atuel River is zero. This assumption is probably reasonable from the point of view of the province of Mendoza; it is not, however, valid from a national viewpoint. Indeed, the water of the Colorado River, which comes primarily from the Grande, is claimed in part by four other provinces and at least two of these, Buenos Aires and La Pampa, are planning major investments to increase their use of these waters.[11] From the national point of view, water diverted to the Atuel has opportunity costs in terms of the land which cannot be irrigated and the power which cannot be generated in the provinces farther down the Colorado River. If the water is to be utilized efficiently from a national perspective, it is not enough to know that the projects under consideration in Mendoza offer a 15 to 20 percent internal rate of return when the water is implicitly given a zero value in other uses. In view of the importance of the Colorado River and the existence of these conflicting regional claims and interests, the national government contracted the

[10] If the same portion of the total costs of both alternative II and the other part of alternative V were attributed to power production, the average power costs associated with alternative II would be only half the average cost of the additional power generated by then transferring 65 m³/second from Bardas Blancas as indicated in alternative V. Consequently, both the power and water costs are much higher for the second than for the first stage of alternative V.

[11] According to an article in *Los Andes*, July 22, 1972, the provinces of Buenos Aires had allocated 17 million and La Pampa 10 million new pesos to works designed to utilize the waters of the Colorado River.

Massachusetts Institute of Technology civil engineering department to examine the alternative uses of the Colorado River.

Comments on Proposed Water Infrastructure Investments

The irrigation infrastructure projects both under construction and under serious consideration represent an enormous investment for the region. The combined estimated cost of the multipurpose dams on the Mendoza, San Juan, Diamante, and Jachal rivers, the two major canal projects within the Tunuyán and Diamante river basins, and the transfer of 40 m^3 of water per second from the Grande to the Atuel rivers (excluding the costs at the Nihuil power station) is about $361 million. If the cost of lining the irrigation canals in the Atuel river basin is included, this total rises to about $403 million.

An evaluation of the overall profitability of these projects as well as recommendations for public investment priorities are beyond the scope of this study. Comments are limited to the likely impact of the proposed investments on the region's future agricultural development and water availability and the range of investment alternatives given serious consideration in the planning process. The major benefits which are claimed for these projects are an increased availability and improved regulation of the region's irrigation water. While these are not the only benefits, it is useful to focus on the implications and alternative means of achieving these benefits. The interbasin water transfer projects would have the most dramatic impact on the availability of irrigation water. The transfer of 40 m^3 of water per second into the southern irrigated zone of Mendoza would increase available irrigation water by over 50 percent in this zone. Such an increase in water would enable agriculture in southern Mendoza to grow for an additional twenty-two to forty-two years if the rate of growth in water use were between 1 and 2 percent per annum.[12] The other projects would do little to forestall any serious water crisis. While the dams should increase agricultural production potential by improving the timing of water receipts, they could actually decrease the total quantity of surface water delivered to farms. A decrease would occur if the increased evaporation losses stemming from the storage of water behind the dam exceeded the water saved by eliminating or reducing the quantity of water which would otherwise run out of the region. Since the surface water is already almost entirely used within the region during years of normal or subnormal river flows, it is

---

[12] A water transfer might slow the growth of water use in other areas of Cuyo by attracting relatively more agricultural investment into the south. However, the transfer would not slow and might actually increase the growth of water use for the whole region.

likely that evaporation losses would on the average be greater than savings. The lining of irrigation canals overlying the confined aquifers increases the total availability of irrigation water in the region. It would be very optimistic to expect the water savings from the projects under construction in the Tunuyán and Diamante river basins to prolong for as much as a decade the advent of a water crisis in these river basins.[13]

None of these projects would significantly affect the inefficient use of water on the farms, nor would they alter the water-intensive agricultural growth pattern. Moreover, they would not directly alter the incentive to drill wells and expand the cultivated lands dependent exclusively on ground water. The combination of all these projects might extend by as much as a decade or more the average time at which the lack of good quality irrigation water forces a reversal of the water-intensive agricultural growth pattern. However, these projects will not eliminate the overuse of ground water stocks nor the likelihood that the elimination of good quality ground water stocks will result in a substantial curtailment of production and large investment losses. This alone does not mean that the investment projects are not warranted. The benefits of an additional decade of agricultural expansion are substantial.

On the other hand, there may be more economical methods of obtaining the irrigation benefits claimed for these projects. All the reasonable alternatives to and implications of these projects have not been considered. There is a tendency to focus on increasing the availability and timing of surface water flows while ignoring the impact on the overall supply of water to the region's agriculture over time. The impacts of the dam and canal lining projects on ground water recharge have been largely ignored in the selection and design of projects. Despite some definite advantages of using ground water instead of surface reservoirs for water storage in an arid environment, this alternative has never been seriously considered in Cuyo. In addition to the elimination of evaporation losses, ground water storage does not flood valuable land. This advantage is particularly relevant for the proposed dam at Potrerillos, which would require a very costly relocation of the railroad and a major road between Argentina and Chile. Moreover, the northern region of Mendoza already possesses more than 13,700 irrigation wells with a total pumping capacity well in excess of the natural recharge to the region's aquifers. The use of ground water instead of a surface water

---

[13] Increased agricultural production resulting from improved water receipts would have indirect effects on agricultural investment and overall water use. Increased production could discourage expansion through lower product prices or encourage more investment by raising profits. The net impact on growth of these offsetting indirect effects would probably be slight.

reservoir would not provide the recreation benefits which are claimed, but never quantified, for the dam at Potrerillos. And, unlike the dam, the ground water alternative would increase the demand for and not the supply of power. We cannot conclude here that artificial ground water recharge would be preferable to construction of the dam at Potrerillos. However, if the primary objective of the Potrerillos project is to improve the timing and flow of irrigation water, the dam may be both more costly and less effective than ground water storage for achieving this. It is likely that the dam would be preferable only if a high value were placed on the projected energy and recreation benefits.[14]

Altering the Conjunctive Use of Ground and Surface Water

Chapter 5 indicated that a change in the conjunctive use of ground and surface water could increase the quantity of water delivered to the farms by reducing water distribution losses.[15] To the extent that such a change reduced evaporation losses and water infiltration in the areas where infiltration would not recharge the region's usable aquifers, the change would also increase the total quantity of water available to the region's agriculture over time. In addition, a more efficient conjunctive use of ground and surface water would reduce the costs of delivering a given quantity of water to the farms.

In general, a more efficient conjunctive water use would require greater concentration of surface water deliveries in the upper reaches and greater pumping in the lower reaches of the rivers. The obstacles to achieving such a redistribution are legal and institutional, not financial. For reasons presented in Chapter 5,[16] the best means of improving the conjunctive use of ground and surface water would be to internalize the full social costs of water deliveries and allow the sale of surface water rights independent of the land. Internalizing the social cost of water use would have the important additional advantage of providing greater incentive for improving on-farm water use efficiency.

Other Alternatives

Weather modification is being studied as an alternative means for increasing the availability of irrigation water in Cuyo. An institute established in July 1972 will undertake research on increasing Cuyo's

[14] The use of surface storage tends to favor the holders of surface water rights as opposed to farmers pumping ground water. However, even a preference for the owners of land with surface water rights could be satisfied through government pumping and controls over ground water use.

[15] See the discussion in Chapter 5, pp. 78 and 86–88.

[16] See Chapter 5, pp. 99–105.

river flows through weather modification.[17] The impact of these research efforts on the future availability of water within Cuyo is highly uncertain. While significant short-run results should not be expected, results in other places offer hope for success. Howe and Easter state:[18] "With regard to precipitation, the result [of two major reports dealing with the state of the art of weather modification] appears to be a cautious acceptance of the hypothesis that, under some circumstances, precipitation can be increased 10 to 20 percent." If conditions proved favorable in Cuyo, such an increase in precipitation would have a significant impact on water supplies. For example, if precipitation rose 15 percent and 75 percent of this increase found its way into the region's stream flows, it would add about 23 m^3 of water per second to the combined average annual flows of the Mendoza, Tunuyán, Atuel, Diamante, and San Juan rivers. This is only about 5 percent less water than would be transferred from the Grande to Atuel rivers under the first interbasin water transfer alternative discussed above. Since the transfer of 24 m^3 of water per second at an estimated cost of $76.9 million (exclusive of the costs related solely to power production) is considered an attractive investment for the province of Mendoza, the potential returns to cloud seeding or some other form of weather modification could prove to be very high.[19]

Evaporation losses will become an increasingly important factor in the region's water supply as the number of dams and quantity of water stored on the surface increases sharply in the coming decades. Currently there is no information available on the costs of or benefits from alternative methods of reducing evaporation losses in Cuyo. Moreover, experiments in other countries offer no immediate prospect that reducing evaporation losses will become an important source of relatively inexpensive water savings in Cuyo. For example, Howe and Easter conclude that "there is no practical economic way of controlling evaporation from large bodies of water at the present time." They add that

[17] The new institute, Instituto Argentino de Nivología y Glaciología, is supported jointly by the National Council for Scientific and Technical Research, the National University of Cuyo, the Government of Mendoza, and several other government agencies and institutions. Prior attempts at weather modification in Cuyo have focused on reducing the damage to the region's crops caused by hail. These efforts are discussed later in this chapter.

[18] Charles W. Howe and K. William Easter, *Interbasin Transfers of Water: Economic Issues and Impacts* (Baltimore: The Johns Hopkins Press for Resources for the Future, Inc., 1971), p. 127.

[19] Very rough estimates of the costs per unit of water gained through cloud seeding in the Upper Colorado river basin in the United States indicate cloud seeding may be one of the cheapest sources of additional water for the western United States. The cost estimates include only the operating costs of a cloud seeding program; the development and research costs are excluded. See Howe and Easter, *Interbasin Transfers*, pp. 127 and 134.

"retardation of evaporation from small ponds may, however, be a worthwhile endeavor in some areas, for costs of water saved appear to range from low to moderate in terms of alternative sources."[20] The relatively high evaporation rates and increasing use of surface water storage in Cuyo suggest the desirability of research into practical methods of reducing evaporation losses within the region.

Other possibilities exist for increasing the availability of irrigation and potable water. The reuse of treated sewage flows has proved an economically attractive alternative in some areas. For Cuyo, however, even if water reclamation proved cost competitive, the quantities of water involved are currently small, and savings could not exceed more than 1 to 2 percent of current water use. Studies for the western United States suggest that the potential water savings can be substantial and the per unit water costs low to moderate from controlling the growth of vegetation with no economic value.[21] The potential water savings and the costs of controlling such plant growth in Cuyo are unknown. Cuyo has some ground water deposits located relatively close to the surface that are considered unusable because of high salinity. While the costs of desalinization with current technology would be well beyond the levels that could be absorbed by the region's farmers, it may be economically possible to use this water to grow some crops with a very high tolerance to salinity. The practical relevance of these water-saving methods is currently highly speculative within Cuyo. Yet, the diminishing returns that are likely to set in if the region continues to look almost exclusively to large-scale investments in dams, canals, and interbasin transfers for increasing water supplies suggest the region might do well to broaden its search for alternative sources of water.

INCREASING THE RETURNS TO WATER

This section examines two subjects: first, the possibilities for and the profitability of increasing the value of production per unit of water at the farm level; second, the possibility that preemption of the region's water for irrigation may prevent nonagricultural development. A wide variety of changes in farming practices might increase the returns to water. The most important of these for Cuyo are considered below under two broad categories: (1) adopting new irrigation techniques and (2) increasing the use of other productive inputs.

[20] Ibid., p. 118.
[21] Ibid., pp. 130–131. The book by Howe and Easter contains a section on alternatives to interbasin transfers, pp. 111–135, which examines the estimated impact on water supplies and the costs of various methods of increasing water supplies in the western United States.

Irrigation Techniques

Water in Cuyo is generally applied to the land through furrows or, less frequently, by flooding.[22] Both irrigation methods are relatively inefficient. Farm irrigation efficiency with furrows generally ranges between 50 and 70 percent in Cuyo; with flooding, efficiency is only 40 to 50 percent.

The type of soil and slope of the land are the major factors affecting irrigation efficiency with these two methods. Efficiency falls where the soil is more porous and the gradient steeper. The national agricultural research and extension service offers farmers courses on irrigation techniques. These courses alone, however, are not likely to generate more than small increases in the overall farm irrigation efficiency. Given the basic land conditions, major expenses are usually required to make significant changes in irrigation efficiency. For example, it might cost $500 per hectare to level land with a 2- to 3-degree slope. Other systems offering substantially higher irrigation efficiencies cost even more. Farmers are likely to undertake such investments only if they expect the costs are justified by the value of the water saved plus other benefits of a change.

There are likely to be important differences between the value of water and efficiencies of irrigation as viewed by individual farmers and a society as a whole. Chapter 5 discusses the sources of differences between private and social values of water. Sizable discrepancies are also likely between private and social views of irrigation efficiency. For example, water which infiltrates below the root zone of the crops or runs off a farmer's land is lost to a particular farmer. However, if this water recharges the usable aquifers or flows directly to other land, the water is not lost to society.[23] The important loss factor for determining which irrigation techniques are adopted is the loss as viewed by the farmer; the important loss factor for obtaining an efficient use of the region's overall water supplies is the loss to the society. The following discussion first examines the farmer's profitability of alternative irrigation techniques under a variety of circumstances; these results are then qualified for the likely impact of differences between private and social water costs and irrigation efficiency rates.

Irrigation with sprinklers or pipes designed to deliver a well-

[22] Of 132 farms surveyed in eastern Mendoza in the late 1960s, 60 percent irrigated through furrows, 23 percent by flooding, and 17 percent used both methods. See Torrontegui and Tonina, "Análisis económico de fincas vitifrutícolas en tres departamentos de la provincia de Mendoza," *Revista de investigaciones agropecuarias* (Buenos Aires: INTA, 1969), Serie 6, Economía y Administración Rural, Vol. 3, no. 3, p. 91.

[23] There are, of course, costs for pumping the water back to the surface, and the quality of the drainage and ground water may be lower.

controlled quantity of water to the plants is rare in Cuyo, although it offers farm irrigation efficiencies well above those of the currently popular techniques. Farm irrigation efficiency rises to about 90 percent with sprinklers and 100 percent with drip irrigation.[24] The major factors affecting the profitability of adopting these irrigation techniques are the costs of the equipment, the quantity and value of water saved, the reduction in labor costs, the impact on production, and the saving in land leveling costs. As is discussed below, the importance of these factors and, therefore, the profitability of the alternative irrigation technologies vary substantially among farms and crops.

The purchase and installation of the equipment for delivering the water from the farm gate or pump to the plants in controlled drips would cost an estimated $1,587 per hectare of grapes and would have an expected useful life of about ten years.[25] There are no significant economies of scale associated with these costs. In addition, a water storage tank would be needed. For a farmer irrigating with ground water, the tank could be small since the water receipts are regular and well controlled. Such a tank would cost an estimated $127 per hectare and have a useful life of over thirty years. The tank would have to be much larger for irrigating with surface water since the water receipts at the farm are irregular. The estimated per hectare costs for such a water storage tank would be about $1,047 on 5 hectares, $873 on 10 hectares, and $698 on 20 hectares.

Economies of scale are more important with sprinkler irrigation. If the equipment is sufficient to irrigate 10 percent of the land from a single position, the per hectare cost excluding the pump and storage tank would be $571 for 5 hectares, $548 for 10 hectares, and $444 for 20 hectares. The useful life of this equipment exceeds thirty years. In order to generate sufficient pressure, pumps would be required; with a

[24] The discussion on sprinkler and drip irrigation in Cuyo relies heavily on José Fajgenbaum, "Análisis económico de la introducción de nuevas tecnologías de riego," a paper prepared in partial fulfillment of the requirements for the *licenciado* degree in economics at the National University of Cuyo, Mendoza, 1972. The appendix to Fajgenbaum's study describes these irrigation systems and the general conditions under which they are suited. With drip irrigation, water is applied only to the root zone of the crops. For grapes planted with the overhead-trellis system, this includes only about 25 percent of the land. While the crops may not actually utilize 100 percent of the water applied with drip irrigation, the basic water requirements of a hectare of grapes are less with this system, which keeps a constant moisture level in the root zone, than the 7,230 m^3 of water assumed for other irrigation methods. On balance the assumption of 100 percent farm irrigation efficiency or the application of 7,230 m^3 of water per hectare with drip irrigation is probably a conservative estimate of the water saving of this irrigation system.

[25] Equipment costs would vary with the required spacing of the pipes; costs would be higher for vegetables than for grapes. Table 7.3 indicates the source of the cost data for the sprinkler and drip irrigation systems.

Table 7.3 Additional Annual Costs with Sprinkler and Drip Irrigation[a]

(in 1969 dollars per hectare)

	Farm size (hectares)	Equipment	Energy	Mainte-nance[b]	Total
Drip Irrigation					
Ground water[c]	any size	271.8	—	5.4	277.2
Surface water	5	369.9	—	7.4	377.3
	10	351.3	—	7.0	358.3
	20	332.7	—	6.7	339.4
Sprinkler Irrigation					
Ground water[c]	5	85.1	37.4	1.7	124.2
	10	79.0	33.8	1.6	114.4
	20	67.0	29.9	1.3	98.2
Surface water	5	196.8	37.4	3.9	238.1
	10	169.5	33.8	3.4	206.7
	20	136.4	29.9	2.7	169.0

Source: The costs are derived from data presented in Fajgenbaum, "Análisis eco-nómico de la introducción de nuevas tecnologías de riego," Mendoza, 1972, pp. 5–10. The data are based on estimates for irrigating grapes with the overhead-trellis planting system. The 1972 peso costs are converted to 1969 dollars at 6.3 pesos to 1 dollar.

[a]These costs are additional to those of getting the water to the farm.

[b] Maintenance is assumed to be 2 percent of the annualized cost of the equipment. Fajgenbaum (p. 7) states that his sources indicated that the equipment did not require maintenance. Nevertheless, he included 1 percent of the original equipment cost every three years for maintenance. This is roughly equivalent to the allowance made in this table.

[c] The costs of the irrigation well, pump, and motor and the power to pump the water to the surface are not included in these costs.

useful life of about ten years, a pump would cost approximately $275 for 5 hectares, $321 for 10 hectares, and $532 for 20 hectares. Water storage tanks would also be needed. The tank for sprinkler irrigation should be somewhat larger than the tank for drip irrigation since the water applied per hectare is about 11 percent higher with the sprinkler system. With ground water, the costs of a tank for sprinkler irrigation would be about $143 per hectare regardless of farm size; with surface water, the per hectare costs would be about $1,190 on 5 hectares, $992 on 10 hectares, and $794 on 20 hectares. In addition to the equipment costs above, the electric power required to generate the pressure required for sprinkler irrigation would cost $187 per year for 5 hectares, $338 per year for 10 hectares, and $597 per year for 20 hectares with daytime power rates.

Table 7.3 summarizes the estimated additional annual costs of drip and sprinkler irrigation with a 10 percent discount rate. In order to obtain the total water costs with these irrigation systems, the costs of getting the water to the farms must be added to the costs in Table 7.3.[26]

[26] The annualized ground water equipment costs in Table 7.3 include storage tank costs of $13.6 for drip irrigation and $15.3 for sprinkler irrigation plus an

The costs of the equipment needed for adopting these irrigation techniques would be eligible for official credit and tax investment incentives. A farmer able to take advantage of these credit and tax subsidies would substantially reduce the effective costs of the systems. With a 15 percent bank lending rate, 40 percent nominal discount rate, and 33 percent marginal tax rate, the effective costs of the equipment would be reduced by 24.5 percent by the tax subsidy and 23.6 percent by the tax investment credit.[27]

The costs of these irrigation systems, even when reduced by the tax and credit subsidies, are substantial and cannot generally be justified by the water savings alone.[28] There are, however, other benefits such as reduced labor requirements and higher expected yields associated with the use of these irrigation systems.

Sprinkler and drip irrigation require less labor for both the irrigation and cultivation of the crops than irrigation through furrows. The labor savings are particularly large with drip irrigation since the equipment does not have to be moved and there are virtually no weeding requirements. Since there are economies of scale in performing some of the

---

additional 2 percent of these costs for maintenance. These tanks would not be sufficient to enable a farmer to pump the water to the surface during the hours of low energy rates and then irrigate during the day. However, if the costs of getting the ground water to the farm already allow for a storage tank sufficient for night pumping and day irrigating, the pools included in Table 7.3 would not be necessary.

[27] See tables 3.1 and 3.2.

[28] For example, the estimated annual ground water costs on a 10-hectare farm with a 30-meter pumping depth and 70 percent irrigation efficiency range from $112 to $197 per hectare depending on the availability of the credit and tax subsidies. (See Table 6.3.) Even if we ignore the economies of scale of pumping more water from the same well, the sprinkler system would reduce the annual per hectare costs of getting the necessary quantity of water to the farm by only about $25 to $44. In comparison, the additional costs of the sprinkler system would range from about $55 to $114 per hectare, depending on the availability of the credit and tax subsidies. With the drip system, the comparison of additional costs and savings would be even less favorable. The savings in ground water costs become more important as the pumping distance increases and as private water costs are made closer to social costs. Table 6.5 estimates the average social costs of using 10,330 m³ of ground water at $277 for a pumping depth of 30 meters and $467 for 110 meters. Nevertheless, even with a pumping depth of 110 meters and no economies of scale, the water savings from the sprinkler system would not justify the additional costs unless these costs were reduced by the credit or tax subsidies. Moreover, on most farms the marginal costs of pumping the additional water required for furrow irrigation would be well below the average annual water costs. For example, based on the data in Table 2.10, the average costs of ground water with a 30-meter pumping depth, no tax and credit subsidies, and 70 percent irrigation efficiency, are $197 on a 10-hectare farm and $128 on a 20-hectare farm. However, the marginal costs per hectare are $8.4 for moving from 5 to 10 hectares, $9.4 for moving from 15 to 20 hectares, and $32.00 for moving from 30 to 36 hectares if the changes do not require larger water storage pools. These costs are based on data in Table 2.10.

Table 7.4 Estimated Net Annual Labor Savings with Alternative Irrigation Systems

Farm irrigation efficiency with furrows[b]	Net labor savings in comparison to irrigation with furrows[a] (man days per year and per hectare)					
	Drip irrigation			Sprinkler irrigation		
	5 ha	10 ha	20 ha	5 ha	10 ha	20 ha
50	30	25	21	19	17	16
60	28	23	19	17	15	14
70	27	22	18	16	14	13
80	26.5	21.5	17.5	15.5	13.5	12.5

Source: Fajgenbaum, "Análisis económico," p. 15.

[a] The labor savings are net for all farm tasks, not just the labor required for irrigating.

[b] The assumed irrigation efficiencies are 100 percent with drips and 90 percent with sprinklers.

tasks which are either eliminated or reduced with sprinkler and drip irrigation, the labor savings vary with farm size. Moreover, the labor savings increase with the percentage improvement in irrigation efficiency. Table 7.4 presents estimates of the net annual labor savings when these two systems are used to irrigate grapes in comparison to the labor requirements of irrigation through furrows. The farm irrigation efficiencies for delivering the water through furrows are varied from 50 to 80 percent while the comparable efficiencies are assumed to be 90 percent with sprinklers and 100 percent with drips.

The importance of reducing labor requirements will vary among farms. While the labor savings are greatest on smaller farms, the opportunity costs of labor are likely to be less on these farms. As was noted in the previous chapter,[29] a 5-hectare farm is not sufficient to provide reasonably full employment to a family of four. However, the savings would enable the owner of a larger farm to hire less labor. Assuming a daily wage rate of $3.7,[30] the value per hectare of the annual labor savings on a 20-hectare farm would be $66.6 with drip and $48.1 with sprinkler irrigation in comparison to the costs of furrow irrigation with a 70 percent farm irrigation efficiency. The lower labor costs are well below the cost increases associated with adopting the new irrigation systems. Moreover, even when the labor savings are combined with the water savings, the new irrigation systems are still generally not economically justified. For example, the combined value of the labor and water saving would be about $69.4 per hectare with drip and $50.2 per hectare with sprinkler irrigation on a 20-hectare farm pumping

[29] See Chapter 6, p. 126.

[30] This wage is approximately the legal rural wage rate including the employer's cost of social services. Many employers, however, do not pay the social services, which amount to about 40 percent of the worker's take-home pay. The social opportunity costs of this labor are probably closer to the worker's take-home pay of about $2.6 per day than to the employer's legal salary requirements.

ground water 30 meters. These savings hardly offset the additional costs of $277 per hectare for the drip and $98 per hectare for the sprinkler irrigation systems. Even when a farmer can reduce equipment costs by 48 percent through the credit and tax subsidies and the pumping depth is increased to 110 meters, the labor and water cost savings are not generally sufficient to justify the new irrigation systems. If the water and labor cost savings are the only benefits, the new irrigation systems would be preferable only if farmers paid the social costs (as estimated in Table 6.5) of the water or were in a situation where the new irrigation systems would eliminate the necessity of drilling another irrigation well.

Potentially the most important factor for the profitability of adopting the drip and sprinkler irrigation systems are their impacts on production. Adoption of these systems can affect yields in several ways, both positively and negatively. First, the area devoted to crops can be increased about 4 percent because of the elimination of the irrigation furrows. While this may not be important on land already planted to a permanent crop, it is relevant for annual crops and land to be planted to permanent crops. Second, yields might rise because of the improved control over soil humidity offered by the new irrigation systems. The plants spend less energy obtaining water and have more energy for producing fruit. Third, sprinkler irrigation increases the likelihood of plant fungus and, consequently, may not be suitable for certain crops. Grapes, particularly when supported by low fences, are considered susceptible to this problem. While this problem has not emerged in the few experiments where grapes have been irrigated with sprinklers in Cuyo, INTA does not include grapes among the crops suitable for sprinkler irrigation.[31] Four, long-run yields may decline because of increased soil salinity resulting from the new irrigation systems. However, irrigation specialists in Cuyo currently feel that this problem can be overcome, perhaps through equipment modifications to permit periodic washing of the soils.[32] Such alterations, however, would undoubtedly increase the costs and decrease the total water use efficiencies of the alternative irrigation systems.

Unfortunately, little is known about the probable net impact on the yields of different crops of using these alternative irrigation techniques in Cuyo. However, the few experiments available for Cuyo and results in other countries suggest that large increases in yields may be possible through a shift from furrow to drip irrigation. For example, experimental yields in Israel with drip irrigation were 50 to 100 percent higher

[31] Such recommendations are presented in a joint publication by Departamento General de Irrigación and Instituto Nacional de Tecnología Agropecuaria (INTA), *Curso de riego para agricultores* (Mendoza, 1972), p. 30.
[32] Fajgenbaum, "Análisis económico," pp. 2–3.

for vegetables, 20 to 50 percent higher for fruits, and 30 percent higher for grapes than the yields with furrow irrigation. Experimental yields over a three-year period for old vines in Mendoza averaged from 12.5 to 67.8 percent higher on the plot with drip irrigation than on the plots with furrowing.[33]

The adoption of drip or sprinkler irrigation in Cuyo is dependent on an expectation of receiving a substantially higher yield in comparison to furrow irrigation; in view of the high cost of these alternative systems, the uncertainty surrounding their impact on yields is a major deterrent to their adoption. Nevertheless, the likelihood of favorable yield responses makes it relevant to consider conditions under which the alternative irrigation systems would and would not be preferable to furrow irrigation. In view of the importance of grapes and the knowledge that drip irrigation both is suitable for irrigating grapes and has substantially increased grape yields in Cuyo and other countries, the discussion below focuses on the relative profitability of drip irrigation under a variety of assumptions.

The value of water saved by adopting drip irrigation would vary widely from farm to farm. At one extreme, the water would have a relatively high marginal value if the water saving prevented the loss of permanent crops or the need for installing an irrigation well. At the other extreme, the marginal value of water would be relatively low if a farmer received ample surface water or had an irrigation well with a shallow pumping depth and excess pumping capacity. If a farmer placed no value on the water saving, the expected increase in grape yields on the 10-hectare farm considered in Chapter 6 would have to be at least 29 percent with ground water and 40 percent with surface water to justify the use of drip irrigation.[34] Marginal water costs per 10,000 m^3 of water on farms with excess pumping capacity and a pumping depth of 30 meters would be about $8 to $9 on farms less than 20 hectares, about $20 on farms from 20 to 30 hectares, and about $32 on farms over 30 hectares.[35] A 30 percent increase in irrigation efficiency would imply an annual cost saving of less than $3 per hectare on farms

[33] Ibid., p. 17. The results of the Mendoza experiments were affected in an unknown manner by heavy frost damage during one of the experimental years.

[34] The percentage change in yield required to make the new system profitable would rise as the base yield fell. The basic yields assumed for the above calculations are presented in Table 6.2. The additional costs and labor savings of shifting from furrow to drip irrigation are presented in tables 7.3 and 7.4. The net annual cost increase, excluding the value of the water savings and assuming a daily wage of $3.7, would be $196 per hectare with ground water and $277 per hectare with surface water.

[35] The marginal water costs assume off-peak pumping rates for farms up to 20 hectares and are based on the implied marginal water costs of data in Table 2.10.

less than 20 hectares and about $10 per hectare on farms over 30 hectares. Inclusion of these water cost savings in the benefits of drip irrigation would lower the percentage increases in yields required to make this system profitable by only 0.4 percent on farms less than 20 hectares and 1.4 percent on farms over 30 hectares. Even with a pumping depth of 110 meters, the value of the water saving would be less than $8 per hectare on farms of 20 hectares or less. In this case the expected increase in yield would have to be at least 28 percent to make drip irrigation profitable.

If farmers had to pay the full social costs of the water used, the value of the water savings would rise considerably. Based on estimates in Table 6.5, the marginal social cost of pumping 10,330 m³ of water would be $100 with a 30-meter pumping depth and $262 with a 110-meter pumping depth. At these prices, a 30 percent water saving would save from $30 to $79 per hectare per year. With social water costs, drip irrigation would be profitable with expected yield increases of 24.2 percent on farms pumping 30 meters and 17.1 percent on farms pumping 110 meters. Such percentage changes in yields are well within the experimental results for grapes with drip irrigation in Israel and at least some of the results in Mendoza.

Availability of the credit and tax subsidies would substantially expand the conditions under which drip irrigation was profitable. With no allowance for the value of the water savings, either the tax or credit subsidy would reduce the minimum expected percentage increase in yields required to make controlled-drip irrigation competitive to 19 percent with ground water and 28 percent with surface water. The combined impact of the tax and credit subsidy would reduce the required yield increase to 10 percent with ground water and 16 percent with surface water.[36]

Earlier discussion indicated that it was profitable to install an irrigation well for irrigating as little as 5 hectares if the alternative was the loss of 5 hectares of good yielding vines.[37] Indeed, this "rescue" demand for irrigation was an important factor in the rapid expansion of irrigation wells from about 1967 to 1971.[38] Yet, if the farmers could have counted on yield increases of 10 to 15 percent or more by adopting drip irrigation, many of these farmers might have been better off by improving irrigation efficiency than by increasing the quantity of water with an irrigation well. For example, if a 10-hectare farm with a 50 percent efficiency were confronted with drilling a well or increasing irrigation

[36] These calculations assume equipment costs are reduced 24.5 percent by the tax credit and 23.6 percent by the credit subsidy.
[37] See Chapter 6, p. 115.
[38] See Chapter 2, pp. 30–32.

efficiency to save 5 hectares of good-yielding grapes, adopting drip irrigation would be profitable if this irrigation system also increased yields by 9 percent or more. If a 15-hectare farm with a 66.7 percent irrigation efficiency were faced with the same alternatives for saving 5 hectares, the controlled-drip system would be profitable if the expected yield increase were 15 percent or more.[39] These calculations ignore the potential value of the excess pumping capacity associated with the option of a well. For some farmers this value might be substantial both as a hedge against low surface water receipts and for future expansion of cultivated areas. For other farmers, however, there may be no opportunity to expand the cultivated area, and the improved water use efficiency may provide sufficient safety against unusually low surface water receipts. Indeed, the "rescue" demand for irrigation wells emerged to compensate for unusually low surface water receipts, and the provincial governments are investing heavily in dams, lined canals, and irrigation wells to prevent a repetition of the low water received on land with surface water rights during the recent past.

This discussion suggests that drip irrigation would be a profitable investment on many farms if farmers could reasonably expect yield increases of 20 to 30 percent with the new irrigation systems. Since the costs of sprinkler irrigation are considerably less, the expected yield increases required for justifying sprinklers would be lower. While there are some good reasons for expecting that these irrigation systems could increase yields sufficiently to make them profitable investments, these reasons are either unknown or not good enough (probably both) for most farmers. Before investing heavily in these relatively expensive systems, most farmers require greater evidence of the probable returns. With the current use of and interest in these irrigation systems in Cuyo, it will be many years before the evidence is sufficient to interest most farmers. However, this process could be greatly accelerated by a change in emphasis on government agricultural research stations in Cuyo. Moreover, the prospect that the marginal value of water, especially in social terms, will continue to rise and the marginal returns to continued government investments in water-related infrastructure will fall within Cuyo, suggests that social returns might be higher if greater government emphasis were placed on methods of increasing water use efficiency on the farms.

Use of Other Productive Inputs

In addition to increasing the efficiency with which water is distributed to the plants, returns per unit of water can be increased by reducing

[39] The assumed grape yields with furrow irrigation are those presented in Table 6.2 for years 11 to 30.

crop losses resulting from the weather, insects, and plant diseases, increasing production through inputs such as fertilizer, better seed, new varieties, and improved cultivation practices, and increasing the average price by improving crop quality and marketing techniques and perhaps by planting other crops.

Agricultural research stations in Cuyo conduct experiments examining the impact of various inputs and cultivation practices on the yields of a wide variety of crops. This research has produced some notable results. For example, the introduction of improved tomato seeds in the early 1960s was primarily responsible for nearly doubling tomato yields within several years.[40] And the development of improved cultural practices for orchard management has enabled growers to increase yields by 30 percent.[41]

Much of the agricultural research in Cuyo has focused on grapes. Experiments examining the influence on yields of fertilizers, pesticides, fungicides, grape varieties, irrigation methods, pruning, and the system of supporting the vines have been conducted by the region's research stations. In some cases the results demonstrate significant relationships between yields and a given factor use or cultivation technique.[42] However, demonstration of a production response does not imply profitability. Where alternative growing practices have been economically advantageous, their adoption has been rapid and widespread.[43]

The economic advisability of adopting alternative inputs and techniques varies with factors such as relative prices for grape varieties, soil

[40] Tomato yields in Mendoza from 1964 to 1970 averaged about 18 MT per hectare, 90 percent above the average from 1956 to 1962.

[41] See Darrell F. Fienup and others, *The Agricultural Development of Argentina* (New York: Praeger, 1969), p. 273.

[42] Experimental results involving the impact of these factors on grape yields are summarized in Instituto Nacional de Tecnología Agropecuaria (INTA), *Programa "Vid"* (Mendoza, March 1972).

[43] Despite the wide variations in grape yields within Cuyo, officials at INTA research stations in both Mendoza and San Juan expressed the view that the research stations currently have little to offer the majority of grape growers in Cuyo. INTA's extension program for grape producers is focused on recommendations regarding use of green manure, methods of irrigation, and means of preventing or cultivating with saline soils. (Ibid., pp. 52–57). However, the major factors accounting for variations in grape yields are weather damage, age and variety of the vines, methods of supporting the vines, and soil conditions. INTA can do little about weather losses beyond recommending cultivation techniques that might help reduce fruit losses after a frost. INTA experiments offer considerable evidence regarding the relative yields of various varieties and vine-supporting systems which are probably important in influencing planting decisions. They are unlikely, however, to prompt many growers to eliminate lower producing varieties and growing systems much sooner than they would otherwise be eradicated. Moreover, the varieties with the highest physical yields generally command the lowest market prices, and uncertain market conditions make it very difficult to predict which variety would offer the highest long-run monetary return.

conditions, and factor prices. Of particular relevance for both this study and the future growth of the region are the impacts of the alternatives on returns to water and the economic profitability of alternatives under varying water conditions. These considerations become more relevant for the decision process as irrigation wells and dams provide greater control over farm water receipts. Unfortunately, however, the experiments are seldom designed to shed light on the role of water. The experiments which introduce factors such as grape varieties and fertilizer applications as variables are generally based on "desirable" water deliveries from the point of view of plant growth but irrespective of the social value of water.[44] The quantity of water delivered to the plants is seldom treated as an experimental variable.

The use of leguminous plants for enriching the soil illustrates the importance of the availability and cost of water for optimal farm practices. In general, Cuyo's soils are deficient in nitrogen, and as a result of INTA experiments virtually all INTA agencies in Cuyo recommend the use of leguminous plants with grapes. Nevertheless, this use of leguminous plants dropped off sharply during the recent years of low surface water receipts, and INTA now points out that the use of these plants is inadvisable when water receipts are low and the grapes have to compete with these plants for water.[45] But since the experiments did not systematically take into account the interrelationships between water deliveries and production, there is currently no way of knowing the quantity or price of water necessary to economically justify the interplanting of leguminous plants and grapes.

With water the major factor limiting the region's future agricultural growth and with the social value of water likely to rise further in the future, the water inputs associated with a given cropping pattern, cultivation practice, and factor use are of great importance to efficient farming from both the private and social perspectives. In order to enhance the relevance and potential impact of the region's agricultural research, the quantity of water should be entered as a control variable in virtually all experiments.

Hail and frost are the major sources of crop damage in Mendoza. Grape losses due to hail damage from 1952 to 1965 are estimated to have reduced Mendoza's production by an average of 12.9 percent; among departments frost damage ranged from an average of 2 percent in Las Heras to 17 percent in Tunuyán. The combined grape losses due to frost and hail are highest in the eastern and southern departments of

[44] Although there are no data on the physical relationship between water applications and production, it is likely that these "desirable" water deliveries are close to the point where the marginal product of water is zero.

[45] INTA, *Programa "Vid,"* pp. 32, 33 and 52.

Mendoza, totaling about 38 percent in La Paz, 37 percent in Santa Rosa, 29 percent in San Rafael, and 26 percent in General Alvear.[46] Other fruits grown in Mendoza are also highly susceptible to weather damage. For example, the damage from three consecutive nights of frost during October 1972 was estimated by INTA at 83 percent of the apples and pears, 85 percent of the peaches, 90 percent of the apricots, and 32 percent of the grapes that had previously been expected from the 1973 Mendoza harvests.[47] In comparison to Mendoza, crop losses to hail and frost are relatively modest in San Juan, averaging about 5 percent for the province as a whole.[48]

The magnitude of hail damage has encouraged a search for methods of eliminating or reducing these losses. The government of Mendoza is supporting research to reduce the occurrence and intensity of hail through the use of radar for early detection of hail producing clouds, followed by rockets for cloud seeding to prevent the hail. This technology has not been proven effective in Mendoza. However, these methods reportedly have been 99 percent successful in the Soviet Union. It had been estimated that this system would be economically justified in Mendoza if it were only 20 percent effective.[49]

Currently, the only reliable means of reducing hail damage in Cuyo is a wire mesh or plastic protective covering for the crops. Both methods have proved very successful in virtually eliminating hail damage, and the plastic covering also reduces frost damage. Nevertheless, because of the high costs of the materials and installation, these protective coverings are rarely encountered in Cuyo. A well-constructed, plastic covering costs an estimated $2,300 to $2,500 per hectare of grapes grown with the overhead-trellis system.[50] With a ten-year life the annualized cost would be $245 to $267 per hectare. In order to justify these cost increases, annual yields on the vineyard averaging 17.9 MT per

[46] J. P. Morelli, "Inversión privada en viticultura," *Revista de investigaciones agropecuarias* (Buenos Aires: INTA, 1970), Serie 6, Economía y Administración Rural, Vol. 4, no. 2, Cuadro 5, p. 68. The estimate of average frost damage for the province was calculated from the departmental data presented in Morelli using departmental grape production from 1953 to 1955 as weights.

[47] See "El INTA dio su evaluación de pérdidas por heladas," in *Los Andes*, October 11, 1972.

[48] Farmers in San Juan pay 5 percent of the value of their production into a compulsory farm insurance program to compensate for hail and frost damage; 4 percent is allocated to hail and 1 percent to frost damage. See Gobierno de San Juan, "Proyecto quebrada de Ullum, Estudio de factibilidad" (San Juan, 1969), Book II, pp. A-15–16.

[49] "Iniciarán estudios para luchar contra el granizo," an article in *Los Andes*, January 23, 1972.

[50] "Ensayan formas de protección para los vinedos contra granizo y heladas," *Los Andes*, April 15, 1973. The 1973 peso costs are converted to dollars at the rate of 10 pesos to 1 dollar.

hectare (see Table 6.2) have to rise by 36 to 39 percent for the farmer to break even. Under these conditions, the coverings have little economic appeal in any part of Cuyo. However, for a farmer able to benefit from the credit and tax subsidies, the production increase required to offset the additional costs is much less. For example, with a 40 percent nominal discount rate, 15 percent bank lending rate, and 33 percent marginal tax rate, the effective cost of the equipment to a farmer benefiting from both the credit and tax subsidies are offset by yield increases of 17 to 19 percent.[51] Under these conditions, the protective plastic covering for grapes is an attractive investment in many areas of Mendoza; the combined grape losses to frost and hail in eight departments, accounting for about half of Mendoza's production, have averaged over 23 percent.[52]

Nonagricultural Water Use

Since agriculture offers the lowest economic returns to water of any major user, another means of increasing the overall returns to water would be to expand some nonagricultural water uses. Moreover, as total water availability becomes a serious constraint on the region's economic development, efficient water use requires a relative shift in use toward sectors offering higher returns.

With irrigation currently acounting for over 95 percent of total water use in Cuyo, relatively small percentage declines in agricultural water use would enable substantial expansion of nonagricultural sectors. However, just as the current laws and institutions governing surface water use prevent a reallocation of surface water to its most productive agricultural uses, they also prevent a reallocation from agriculture to any other use except potable water. Surface water is allocated according to previous grants of water rights, and potable and irrigation requirements have already preempted the rights to the region's surface water. Ground water, the use of which remains uncontrolled, is the major source of water for new users. Initially, uncontrolled use of ground water results in an expansion of water use, not a reallocation. However, if such an expansion were permitted to continue, a reallocation of ground water use would eventually emerge. The declining quantity and quality of ground water use would raise water costs and eliminate users who could not afford the higher costs. The first victims would be farmers with relatively high pumping costs and low returns to water. This method of reallocating ground water to higher productivity users would be both economically inefficient and politically unpopular. Economi-

[51] The operation and impact of the credit and tax subsidies are explained in Chapter 3, pp. 47–50.
[52] Based on the data in Morelli, "Inversión privada," p. 68.

cally, the commonality problem and other discrepancies between the private and social costs associated with ground water use would cause the rate of use of ground water stocks to surpass socially optimal levels.[53] Politically, current users of ground water want to preserve the value of their investments dependent on ground water. In the past, policies have been shaped largely by political concerns with efficiency considerations ignored; there is little reason to expect that future policies regarding ground water use will be any exception. Demand for controls over ground water use are already being made by current users. Such demands will undoubtedly increase as the number of users increases and the available stocks decrease. Legal precedent and the political importance of existing users indicate that pumping grants will be issued on the basis of past use, perhaps with priorities for potable water followed by irrigation. From an efficiency point of view, the imposition of such controls could be worse than the reallocation that would emerge from uncontrolled exploitation of the ground water stocks. If ground water use followed the pattern of surface water, controls would eliminate the opportunity for introducing higher productivity uses of water.

While the lack of available water has not yet been a significant obstacle to the region's nonagricultural development, current trends and legal precedents could well place water in such a position within a decade or two. Petroleum has been the region's fastest growing industry over the last decade, and significant quantities of water are used both in the extraction and refining of the oil. Oil drilling in the region continues and, if successful, would place further demands on water supplies. Morcover, the region reportedly has rich mineral deposits,[54] the exploitation of which would require significant quantities of water. If ground water succumbs to the same controls placed on surface water (which both ration the water through water rights and attach the rights to the land), lack of water would become a major block to continued development of industry and mining within Cuyo.

The best means of preventing such a barrier to nonagricultural development would be to allow for the marketability of water.[55] By assuring new investors of an adequate water supply, water marketability would permit both agricultural and nonagricultural investments with high returns to water; such investments are essential for the continued economic development of the region.

[53] See the discussion in Chapter 5, particularly pp. 90–92.

[54] For example, San Juan reportedly possesses large copper deposits in concentrations well above levels currently being profitably mined in other areas of the world. See "Podría autobastecer al pais de cobre provincial," *Los Andes,* May 2, 1973.

[55] There are various alternatives for introducing a market in water. The most promising alternatives are examined in Chapter 5, pp. 97–102.

CONCLUSIONS

While we have not demonstrated that a particular government program would maximize social returns over time, we have demonstrated that current policies are biased in their conception and, therefore, likely to fall well short of any social optimum use of the region's resources. Government policies manifest an asymmetry regarding water. On the one hand, the government is undertaking and proposing projects costing hundreds of millions of dollars primarily to increase the availability of water. On the other hand, the laws, institutions, and pricing policies affecting water use and even the government's agricultural research program are based on an apparent assumption that water is not a valuable resource.

Government water projects are designed to prolong, not alter, Cuyo's historical, water-intensive agricultural development. There is a tendency to look to costly, but highly visible, public works projects for solving the problems of the agricultural sector. These projects, however, will at best postpone the advent of serious problems stemming from the limited supply of water. Indeed, the investment of hundreds of millions of dollars in water infrastructure will only postpone for about a decade the time when low ground water stocks force a decline in agricultural water use and perhaps limit the region's nonagricultural growth. Moreover, the projects are focused primarily on improving and increasing *surface* water supplies with little concern for their likely effect on *total* water supplies. Consequently, some of the agricultural benefits claimed for the projects are suspect, and some potentially attractive means of improving water availability, such as using ground instead of surface water storage, have not been considered.

Changes in the laws, institutions, pricing policies, and research efforts to reflect the importance and social costs of water would alter sharply the region's development. For reasons elaborated in Chapter 5, the changes should move toward greater water marketability and closing the gap between private and social water costs. Such changes would encourage greater on-farm investments to increase the returns to water and direct more water from relatively low to high productivity uses. The need for some of the expensive government water projects might be postponed or obviated. And there is no reason why such changes would require a redistribution in relative incomes or wealth. Any changes toward greater resource use efficiency would increase the total income of the region, enabling any potential losers to be fully compensated.

summary and conclusions

The past several decades have brought a sharp rise in the value of water in Cuyo. The region has passed from a situation in which surface water flows exceeded water use to a situation in which a farmer's surface water receipts are uncertain and generally insufficient for the minimum needs of land possessing legal rights to this water, and a sizeable portion of the region's agriculture is dependent on a diminishing supply of ground water.

The higher value of water has slowed the overall rate of agricultural growth, and altered the sources of this growth. Agricultural expansion in the first half of this century was largely the result of increases in cultivated areas. In contrast, the change in the relative product mix accounted for over 50 percent while the increase in cultivated land accounted for only about one-third of the growth in the value of agricultural production in the region during the last twenty to twenty-five years. The relative quantity of land planted to permanent crops, especially grapes, rose sharply; permanent crops now account for over 75 percent of the cultivated land and 87 percent of the value of agricultural production.

170

The national and provincial governments have assumed a more active role in Cuyo's economy since recent water shortages have threatened the region's agricultural prosperity. The governmental role has tended to offset the increasing costs and uncertainties of water receipts stemming from the changes in the relative supply and demand for surface water and the increasing dependence on ground water. Substantial government expenditures on dams, lining of canals, and irrigation wells to supplement surface water flows have increased the usable flow and reliability of surface water receipts. Government credit, tax, and power pricing policies have reduced the real costs of ground water by 50 percent or more to many farmers, and government pricing of surface water has not taken into account the increasing value of water.

While government policies have cushioned the short-run impact of the rise in relative water scarcity, they are likely to hamper the adjustment that eventually must be made to the realities posed by the supply of this essential resource. Government investment incentives, high grape prices, and relatively low marginal water costs confronting most farmers are encouraging the expansion of cultivated lands and water use. The implications of these growth forces and trends are alarming. Eventually, water use must be reduced to levels that can be supplied by annual rainfall, river flows, and ground water recharge. While water use can exceed these levels in the short run as ground water stocks are utilized, the adjustment to the long-run sustainable water use levels would be very costly and disruptive if these stocks are utilized too rapidly. Continuation until 1985 of the recent modest growth of total water use would generate ground water use levels that could fully deplete Mendoza's principal aquifers before the turn of the century and San Juan's within an additional sixteen years. The investment of hundreds of millions of dollars in water infrastructure would extend these dates only about a decade. Moreover, these estimates may overstate the usable time horizon of the aquifers. Well before the aquifers are fully depleted, higher pumping costs, lower ground water quality, and dry wells would be reflected in lower agricultural yields, higher production costs, and crop losses. The resulting decline in water use could be precipitous if the region were hit by an untimely dry period. The economic losses and disruption to the region's economy that would result from a sharp decline in water availability would be enormous. A substantial portion of the investment in permanent crops and irrigation wells would never be recovered if the availability of good quality ground water declined rapidly. Given the importance of the agricultural sector in the region's economy, the investment losses and economic and social disruption would be felt by all sectors of the region's economy.

There are no apparent social or economic objectives that justify the current policies encouraging water use inefficiency. Nonefficiency objectives such as rural and regional development, aid to small farmers, and rural income stability, could be achieved equally well and probably much better through policies that do not squander the region's most essential, scarce resource. Current policies must be attributed to ignorance of their long-run implications or to an unwillingness or inability to impose the measures required for a more efficient water use.

While major changes in water use patterns and growth trends in Cuyo will occur within several decades, the development scenario just depicted is not yet preordained by past events. The unknown is whether the change in water use will result from a crisis imposed by sharp reductions in water availability, government controls limiting increases in water use to protect the position of current users, or an effort to alter current trends and incentives to promote a more efficient and sustainable development of the region. In developing a strategy for altering the use of Cuyo's water, there is likely to be a trade-off between the impact on the region's growth and the changes in the current distribution, costs, and use of water. An emphasis on improving water use efficiency would permit a higher sustainable economic growth but require more drastic changes in current water use.

Any serious attempt to improve upon current trends is likely to encounter considerable resistance. All serious efforts to avert a crisis resulting from an excessively rapid use of ground water stocks would involve a reduction in the region's short-run growth, an outcome not generally advocated by politicians nor readily accepted by the people. Farmers expect governments to offset the ill effects of factors outside an individual's control and to provide an environment conducive to growth. Thus, the maintenance of low surface water prices despite the rising value of water, wells to reinforce surface water flows, and subsidies to offset the higher costs associated with ground water use are viewed as normal and necessary government actions to protect the region's prosperity. Farmers cannot be expected to foresee that these policies are inconsistent with the long-run economic prosperity and stability of the region. Farmers, however, are more likely to favor a reduction in growth prospects than they are to accept changes threatening their current economic position. Thus, if they recognize that current water use trends cannot be maintained and are likely to lead to major economic losses in the not too distant future, farmers would support measures curtailing growth but protecting their present position.

The strategy least disruptive to existing water use patterns but consistent with curtailing the rapid increase in water use would be to impose restrictions on increases in ground water use. Restrictions on pumping and drilling new wells coupled with the water infrastructure investments under construction and serious consideration would greatly extend the life of the aquifers and perhaps enable the region to maintain current or even somewhat higher water use levels indefinitely. Restrictions on new wells would be relatively easy to enforce and generally popular since they would help protect prior investments in wells. While pumping restrictions would be more difficult to enforce and less popular, they would be essential if direct controls are relied on to curb the growth of ground water use, since the pumping capacity already exists for a rapid drawdown in the region's major aquifers and farmers' pumping costs are much less than the social costs of ground water use. The use of such controls over ground water use are the most likely response when concern over water use forces government action. Moreover, precedents, both in the regulation of surface water and in the tendency for policy to protect historical patterns and interests, indicate that ground water rights probably would be tied to the land previously using ground water. Such a restriction would seriously limit the region's ability to respond to changes in conditions affecting the profitability of water use. Water use inefficiency would increase, and the region's agriculture would tend to stagnate or even decline as water could not be shifted from lands with declining productivity to lands with greater current potential. Under these conditions, it would be a moot point whether such controls would be preferable to the current situation of rapid ground water use.

The continued prosperity and economic stability of the region depend on the ability to develop and implement a comprehensive strategy to replace the current water-intensive growth with a renewed growth that reflects the higher value of and supply constraints on water. The measures required to ensure a more efficient and sustainable development of the region are neither self-evident nor likely to be politically popular; the development and acceptance of such measures would require a broad recognition that current policies and growth trends are detrimental to the long-run development of the region and greater efficiency in the use of the region's water is essential to continued agricultural development and prosperity. Without this recognition, policy will continue to be tailored to protect vested interests and inefficient water use patterns to the detriment of the region as a whole. Currently, however, outside of the universities there is no significant support for nor recognition of the need for major policy reform. While low surface water receipts, rapid increases in ground water use, and falling water tables from 1967–68 to 1971–72 made the availability of water a prime development issue in Cuyo for five years, the fears of inadequate water have been calmed by the unusually high water receipts during 1972–73, huge investments in ground water pumping capacity, and past and promised investments in dams and lined canals. Even during the years when water shortages were causing substantial crop losses, there was no indication in planning documents or policy measures of an awareness of the long-run nature of the problem nor any indication how it should be solved. A recent major study of the Cuyo region by CONADE, the national development council, concluded that the economic structure of the region must be gradually changed because of the inelasticity in the demand for wine and grapes, oscillations in agriculture, and the great mineral prospects.[1] There was not even any mention of changes in the relative supply and demand for water nor of the importance such changes might have on the region's economy. The major policy response to the recent water shortages was the construction of large-scale water infrastructure projects, the design, selection, and operation of which have been biased by an outdated conception of the value of water in the region. Alternative investment patterns which might have provided higher returns were ignored and the search for new irrigation and cultivation methods offering higher returns to water and greater long-term growth potential for the region were discouraged because of their relative neglect in government research efforts and the lack of private economic incentives to test water-saving methods.

A new development strategy focusing on improving the use of water over time is needed for Cuyo. The first stage of such a strategy should (1) eliminate the credit, tax, and power pricing subsidies for irrigation wells and ground water pumping; (2) increase the annual cost of surface water use to more closely reflect social costs; (3) legalize the sale of surface water rights independent of the land but subject to approval by the provincial irrigation departments that such sales would not create significant damage to third parties and that the new legal water distribution could be accommodated by the irrigation infrastructure; (4) undertake major research projects on the potential benefits and costs of new irrigation techniques and water-saving cultivation practices and strengthen extension survices for transferring this knowledge; (5) examine the costs of implementing and the magnitude of a user tax on ground water to equate the private with the social costs of ground water use; (6) eliminate the bias in the design and selection of water-related public works projects which currently favor the costly, highly visible projects and focus on increasing surface rather than total water supplies; and (7) establish central agencies in both Mendoza and San Juan with the capacity to develop plans for improving the long- and short-run uses of water in each province and the power to coordinate

[1] Consejo Nacional de Desarrollo, Oficina Regional de Desarrollo Cuyo, *Análisis y diagnóstico regional,* Documento de Trabajo (Mendoza, 1969) Vol. 1, pp. 6–7.

and control the water-related activities of all other agencies to ensure the water use plans are fulfilled.

These measures would slow but not eliminate the excessively rapid use of ground water and provide greater incentive for a more efficient water use but not eliminate the gap between private and social water costs. Moreover, the measures would provide some incentive for and a means of improving the conjunctive use of ground and surface water. Many farmers would have little trouble adjusting to these policies. The resulting cost increases for surface water and ground water pumped from 30 meters or less would not amount to more than 3 percent of the revenue from a good-yielding vineyard. Moreover, some farmers would benefit by the sale of surface water rights. However, for farmers with higher pumping distances and lower yields, the cost increases would represent higher percentages of farm revenue. For example, the cost increases would amount to 8 percent or more of the gross revenue from good-yielding grapes when water is pumped 70 meters or more, and the cost increases as a percentage of farm revenue would double on farms with yields comparable to the Mendoza average. To cushion the impact and allow time for research and extension efforts to develop and implement new irrigation techniques and water-saving cultivation practices, the cost increases might be phased in over several years. Nevertheless, the strategy for improving Cuyo's water use must be prepared either to accept or to provide compensation for the negative repercussions that would be felt by some farmers.

The satisfaction of political and social criteria is likely to require either special assistance to facilitate the adjustment to higher water costs or compensation to those who would not adequately adjust on their own. Although their cost increases would be higher than the average, farmers with greater pumping depths may not pose any special problem since ownership of a well indicates a prosperity and access to credit above that of the average farmer. Moreover, such a farmer may be able to keep water costs down by purchasing rights to additional surface water and pumping less. The real adjustment problems are likely to be encountered among the small and inefficient farmers. These marginal farmers would probably be the last to innovate in response to higher water costs and would have difficulty making a decent income even without the burden of higher costs. They would also be the least likely to benefit from general measures designed to encourage the adoption of new irrigation techniques. For example, since marginal farmers usually cannot obtain bank credit and do not pay income taxes, they would not benefit from credit subsidies and tax investment incentives designed to offset the high costs generally required to significantly improve irrigation efficiencies. While the plight of marginal farmers is worthy of special consideration by policy makers, this should not deter the introduction of a strategy to improve water use. If the government decides to preserve the small and inefficient farmers, assistance measures should be directed to offset the causes of the problems of specific groups. For instance, special credit, marketing assistance, or extension services might be provided on a selected basis. Assistance should not be provided through the current system, which undervalues the region's scarcest agricultural resource, and threatens the prosperity of all farmers. On the other hand, if the government decides not to adopt special measures to preserve marginal farmers, their transition to the status of rural or urban wage earners should be facilitated.

From the point of view of improving water use efficiency, it would also be highly desirable to impose a user tax to account for the external diseconomies and user costs associated with ground water use. According to the very rough estimates of this study, the optimal user tax would initially amount to about 5 percent of the revenue from a good-yielding vineyard. The combination of this tax and the higher power rates would substantially reduce the profits of farmers using ground water, even on a relatively efficient farm. While there would necessarily be some lag before a user tax could be effectively implemented, it might be desirable to delay further the imposition of a user tax if additional time were necessary for the research and extension efforts to provide farmers with an economically attractive means of adjusting to higher water costs. Although further research is needed, sprinkler and drip irrigation systems are promising alternatives for some crops. In the meantime, it might be desirable to limit investment in new irrigation wells by requiring drilling permits which would be sold or auctioned by the government.

While decisive measures are required, there is still time to phase in over several years the water cost increases required to encourage on-farm water use efficiency and develop alternative irrigation technologies and cultivation practices which would enable farmers to respond more constructively to higher water costs. The longer the delay, however, the more disruptive and costly the transition will be, since current incentives and growth patterns are increasing the dependence on and decreasing the supply of ground water.

This study has focused on water use efficiency and economic development within the Cuyo region; the analysis and conclusions indicate how resources might be more efficiently utilized within the region. The study does not, however, indicate how much of Argentina's resources should be directed to Cuyo from the point of view of national welfare. The national perspective becomes particularly important in the evaluation of the major water infrastructure projects underway and contemplated for Cuyo. Financing of these multi-million dollar water projects would affect the availability of development funds for other regions and sectors within Argentina, and the proposed interbasin water transfer would also affect the availability of water in other regions. The benefits and costs of these projects differ when viewed from the national as opposed to the regional perspective.

While it is beyond the scope of this study to evaluate specific projects from the national perspective or to offer guidelines for the regional and sectoral distribution of Argentina's resources, it is relevant to point out the contrast between the agricultural situation in Cuyo and that in Argentina's richest and most important agricultural region, the humid Pampa. Studies by Fienup and Reca have indicated how Argentine policy over several decades has squandered the great, natural agricultural assets of the Pampa by discouraging agricultural investment in the region.[2] Yields and overall production in the Pampa have stagnated. While price controls on beef and grains have been the primary cause of this stagnation, artificially high prices for key agricultural inputs such as fertilizer, insecticides, and farm machinery have also contributed. Reca concluded:

> The lesson furnished by the performance of the agricultural sector of Argentina is clear: there was progress in the Pampas as long as economic incentives were present. Once public policy failed to provide them either in the short run (as exemplified by the grain price policy) or in the long run (development of new varieties and techniques of cultivation), agricultural production stalled in the Pampas. In the rest of the country [specifically grapes in Cuyo] agriculture was not discriminated against as in the Pampas and the rate of growth attained there was comparable to that of countries whose agriculture has been making satisfactory progress.[3]

The absence of planning and policies which take adequate account of the potential as well as the limitations of Argentina's basic natural agricultural resources and the long-run implications of policies on agricultural growth and resource use have been clearly demonstrated. In Cuyo policies encourage an inefficient, overutilization of water, the natural resource which most constrains the region's development and

---

[2] Darrell F. Fienup, Russell H. Brannon, and Frank A. Fender, *The Agricultural Development of Argentina: A Policy and Development Perspective* (New York: Praeger, 1969), and Lucio Graciano Reca, "The Price and Production Duality within Argentine Agriculture, 1923–1965" (Ph.D. dissertation, University of Chicago, 1967).

[3] Ibid., p. 97.

SUMMARY AND CONCLUSIONS 177

prosperity; in the Pampa policies encourage an inefficient, underutilization of the rich, well-watered plains which represent one of the world's richest, natural agricultural resources. Failure to make good use of their relatively ample, natural assets has been a primary cause of Argentina's history of low overall economic growth.

APPENDIX

The available data relevant to a study of agricultural development and water use in Cuyo leave much to be desired. Frequently the researcher is confronted by either an absence of desired data or a bewildering abundance of conflicting data. For example, data on the use of water and other productive inputs for individual crops or farms are not available while one must select among several alternative and conflicting series for data on the land planted to and the production of various crops. Offices of both the national and provincial governments collect and publish annual data on the area under and the total production of individual crops on a departmental level within Mendoza.[1] The data from these two sources are not consistent, nor are they consistent with the production and planting data for grapes collected and published

[1] Offices of the Dirección de Estimaciones Agropecuarias of the Ministerio de Agricultura y Ganadería de la Nación use field agents to collect acreage and production data for both Mendoza and San Juan. These data are published in various issues of *Revista de la bolsa de cereales*, Buenos Aires. Time series data of the provincial government are published in Asesoría de Desarrollo, Gobierno de Mendoza, *Series estadísticas*, Vol. 5, Sector Agricultura, 1970.

Table A.1 Wholesale Price Indices and Theoretical Parity Rates

Year	Argentine pesos[a] (1969 = 100)	U.S. dollars[b] (1969 = 100)	Theoretical parity rates[c]
1960	20.1	88.7	0.79
1961	21.7	88.7	0.86
1962	28.3	88.7	1.12
1963	36.5	88.7	1.44
1964	46.1	88.7	1.82
1965	57.1	90.5	2.21
1966	68.5	93.7	2.56
1967	86.0	93.9	3.21
1968	94.3	96.3	3.43
1969	100.0	100.0	3.50
1970	112.7	103.6	3.81
1971	159.2	107.0	5.21
1972	281.2	111.8	8.82

[a] The Argentine wholesale price indices from 1960 to 1970 are based on unpublished work sheets of Dr. Claudio Loser, Instituto de Economía, Facultad de Ciencias Económicas, Universidad Nacional de Cuyo. The 1971 and 1972 figures were calculated from data in International Monetary Fund, *International Financial Statistics*, October 1973, p. 46.

[b] The United States wholesale price index was calculated from data from various issues of IMF, *International Financial Statistics*.

[c] The theoretical parity rates for each year are calculated as (column 1 ÷ column 2) × (3.5). This assumes that as of 1969 3.5 new pesos were equivalent to 1 dollar. The 1969 exchange rate was used as a base for computing the theoretical parity rates since the rates at that time were relatively stable and free of controls. It should be noted that the parity rates are all in terms of new pesos; one new peso (created by ley 18188 in 1970) is equivalent to 100 old pesos. Peso costs effective early in 1972 are converted to dollars at the rate of 6.3 pesos to 1 dollar.

by the Instituto Nacional de Vitivinicultura.[2] Moreover, a recent CONADE study of the region provides acreage and production data which differ from the data of the other three sources.[3]

Despite the shortcomings of existing data, this study necessarily is dependent on such data. Time constraints did not permit undertaking extensive on-farm surveys, and the desired time series data could not have been obtained through such surveys anyway. Considerable time, however, was invested in collecting and evaluating the data already available. Nevertheless, the author is not in a position to resolve all the inconsistencies among alternative sources. When presented with alterna-

[2] Data from the late 1940s to 1967 on the production and plantings of grapes are available in Instituto Nacional de Vitivinicultura, *Sintesis de estadística vitivinícola*, Mendoza, 1967. More recent data of the national grape-wine institute are available in their annual publication, *Estadística Vitivinícola*.

[3] Oficina Regional de Desarrollo Cuyo, Secretaria del Consejo Nacional de Desarrollo, *Análisis y diagnóstico regional*, Documento de Trabajo (Mendoza, 1969), Vol. 3, Appendice Estadístico y Gráfico.

Table A.2 Farm Level Prices of Agricultural Products

Crop	Price 1960 pesos per kilo[a]
Grapes	4.08
Cherries	18.59
Plums	4.49
Apricots	3.95
Peaches	3.79
Apples	2.86
Quince	1.35
Pears	3.16
Melon	3.12
Figs	5.06
Tomatoes	2.48
Potatoes	2.25
Onions	2.95
Peppers	3.67
Garlic	10.70
Squash	1.67
Beans	12.32
Green Peas	3.74
Sweet Potato	2.25
Alfalfa[b]	
Seed	21.04
Feed	1.69
Barley[b]	
Forrajero	2.25
Cervecera	2.45
Oats[b]	2.43
Rye[b]	2.28
Corn	2.79
Wheat	2.96
Olives	6.09

[a] The prices are the average of growers' prices from 1960 to 1962 deflated to 1960 prices by a national agricultural price index. The price deflators are 1960 = 1.000, 1961 = 1.138, and 1962 = 1.684.

[b] It is assumed that the value of a ton of these grains in pasture is equivalent to 60 percent of the value harvested.

tive and conflicting sources of data, several concerns were involved in selecting the data used in this study. The methods used for compiling the data and the reasonableness of the data were assessed. Moreover, when time series were required, the length and completeness of the alternatives were important considerations. While the census data are clearly the most reliable, they are available for relatively few years. These data, however, are valuable for evaluating the accuracy of alternative time series.

The percentage variations among alternative data sources were generally not large. Moreover, when significantly different data were avail-

Table A.3 Land Planted by Crop Groups in San Juan

(in hectares)

Agricultural year	Grapes	Other fruits[a]	Vege-tables[b]	Grains[c]	Olives	Total
1954–55	38,900	3,229	7,017	23,667	7,435	80,248
1955–56	39,500	2,989	6,540	21,460	9,108	79,597
1956–57	40,500	3,195	6,940	19,867	10,608	81,110
1957–58	42,000	3,888	6,777	20,033	10,610	83,308
1958–59	42,600	3,087	5,536	18,600	10,610	80,433
1959–60	43,500	3,087	6,392	18,683	10,609	82,271
1960–61	44,700	3,079	6,742	18,600	8,688	81,809
1961–62	46,200	3,141	5,462	19,150	8,157	82,110
1962–63	47,300	2,919	5,719	16,750	7,727	80,415
1963–64	47,800	3,033	6,994	19,467	7,779	85,073
1964–65	48,500	2,760	7,237	17,450	7,706	83,653
1965–66	49,300	3,312	7,184	18,333	7,630	85,759
1966–67	51,400	3,483	6,744	17,833	7,642	87,102
1967–68	53,300	3,017	6,143	16,383	7,642	86,485
1968–69	53,000	3,179	5,747	14,700	7,650	84,276
1969–70	50,300	3,635	5,848	11,250	7,650	78,683
1970–71	51,321	3,554	5,717	10,417	7,267	78,276
1971–72	51,281	3,662	5,828	11,963	7,343	80,077

Sources: The data are from the following three sources: Banco de San Juan, *Series estadísticas de la provincia de San Juan, Año 1971*, San Juan; various issues of *Revista de la bolsa de cereales*, Buenos Aires; and the files of the San Juan office of Estimaciones Agropecuarias, Ministerio de Agricultura Nacional. The breakdown among the crop groups can be obtained from the author.

[a] Other fruits include apples, quince, plums, apricots, peaches, figs, pears, melon, and watermelon.

[b] Vegetables include tomatoes, potatoes, onions, peppers, garlic, green peas, sweet potatoes, green beans, lima beans, dried beans, artichokes, celery, and squash.

[c] Grains include alfalfa, barley, corn, and wheat. Grains used for green manure are excluded.

able for items central to the analysis of this study, the sensitivity of the conclusions to the different data sources were examined. The use of alternative time series data would not have altered the basic conclusions that a continuation of historical trends would result in a rapid depletion of the region's ground water. To the contrary, the projected rate of use of the region's ground water would be somewhat faster if the projections were based on alternative data series for cultivated land. From the point of view of this study, the most important inconsistency among the alternative data is probably the difference between the alternative estimates of the land devoted to grapes in San Juan during recent years. The Instituto Nacional de Vitivinicultura lists 56,677 hectares of grapes in San Juan as of December 31, 1971, compared to the 51,281 hectares for the 1971–72 agricultural year listed by the San Juan office of the

Table A.4 Value of Agricultural Production by Crop Groups in San Juan

(in millions of 1960 pesos)[a]

Agricultural year	Grapes	Other fruits	Vege-tables	Grains	Olives	Total
1954–55	2,324	86	394	250	108	3,162
1955–56	1,684	85	362	142	36	2,309
1956–57	1,899	56	399	124	102	2,580
1957–58	2,474	100	394	126	22	3,116
1958–59	2,656	84	343	103	114	3,300
1959–60	2,425	94	315	122	102	3,058
1960–61	2,447	95	337	116	34	3,029
1961–62	2,596	94	318	122	97	3,227
1962–63	2,608	85	339	98	91	3,221
1963–64	3,299	87	396	215	123	4,120
1964–65	3,072	80	386	108	81	3,727
1965–66	3,456	112	402	126	121	4,217
1966–67	3,943	106	358	52	144	4,603
1967–68	2,711	73	304	108	32	3,228
1968–69	2,079	63	278	95	102	2,617
1969–70	2,212	66	273	62	35	2,648
1970–71	2,481	66	276	65	145	3,033
1971–72	2,553	72	259	93	44	3,021

[a] The value of production figures are based on the growers' prices listed in Table A.2. The production data by crop used to calculate the production values can be obtained from the author. The sources of the production data are the same as those for the land planted by crop which are indicated in Table A.3.

Dirección de Estimaciones Agropecuarias of the Ministerio de Agricultura y Ganadería de la Nación. The latter estimate was used in this study. According to Ing. Alé, the official in charge of Estimaciones Agropecuarias in San Juan, there are several explanations for the differences among these figures. The higher estimate apparently includes land devoted to access roads under the grape acreage estimates while the smaller figure does not include this land. However, the major difference between the two estimates may be the failure of the higher figure to take adequate account of the vineyards that became completely unproductive due to inadequate water and rising soil salinity. Ing. Alé argues that restrictions on grape planting, and fears that these restrictions might be expanded, led many farmers not to report land taken out of grapes in this period since this would have left these farmers the option of returning the land to grapes without first obtaining a permit to plant grapes. To the extent that this did occur, the grape acreage estimates of the grape-wine institute, which are based on registered vineyards, would be too high. Although the author is not in a position to judge which figure is more accurate, it should be noted that use of the higher figure would have increased the estimates of the growth in land cultivated and

Table A.5 Land Planted by Crop Groups in Mendoza

(in hectares)

Agricultural year	Grapes	Other fruits[a]	Vege-tables[b]	Grains[c]	Olives[d]	Total
1946–47			28,396	93,175		
1947–48	108,347	35,269	35,345	100,862	18,367	298,123
1948–49	113,998		33,224	100,651		
1949–50	119,649		35,277	93,563		
1950–51	125,301		25,211	76,743		
1951–52	130,952		23,297	73,757		
1952–53	136,603		24,750	59,673		
1953–54	142,254		24,495	66,453		
1954–55	147,500		25,915	69,986		
1955–56	151,300		22,650	74,030		
1956–57	155,000		22,278	86,394		
1957–58	158,500		21,620	78,070		
1958–59	160,900		21,186	64,611		
1959–60	164,000		23,253	63,973		
1960–61	168,300	38,858	25,897	66,814	26,435	326,304
1961–62	173,700		19,412	73,289		
1962–63	180,900		17,892	71,150		
1963–64	185,500		19,345	70,902		
1964–65	190,500		21,460	71,197		
1965–66	195,300		20,620	72,547		
1966–67	199,600		21,460	72,280		
1967–68	202,300		21,032	73,711		
1968–69	209,500		22,169	67,515		
1969–70	209,500	51,974	20,519	68,124	17,068	367,185
1970–71	209,500		22,151	65,919		

Sources: The data are from the following sources: Asesoría de Desarrollo, Gobierno de Mendoza, *Series estadísticas* Sector agricultura (Mendoza, 1970), Vol. 5; various issues of *Revista de la bolsa de cereales,* Buenos Aires; Dirección de Estadísticas e Investigaciones Económicas, Gobierno de Mendoza, *Registro permanente de uso de la tierra, Estadísticas agropecuarias—1969,* Mendoza, 1971. The breakdown among the crop groups can be obtained from the author.

[a] Other fruits include peaches, apples, plums, cherries, apricots, quince, pears, nuts, and a small category listed in the sources as others. Data on the number of trees were converted to hectare equivalents by assuming one hectare contained 400 peach trees, 340 plum trees, 200 apricot trees, 180 apple trees, 180 pear trees, or 330 trees of any other fruit. Data were available only for 1947, 1960, and 1969.

[b] Vegetables include only tomatoes, potatoes, onions, peppers, garlic, beans, peas, and sweet potatoes. Other vegetables which probably account for about 5 percent of the land planted to vegetables were excluded because of insufficient data.

[c] Grains include alfalfa, barley, oats, rye, corn, and wheat. Grains used for green manure are excluded.

[d] This assumes 115 olive trees per hectare.

Table A.6 Value of Agricultural Production by Crop Groups in Mendoza

(in millions of 1960 pesos)[a]

Agricultural year	Grapes	Other fruits	Vege-tables	Grains	Olives	Total
1947–48	4,696	511	633	772	76	6,688
1948–49	4,020	513	528	770	68	5,899
1949–50	5,113	720	695	736	93	7,357
1950–51	4,566	498	562	645	71	6,342
1951–52	4,201	517	564	607	108	5,997
1952–53	4,960	605	703	535	111	6,914
1953–54	3,674	453	745	584	123	5,579
1954–55	6,624	585	798	606	200	8,813
1955–56	5,245	553	668	570	170	7,206
1956–57	2,274	505	730	570	204	4,283
1957–58	4,396	668	651	532	189	6,436
1958–59	6,186	749	634	545	133	8,247
1959–60	5,558	596	629	512	213	7,508
1960–61	5,576	730	729	524	95	7,654
1961–62	6,501	811	621	566	168	8,667
1962–63	7,382	765	637	553	128	9,465
1963–64	6,363	985	727	544	154	8,773
1964–65	5,733	811	963	538	129	8,174
1965–66	7,006	686	846	555	139	9,232
1966–67	9,468	833	890	561	148	11,900
1967–68	6,972	969	858	614	146	9,559
1968–69	6,768	612	820	540	144	8,884
1969–70	7,013	585	904	537	212	9,251
1970–71	7,765	1,106	853	548	274	10,546

[a] The value of production figures are based on growers' prices listed in Table A.2. The crops included and the sources of the underlying production data are the same as indicated in the notes to Table A.5. The production data by crop used to calculate the production values can be obtained from the author.

water use in San Juan and shortened the life spans of the province's principal aquifer when historical growth rates were projected into the future.

The data listed in this appendix include only a portion of those used in the study. Data are included here only when alternative and inconsistent data are readily available, when data essential to the analysis are not readily available in published sources, and when it was felt that the accompanying data might be particularly valuable for following the analysis of this study.

As a final conclusion of this study, the author feels there is a great need for a thorough reevaluation and reorganization of the data gathering and publishing in the region. The value to future planners and researchers of the published agricultural data could be greatly increased

Table A.7 Data Used for Analyzing Agricultural Growth in San Juan from 1954–55 to 1971–72

	Land planted (hectares)	Yield[a] (1,000 1960 pesos)	Estimated value of production[b] (millions of 1960 pesos)
Grapes			
1971–72	51,281	56.59	2,902
1954–55	38,900	54.46	2,118
Other Fruits			
1971–72	3,680[c]	23.59	87
1954–55	3,090[d]	24.74	76
Vegetables			
1971–72	5,772[c]	51.60	298
1954–55	6,732[d]	50.57	340
Grains			
1971–72	11,190[c]	7.24	81
1954–55	22,887[d]	5.44	125
Olives			
1971–72	7,343	12.26	90
1954–55	7,435	8.46	63
Totals			
1971–72	79,266	43.62	3,458
1954–55	79,044	34.45	2,723

Sources: The sources of the basic planting and production data are indicated in Tables A.3 and A.4.

[a] The yields are calculated as follows: the physical yields are calculated from a least squares regression of yields over the entire period; these physical yields are then multiplied by the appropriate prices from Table A.2. The yields for the crop groups with more than one crop are calculated by dividing the number of hectares into the estimated value of production for the entire group.

[b] The estimated value of production for any crop is calculated by multiplying the value per hectare of the crop (derived according to note a) times the number of hectares planted to the crop. The value of production for a crop group with several crops is the sum of the values of each crop in the group.

[c] The 1971–72 land planted to nonpermanent crops which includes the vegetables, grains, and some of the fruits are an average of actual data for 1970–71 and 1971–72.

[d] The 1954–55 land planted to vegetables and grains are three-year averages centered on 1954–55; the figure for the nonpermanent fruits is an average of 1954–55 and 1955–56.

through centralization of the compilation and publication of the data and the adoption of more scientific estimation techniques. Moreover, greater centralization should make lower total costs for the compilation and publication of the data consistent with an improvement in the usefulness of the final product. In view of the rising importance of water in the region's economy, emphasis should be given to collecting data on water use and the sensitivity of agricultural production under alternative techniques to the quantity of water used.

Table A.8 Data Used for Analyzing Agricultural Growth in Mendoza from 1947–48 to 1969–70

	Land planted (hectares)	Yield[a] (1,000 1960 pesos)	Estimated value of production[a] (millions of 1960 pesos)
Grapes			
1969–70	209,500	35.05	7,343
1947–48	108,347	35.15	3,809
Other Fruits			
1969–70	51,974	15.77	819
1947–48	35,269	15.09	532
Vegetables			
1969–70	21,613[b]	43.98	950
1947–48	32,322[b]	18.95	613
Grains			
1969–70	67,186[b]	7.20	483
1947–48	98,229[b]	8.07	793
Olives			
1969–70	17,068	9.17	157
1947–48	18,367	3.01	55
Totals			
1969–70	367,341	26.56	9,752
1947–48	292,534	19.83	5,802

Sources: The sources of the basic planting and production data are indicated in tables A.5 and A.6.

[a] The yields and estimated values of production are calculated as indicated in notes a and b of Table A.7.

[b] The 1947–48 and 1969–70 figures for land planted to vegetables and grains are three-year averages centered on the indicated years.

THE JOHNS HOPKINS UNIVERSITY PRESS

This book was composed in Times Roman text
and Alternate Gothic No. 2 and Permanent
Headline Open display type by Monotype
Composition Company, Inc., from a design
by Patrick Turner. It was printed on 60-lb.
Warren 1854 paper and bound in Holliston
Roxite vellum cloth by Universal
Lithographers, Inc.

Library of Congress Cataloging in Publication Data

Frederick, Kenneth D.
    Water management & agricultural development.

    Includes bibliographical references.
    1.   Water resources development—Cuyo (Province)
2.   Water-supply—Argentine Republic—Cuyo (Province)
3.   Viticulture—Argentine Republic—Cuyo (Province)
I.   Title.
HD1696.A73C883   333.9′1′009821   74-24402
ISBN 0-8018-1701-3